To Bob

Enjoy

Trish Dugger

THE
TRISH DUGGER
COLLECTION OF
POETRY

FROM 1948- 2019

PUBLISHED BY MIMI ESTELLE

Copyright © 2019 MIMI ESTELLE
San Diego, California

Illustrations Copyright © 2019 MIMI ESTELLE
San Diego, California

ISBN 978-0-578-57911-5
eBook ISBN 978-0-578-57912-2

Title: The Trish Dugger Collection of Poetry
from 1948-2019

Book Design by MIMI ESTELLE

Printed and bound in the United States of America

{ TABLE OF CONTENTS }

1948 to 1999

Cigarette Smoke

silent loveliness rises
leaning on air
spirals of liquid velvet
ever changing
escape my grasp
an intangible dream
melting into space
leaving behind
reality and ashes

1948

Twenty-five and Still Alive

Today is the twentieth day of Jan.
It's the birthday of a lucky man.
Today Kevin Michael is twenty-five.
It's a wonder that he's still alive.
To perils he is not a stranger.
His early years were full of danger.
When he was just a little tyke
His folks tried losing Kevin Mike.
They took the family for a ride
And left poor Kev in Oceanside.
Alone at the beach and full of fear,
He saw the waves dash at the pier.
Though he was just a little shaver,
Nowhere would anyone be much braver.
Then later on when Kevin Dug
Spilled red paint on the living room rug,
Mom glared at him, all evil-eyed.
If looks could kill he would have died.
There was a time in the schoolyard when
Kev was playing with his buddy Ben.
He fell off the slide and conked his head.
And lay on the ground like he was dead.
He used to play mock war with Dale.

And both survived to tell the tale.
Remember the cage he had to make
For his very own baby rattle snake?
He caught it with his own two hands
And kept it til his folks commands:
"That snake must go! This is it!"
"One of your buddies might get bit!"
Then Doug and Kev, those little jerks,
Got into homemade fireworks.
And strange to say, it is a fact,
They've still got all their limbs intact.
Of course, it's hard to beat the time
He met up with a man of crime.
An escaping convict on the run
Held Kev a hostage with a gun.
They interviewed him on TV.
That's really big time you'll agree.
The episodes go on and on ----
A regular close call marathon.
Maybe the reason he's so lucky
Is that his dad is from Kentucky.
Give him a great big kiss and hug.
Happy Birthday Kevin Michael Dug.

1981

Darkness

Finding my way
down familiar halls,
fingering walls,
wearing a gown
smudged with jam,
dotted with crumbs,
leaving a trail of
disarray, I plow
through pillows
scattered about,
tossed and hurled,
pillows of
forgotten colors.
Before Darkness,
a particular pillow
of subtle shade
was carefully
casually tossed
on a chair of
harmonious hue.
Interior decoration
is lately more
interior.
Aromas, textures,
sounds decorate
my dark areas,
(living, dining,
sleeping)
everything in
your basic black.

1985

Abracadabra

His bare feet giggle
and his smile dances.
His pocket's full of
gravel and of course,
he is precocious.

He has a book of magic
tricks and waves a wand.
He wants to show me
magic, and of course,
he already has.

1993

Such Sweet Sorrow

Something of which
I seldom speak:

she came to visit us
once a week
in good weather,

but I never

I never saw her cry.
I used to wonder why
I never saw her cry.

I never heard her weep.
Did she cry herself to sleep?
I never heard her weep.

But I can tell you this

when she offered her
cheek for a kiss,
she didn't cry
when we said goodbye.

And I will always hear
her words soft by my ear,

Honey, don't smear
my lipstick.

1993

My Love

You are
my rose my
sunset my
chocolate.
You are my
bubblebath
my rainbow
my song.

1996

Portrait of My Father and Me

Here is the portrait.
It's not quite finished,
of course, but I'm pleased
with the work of the artist.
He has the finest credentials,
the highest recommendations.
All in all, he has treated me
kindly. Don't you find it
a flattering likeness?
The flesh tones are lifted
from life, the colors sublime.
And I'm happy he painted
a sparkle in both of my eyes,
though the right one is blind.
Study the negative space,
how the outline of image,
of positive form, my face,
is defined by this shadowy
background. It appears
to be two-dimensional
and confined to the canvas,
but this is a misconception.
The negative space is vast
and deep and dark
and mysterious, and full
of what is not there.

June 1997

Full Moon Lament

Lovely lady, silvery cool
and distant, aloof in your
roundness, you glide into
my bedroom, keeping me
awake and little care. Why
must you be so heartless?
Where were you earlier when
romance was left wanting?
Go away and leave me
alone with my insomnia.
Let the darkness cradle me.
Let the hush of night
lull me to sleep. I am not
ready for reality of day
that comes too soon.

June 23, 1997

Home Sweet Home

I am large in a land
where lean and supple
reign supreme and
a fat lady has no face
and I have wondered
if I am lovable.

Yes, there is someone
who responds to my
willowy spirit,
a wizard with magical
powers to wave away
my outer layers. For a
while I am weightless

Floating

over the Valley of Slender,
which I have visited from
time to time. It was here
I met my true love in his
native area. and we have
been together ever since
in thickness and in thin.

Yes, he has been aware
of my solitary travels
on the back-roads of bullimia,
and my endless crossings of
the great barren diet plateau
And he waits for me to be
at peace in the place
where I reside.

August 15, 1997

R.S.V.P.

Our tacky folding aluminum chairs
with seats of faded plastic strips
are stored in a hollow under the stairs,
displaced by a couple of rockers,
(white wicker).
More of our family's overflow furniture.
We put them out on the upstairs porch,
(renamed veranda).
Like refined old-fashioned visiting kin,
they summon forth mannerly ways,
evoke the social graces, slow us down.
We dine by candlelight, then respond to an
imagined invitation from a couple of charmers:

The rocking chairs on the veranda
request the pleasure of your company
for after-dinner rocking
and quiet contemplation.

And so we retire to the veranda
(back and forth and back and forth)
and sit and rock and contemplate
(back and forth and back and forth)
two fat crows in the tallest treetop
(back and forth and back and forth)

September 1997

LEVI STRAUSS & CO W34 L36

Her generous derriere
was settled on the middle chair
of the black jack table,
better to see the dealer's cards
with her half-blind eyes, when
long and rangy
Stetson-topped, big silver buckle
belted jeans with rear leather patch
leaned into the table beside her.
and she read with miraculous ease:

LEVI STRAUSS & CO W34 L36

as her insides fluttered like a petticoat
hung out to dry in the breeze.
He placed his bet, made the offered cut,
and the dealer dealt around.
He doubled down.
Hit a niner and a deuce
with a one-eyed jack, turned to leave
with his winnings and,
tipping his hat, he smiled at her.
She was ready to ride,
were he to ask,
when the dealer flipped over
his down card and she was busted.
Sure enough, right about then,
old familiar
LEVI STRAUSS & CO W38 L31,
baseball cap and a gray moustache,
showed up to do-si-do her back to the barn
with a steady hand and a practiced arm.
He had signed on in the springtime
for the round-up

1997

The Rustle of Petticoats

She wears a new hearing aid,
it's her magic vessel
through canals of sound.
Surprising noises, formerly muffled,
strike the startled drums of her ears.
But it is the faint fragile sounds
that so entrance her.

She was my mother
and she would later say...
*You cannot imagine
how wonderful to hear
the rustle of petticoats!*

swoosh swish swoosh swish
never before heard
swoosh swish swoosh swish
like the whispered word

But I can imagine this:
She sits in a darkened theater.
A lover, his hand on her breast,
leans and whispers
Baby Oh Baby You feel so good

She has read his lips,
his written lines,
but now dusty daisies
in the garden of her psyche
lift their faces to the gentle
rain of his whispered words.

1997

Rock On, John Fogerty, Rock On!

Impossible believin' that he's gone.
Puttin' off my grievin' with a song.
Not a love song ..... no romance.
Not gone-away blues ..... no chance.
Only one kind of music suits me now.
Rock 'n Roll's gonna get me through somehow.

Turn it on, crank it up, play it loud.
Only Rock 'n Roll can chase away my cloud.
Gets me up, makes me move, gets me out.
Only Rock 'n Roll can turn my blues about.
Only one kind of music suits me now.
Rock 'n Roll's gonna get me through somehow.

Can't sleep or eat. Can't concentrate no more,
Ever since he walked out my front door.
He filled my heart, he satisfied my soul.
Now I get by with friends and Rock 'n Roll.
Only one kind of music suits me now.
Rock 'n Roll's gonna get me through somehow.

Keepin' track of time just keeps me blue.
Not denyin' life with him was honey sweet,
But I'm movin' on by pickin' up my feet.
Only one kind of music suits me now.
Rock 'n Roll's gonna get me through somehow.

June 1998

Happily Ever After

It's a cotton candy day.
Even the clouds are
spun-sugar swirls
in a crayola-blue sky.
We're going to have fun.
Run to the top
of a grassy hill,
roll all the way down
to the bottom, ride
on a merry-go-round
and lose our shoes.
We'll run away from home,
and join the circus.
At the end of the day
we'll fall asleep
on cotton candy pillows,
sticky and pink, stuffed
with sweet dreams.

October 18, 1998

Out-of-Season

Bowl of ruby
nuggets
lumpy bumpy
raspberries
and cream,
out-of-season
ambrosia
in front of me,
makes me purr.
I feel stroked
in a special way
as once I was,
in season.

October 18, 1998

Revelations

I sit on the side of my bed,
less resilient than it used to be.
My hand follows the worn

routed edge of a cherry wood
bed-side table made
by my middle-aged son
in high school wood shop.

I pull out the drawer
of the bed-side table
and study its contents
and I realize my seniority
is revealed by
an array of ointments:

anti-wrinkle
anti-itch
anti-sunspot
anti-ache

and I wonder .....
whatever happened
to a little book of

love sonnets and a vial
of aromatic oil?

Well,
I really can't remember,
and anyway

where the hell is my anti-acid?

October 19, 1998

Small Comforts

Evenings would find
my husband stretched out
in his vintage recliner,
while I, nearby,
could be found
curled up on the couch.

Nine o'clock:
A whippoorwill calls.
My husband lifts up to
look at a bird clock on
the opposite wall.
It was a very sweet time.

Now the man and
the chair are gone, but
time is eternal with
the help of a couple of
double A batteries.

And evenings find
my cat and me
passing time together,
curled up on the couch.
Big hand, little hand.
Stroke by stroke.

Nine o'clock:
A whippoorwill calls.
Willy's ears perk up and
my heart quickens.
It is a very sweet time.

March 1999

To Mrs. Erickson

What do kids know?
Kids know everything.

They know who to trust
and who will give them away.
They know when to keep their
mouths shut and when to run.

Kids know how to disappear
behind their eyeballs and
they know how to keep from
crying even when they hurt.

I knew right away my
life was changing when
Mrs. E
came to be the new
superintendent of the
children's home.

Splendid and tall as a
Christmas tree, she walked
among the tables of kids
at supper, smiling, loaf of
bread under her arm,
passing out slices
to anyone still hungry

and Mrs. E paid attention.
Paid attention to me to *me*.
I became the star of my own life.
I tiptoed out from the side wings
into center stage spotlight,
and her applause for me was like
cold lemonade and ginger snaps
on a sultry summer afternoon.

Hot chocolate in the middle of
a stormy night when some
of us couldn't sleep: Mrs. E
silently beckoned and we,
rising like ghosts from our
dormitory beds, followed her
downstairs to the kitchen,
a warning finger to her lips:
ssh ssh

And I knew this was like
being in your own family,
with your own mother.
And I knew I was safe.

April 1999

Written in Stone

Mind debris surrounding me
like litter after a remodel,
and I am left alone to deal
with the clutter, sort out
the chaos, empty the trash.

It takes a measure of time
to pick up the wheel barrel.
strength to shovel scattered
thoughts and images into it,
to wheel them into the left side
of my brain, dump them out,
and let them roll around like
cement in a cement mixer.

It takes a simple acceptance
to tamp them smooth, then
to pick up my pen and draw
our initials in the middle of
a heart, finally to allow
thoughts and images to cure.

I close my eyes and see.....
a chain link fence around a
kindergarten yard across the
street from the spot where our
new dumpster would be placed.

.....a cement mixer pulls up
along side of the designated
spot to pour a slab. All the
kindergarten kids are lined up,
leaning against the fence,
watching in fascination.

.....he picks up a stick and
draws a heart in the wet
cement, our initials in the
middle of the heart and
underneath, the date: *3-31-98.*
An event written in stone.
And two weeks later he died.

An event written in stone.
Little did I know it was to be
a monument, a legacy.

May 1999

The Fog

furry soft
enfolds,
feather fluff
blurs
sharp curves,
like a plural
of dry martini
and almost
as darkly
dangerous.

June 1999

In a Jellybean Jar

Ashes to ashes
and dust to dust and
left-over flowers
to the Children's Home.

When somebody died,
somebody important,
tons and tons of left-over
flowers in baskets
and vases by the million
were sent around
to the Children's Home.

Red, yellow, orange
and pink and purple.
every single color in
a jellybean jar.

We set them out on
the porch in back where
the heavy spicy sweet
smells made us gag
and pinch our noses,
all of us kids
at the Children's Home.

One of our matrons, Mrs. B,
whacked off all the long stiff
stems and then she made a
mountain of fist-sized bunches,

every single color in a jelly-
bean jar, for all of us kids to
take to school, all of us kids
at the Children's Home.

And off we went the very
next morning, carrying
bunches of pretty flowers,
every single color in a jelly-

bean jar, carrying flowers to
our teachers, some to the
nurse and best friends
too, from all of us kids
at the Children's Home.

And if you walked down those
long halls at the school, and
opened all those doors and
saw all those bunches of pretty
flowers, every single color in

a jellybean jar, you might even
be glad that somebody died,
somebody important. and
that the funeral parlor owner
was the uncle of Mrs. B
at the Children's Home.

July 1999

Luna Loca

When my husband was alive
and the moon was full,
we sang all the moon songs,
lying in each other's arms,
singing in the moonlight.
He knew all the verses and
sang off-key. I supplied the alto
to our luna harmony, and now,
singing solo is lonelier than
I can say. But just the other day,
riding in the rain, windshield
wipers swishing, I said to
a grandson, *Hey! Let's sing.*
Do you know any rain songs?

August 1999

A Time for Everything

Evening slips in at end of day
like a latecomer to a concert,
and stays through the Sunset finale,
until the last blazing notes fade
into the dark descending curtain
of Night. Stars nodding at applause,
assume their lofty position,
while Dawn waits in the side wings.
of heaven. She will have her day.

September 1999

Mimi Smiles

and she is color,
day glo bright.
She is a rainbow
of delight.

I am her Nana
and she wants me
to paint her tiny
fingernails.

Yes, honey.
I will paint your nails.
I have a pretty pink
for you.

It is a not a fair trade.
She paints my
whole world
red, yellow, orange.
green, violet, indigo
and blue.

December 30, 1999

2000

Saved Again

First the wafer
and then the wine.
And then the wine
an unexpected gulp.

And then the wine
so warm and seductive
all the way down
to my stomach:
HELLO!
Here you are again
after all this time.

And then the wine
in a flash to my brain:
How about
another slug of
the Blood of Christ?

RATS!
No second rounds
for the communion rail.

Saved again.
Thanks be to God.

January 2000

Loneliness

Loneliness is not blue
like the sad man sings.
It is not gray like a rainy day.
Loneliness is white
pouring from a full moon bucket,
white flooding a tidy room,
white spilling on empty chairs,
into empty shoes, gleaming
luminescent moonbeam white.

Loneliness is camouflaged
by conversation with
attentive friends who
do not want you to be lonely.
Loneliness waits
for their departure and
then takes its place
beside you on the sofa.

Loneliness turns on the TV,
feeds the cat,
settles into bed beside you,
embraces you and
you do not know if you want
loneliness to go away.

April 2000

The Quilt

Born from the labor
of gathered women
bending over stretched
fabric on a frame.
Thimbles on finger tips.
sharp needles flashing.
Precise tiny tracks trace
flamboyant patches.
Plainly dressed women
plied their craft to
keep me warm at night.
I dream in color, see
kaleidoscope patterns,
but not the quilters.
They're invisible like
nesting mother birds
in protective colors,
drab brown and gray,
laying eggs that will
crack open to reveal
a riot of bright parrots.

April 2000

Justifiable Homicide

A poem got a hold of me
got a hold of me
and it won't let go
the poem knows well
how to handle me
how to grab my mind
hook my heart
rev my engine
something fizzy
sliding down to my gut
pinches my butt and
it won't let go
snakes me in with
a slithery move
sucks me in with
a flash of its sash
it's a grabber
yanks me into the
rumble tumble roll of it
the endless automatic
drone of it
shoving aside soft
fluffy puffs of sleep
unattainable
pillows of trance
sweetness of lullaby
cradle of dreams
oh man that poem
got a hold of me
and it won't let go
stuck under my fingernail
a sliver under the quick
can't get it out and
it festers it wants my attention
seizes my attention
smarts and smarts
all red and puffy and
I can't get it out
go away pesky poem

get out from under
my fingernail
give the words a rest
let them run away and hide
I've played this game before
and I don't want more
it tosses its razzle-dazzle
words in the sky
catches my eye
with a shake of its neon
kaleidoscope tail
it knows me well
how to sucker me in
seduces me with
its loose open vowels
allure of assonance
drops buttery toasted
bread crumb words
along my path
sweet spicy cinnamon
words words words
down a tangled path
to a dreary rewrite road
"the" or "a" ? "the or "a" ?
Who the hell gives a shit anyway?
oh god I'm so tired
I need to lie down and
I'm desperate to lie down and
OK OK I give up I give in
bring me some paper
and a ball point pen
and I'll write the fucking poem:

Summer of Sadness

Weep, weep for wasted words.
A poem died this summer.
Weep, weep for murdered metaphors.
A poem died this summer.

Yes, yes, I confess.
I confess I killed it.
Yes, yes, I shot it dead.
It dropped and slid right out of my head.
What else could I do? I needed sleep,
And now I weep. Now I weep.
A poem died this summer.

Then the tired poet said:

Good night everybody.
I'm going to bed

June 18, 2000

Perspective

My mother died when she was 67.
She went to heaven.
In the coffin her skin was cold.
She looked old.
But now that I am older than she,
Where in my life does that put me?
According to calendars it appears
I'm in the autumn of my years.
What does it matter,
This thing called time,
When I'm writing a poem,
Searching for rhyme?
What does it matter,
This thing called age,
When every day
Is a brand new page?
I won't go to heaven.
Don't ask why.
Not many good times
Passed me by.
My heaven is here
On a sandy beach
With the sun and surf
Within my reach.
There's still much to do,
So much to see.
Do you want to have fun?
Come along with me.
I'll never ask
How old you are,
Just how fast you want to go
And how far.

July 14, 2000

The Last Dance

When did I start to get old?
Was it when I stopped
reading daily comic strips?
Was it when I started
reading obituaries?

If I were a bottle of brandy,
say Courvoisier cognac,
I would be expensive.

My sex appeal started
slipping away with barely
my awareness,
leaving at a steady pace,
way out in front of desire.

When my youth disappeared,
my sex appeal
kept on slow dancing.
My body moved to
throbbing low notes.
Where is the music now?
It is harder to hear.

Where is a man
swaying to a waltz
who will spin me
around once again?
It is harder to see.
There he is!

An older man looking
around for a partner
with sex appeal.
He will pass me on
the dance floor and not
even know I am here.

Well anyway,
that's OK. I have my eye

on a much younger guy
with dark wavy hair and
the devil in his smile
and lots of sex appeal,
though the older man
and I may both
end up sitting out
the last dance.

August 2000

Hope

The lowly yellow dandelion
is lifted up to his chin.
A yellow glow reflected there
says, Yes! He loves butter.
Yes! He loves the impish
dandelion invading his
serious lawn. Yes!
He loves a lady standing
straight up to his chin,
her yellow tuft on top
a slender stem.

Yes, he loved her sunshine
until the day he died,
the day sorrow slowed
her step, turned
the yellow tuft to silver.
But weeds are resilient.

They persist and grow,
instinctively know hope
is the puff of wind
that scatters seeds
in new directions.

October 7, 2000

2001

Valentine's Day

Valentine's Day
Lovers' Lane
Cupid's arrow
It's a pain.
If a lady doesn't have
A sweetheart too,
She's out in the cold
Turning blue.

I don't have a lover.
I *do* have a muse,
Not exactly
What I'd choose.
But I shed no tears.
I have a good time.
Though my bed is cold,
I have a hot rhyme.

Roses are red
And roses are thorny.
If you don't have a lover
And you feel horny,
Rely on yourself.
Don't despair,
And don't run out of batteries.
You'll get there!

February 2001

Moon Madness

Full moon.
Full moon *again.*
Wretched moon!
What have you done to me?
You have ruined me
for the new moon,
once a sight of delight,
silvery slice of a curve
cupped to hold my wonder
in the night sky.
But you!
So roundly round
and fully full.
I am a captive in your spell,
even though you never stay
to keep your promises.
A pox on your pull!
Let others howl.
I shake my fist at you.
You keep me awake
and drive me crazy.
To hell with your phases
And another thing.....when
will you be back here *again*?
Hurry!

February 8, 2001

Love Letters on Postcards

We are all survivors
of promises made
and promises broken.

Hello, my little girl, Daddy is
on a month's trip to Florida
and when I come home
I'm coming for you dear.
(He never came home.)

We are all lonely heroes on
a hazardous journey, ETA
uncertain, destination unknown.

Hello Patty, Daddy is still
down South. I certainly do wish
I could have you here with me.
Do you still love your daddy?
(She still loves him.)

We are all gifted stars
in a realtime melodrama
longing for applause.

How is Daddy's girl today?
I sure wish you were here with me.
You must be a good girl.
(She was a good girl.)

We are all searchers
looking for a lost love
from another lifetime.

Hello little sweetheart,
Aren't these oranges grand?
You must save all the cards
you get from Daddy.
(She saved all the cards.)

March 8, 2001

Frog Festival

Frogs are having fun,
whooping it up
down at the Frog Fest
in the creek,
while I am struggling
in my thought kitchen,
trying to boil up a batch
of words, snapping them
off like green beans...
ping ping ping
into the bottom
of an empty mental pot.

Spring has sprung.
Frogs are croaking.
I want to cook up a poem
but the fire's not smoking.

Guess I'll kick off my shoes
and get a bucket
and go on down to the creek
and catch me a few.
Frogs are not
as slippery as words.

March 19, 2001

Bottoms Up

Pour me a poem.
Make it a tall cool one
with a twist.
Pour out what
you're going through,
how it looks to you,
but please go light
on bitter brew.
If that is all
you have to offer,
make it a short one
on the rocks.
I'll toss it back,
settle up and leave.
I'm on the downside
of life and that's
enough down for me.

April 4, 2001

waiting

counting
seconds on a clock
tick tock tick tock
counting
tiles on the floor
hundreds and more
counting
cracks on the wall
pictures in the hall
counting
chairs in a row
people come and go
counting
nurses with charts
meds on carts
counting
waiting

April 7, 2001

Cool Moon

Polished silver in a pale morning sky.
You waited to say goodbye,
having seen me pass out,
high on the sight of you last night.
I wonder that my eyes are large enough
to drink in your fullness.
And the meaning of your stay-over?
Let me guess. Ah yes!
Your lunar ego *requires* my adoration.
But look! Over there in the east:
Here comes the sun! It's time for
your disappearing act.
A wink at me, then off you go
on your merry orbit.
I wouldn't want you to catch me
doing my Sun Worship Dance.

May 7, 2001

Nana Rules

Nana has a house
right near the ocean
and teen grandsons
with a vacation notion
and her house is rockin'
with a hip hop beat
and everybody hears it
out on the street
it's a rap vibration
from a teen invasion
for a summer vacation
with rap
it's the younger generation
with rap
the boys 'n the hood are back
with rap
it's a hip summer trip it's rap
and Nana's not gettin' her nap
'cause the hip hop noise
from the summer boys
has a heavy pounding beat
and the boys 'n the hood
have sandy feet
and they're sittin' on their asses
while the sink is full of glasses
and the bed's not made
'cause they'd
rather listen to rap/hip hop
what ever happened to bop?

Nana had swing/she had doo wop
now she got rap/she got hip hop
from a teenage invasion
for a summer vacation
yeah the boys 'n the hood are back
where's eensy teensy spider
twinkle twinkle little star?
this turn of events is really bizarre
but the boys are sweet

with their hip hop beat
and their sandy feet
and they think Nana's cool
as a general rule
'cause she spoils them rotten
and look what it's gotten
hey hey Docter Dre Eminem
lotta controversy 'bout him
he is a dude with attitude
but the boys with their sandy feet
can listen all they want to his beat
but not when Nana
wants to take a nap
that's when they know
they better can the rap!
Nana is cool
but the kids are not fools
NANA RULES!

June 19, 2001

Identity

Patricia Ann Dugger,
neé Saunders,
doesn't cook, but
frequently launders.
She lives in
Cardiff by the Sea,
zip code 92007.
Her house is
in a canyon.
her slice of heaven.
She is a woman,
a mother, a mom,
She's tdug102@aol.com.
She's also Nana who's
known to rave about
Andrew, Grant, Mimi.
Timmy, Jeff and Dave.
Last but not least,
for those who
don't know it,
this mother and nana
is also a poet.
You may know her as
Pat or Tricia or Trish.
Read and enjoy.
Love to all,
Trish the Dish

August 2001

Power of the Wind

Trying to lose
Sunday morning blues,
I go for a walk
and see a boy running,
coming undone
from Sunday clothes.
Hair slicked back.
White short-sleeved
button-down shirt
pulled out from
dark pressed pants.
Oxfords untied.

He runs laughing,
eager to be free
from confines
of Sunday clothes.
Arms outspread,
he runs.
He runs like the wind.
He howls.
He howls like the wind.
He is the wind.

I feel a rush of him
against my face.
He gathers up tears
in his current.
He scatters them
like dry leaves.
I hear the crunch of
dry tears under my feet
and I rejoice
in the power of wind.

Septemeber 2001

Words from the Deep

The ocean of this morning
washes over me. I float
out on the day, my skin
stinging with the salt
of a lonely night.

I rinse sand from my eyes,
untangle seaweed
wrapped around my waist
I admire a scarf
of white lace foam
on my shoudlers.

Already I am caught
in the rip pulling me
away from the words
I bargained for.

The table is set
with paper and pen.
Uninvited guests
are starting to arrive:
Moray eels of doubt
snake across the table.
Sea urchins weep
over inadequate words
and crabs claw at paper.

Oh! Neptune! I moan.
I never wanted
to be a mermaid,
only to swim like one
through inky black seas.
Where is the oyster
you promised me?

Ahhh! I spy it
and pry it open,
and behold a pearl:

Creamy satin white,
Lustrous in the light.

I have not lost
my legs in vain.
I cannot walk
but I can write again.

October 21, 2001

Book Press

Another poetry reading last night.
Becky's back. I've missed her.
Scott too. Cool. And that guy
with long hair and long poems.
Me looking at my watch.
Another poetry publication.
Couple of bucks.
Or was it a chap book?
I get confused.
They are piling up.
I toss them into baskets,
on shelves, stack them
on end tables.
Perhaps the weight
of words upon words
will press out essence
of simile. I'll anoint
myself with oil of lyric.
Luminous lines will appear
like gold fish flashing
in my thought stream.
I'll snag them with
a ball point, put them in
a poem that swims
free style with fins.

December 1, 2001

The Woman for Him

Let me see if I have this right...
The woman for him
(as he tells it)
is, of course, beautiful
and her smile,
oh my! her smile with a flash
of teeth, (sharp teeth, by the way),
the woman for him
shreds him into coleslaw,
drizzles vinegar over him,
chews him up, swallows him,
and eventually
flushes him out of her life.
What does he have
to say about that? Well...
it was one hell of a ride
through the canal,
darkly basic, intimate.
He hopes she will be back,
that she has a taste for him.
Maybe so.
She is already thinking:
balsamic!

December 16, 2001

2002

Dry Season

My Sahara craves
your flood of caresses.
Inundate me. Flow
into my every crevice.
You will be amazed
at the flowering
of my arid land.
I will delight you
with exotic flowers.
Sweet fragrance
of desire, exciting
colors of passion:
cerise and scarlet
await your arrival.
We will create
our own phenomenon:
desert in bloom
in erotic season.
You don't have to love me.
Just pretend you do...
infinitely more rewarding
than my pretending
you are here with me now.

January 6, 2002

Louder Than Words

It doesn't seem to matter if it's love,
And I could hardly care if it's just sex,
As long as you and I fit like a glove,
Why analyze our feelings so complex?

Our little time together is best spent
In exploration physical, not talk.
Without discussion show me your intent.
Take me in your arms or take a walk.

My heart beats fast and so does yours, I trust.
You touch me and it takes my breath away.
Call it what you want...it's love or lust.
Dispense with words! Let's get it on, I say.

In matters relating to sexual attraction,
Words are nice but what counts most is action.

February 2002

Foster Home

children placed in a home
strange lady leads them to a room
speak when spoken to

kids in strange new home
scary lady tells them rules
speak when spoken to

February 26, 2002

HAIKU

Raindrops scampering,
chase away the dry season,
rushing to puddle.

Soft violin breaks
the stillness with melody,
the heart with minor.

Sweet abandon of
freesia chaperoned by an
iris color guard.

Bird nest in basket
hanging by the front door. Slam!
Mother bird takes flight.

Electric fingers
touch me where I'm bare, set my
tinder box ablaze.

My plate is empty,
belly full, pants tight. I feel
fat ... until dinner.

Her knives are sharpened.
They slice cleanly and she is
wearing a band aid.

I write haiku, read
short stories, eat fast food, can't
sit still. Gotta go!

February 26, 2002

Walking It Out

Springtime surprises me
on a March morning walk,
scent of freesias in the air.
Sassy breezes erase
worry lines on my face.
What was I worried about?
Oh yes ... I took my cat back
to the Humane Society.
Relinquish
is their nice word for *return*.
Euthanize
is there nice word for *kill*.
He bites. Or did.
I work things out on walks.
Left Right Left Right
Left my cat. Right thing to do.
Left my cat. Right thing to do.
Ahead lies the ocean, broad band
at the edge of land.
Solid dark blue topped by
an expanse of sky,
milky blue, wide and high,
like a first grader's artwork,
simple and clear.

March 3, 2002

After a Dry Spell

Reticent rain
tiptoes down from
a pregnant cloud.
pit pit pit pit
Water breaks,
drizzles a glaze
over roads.
Everything,
leaf and tree,
glistens.
Listen ...
a splash!

March 7, 2002

Elegy for My Cat

The scar
from your bite
gleams white
on my tan arm.
You were
only playing
in a wild way,
crossed over
an invisible line.
My own heart
is so inclined
in fierce affection.

March 16, 2002

The Forever Factor

Some things are forever,
or seem to be ...
Bobby turning up again
and grandpa taking him in.
Harvest time on the farm.
They could use an extra hand,
even a shaky one.

Always a bunk for Bobby,
another chicken to fry,
biscuits in the oven,
a big blue enamel coffeepot
on the wood-burning stove.

Always an etched glass jar
of soda crackers in the middle
of red-checkered oil cloth
on the kitchen table and always
a flask in Bobby's hip pocket.

We sat around the table,
grandpa and grandma,
me on Bobby's knee.
I leaned against his soft
flannel shirt, gazed
at the lines on his rough face,

like a map of the roads
he had traveled.
His light blue eyes brimming
like lakes after a rain,
looked down on me.

Now there was folk talk...
the folks in Kentucky,
how are they doing?
Bobby's voice droned
on with news from the south.

I watched his lips move.
He chuckled, smiled.
The Tennessee folks,
what about them?

Bobby reached behind
for his flask, uncapped it,
took a sip, poured a
spoonful, and lifted it
to my lips. Baptism by spirits.

Fire in my throat and my lips
parted for more. Grandpa
laughed. Grandma laughed.
Bobby laughed and me too.
I laughed and clapped my
hands.

Everybody glowed
in the warm cozy kitchen.
Some things are forever,
or you want them to be.
And when they are gone...

grandpa, grandma. Bobby,
the warm cozy kitchen,
you might try to find them
in the only forever...whiskey.

But all you will find is an
unending thirst for whiskey.

March 30, 2002

What When Where How and Why

I lost my shoes
last night
at a party somewhere.
I took them off
with the rest
of my clothes
and I sure as hell
don't want
to know why.

April 2, 2002

Amaryllis in April

They are resurrected
from warm spring soil.
I cut four tall hollow stalks,
five blood-red blossoms
to a stalk, each so large
it overflows the cup
of my two hands.
Hallelulia trumpets
silently proclaim
their own perfection.
I place them in a white
vase on the coffee table
where they preside
over the living room.
What a paradoxical
and versatile God who
watches over blood
spilled in war and
at the same time
allows me solitude
to write words
in praise of amaryllis.
It does. More than war.
Maybe because of war.

April 9, 2002

I Have a Voice

I have a voice.
It must be heard.
My song is not
The song of a bird,

Canary or lark,
A sweet refrain.
I sing a song
Of joy and pain.

My voice is mine.
It tells my life.
I am a mother.
I've been a wife.

You may not like
The words I say,
The sound of my voice,
Or even the way

I write and I rhyme,
How I sing my tune.
You don't have to listen.
My song ends soon.

But I have to sing.
I have no choice.
I sing because
I have a voice.

April 16, 2002

Haiku

old vine climbs slowly
clings to cracks in ancient wall
together they stand

sinking paper rafts
carry words not said to sea
regret weighs heavy

cold stone beauty lasts
forever   aging flesh is
wrinkled but gives warmth

beauty is in fall
of petals   fading blossom
bare stem leans with grace

full moon reveals
all secrets   crescent moon glows
mysteriously

trumpet solo soars
transports my spirit skyward
flying with angels

May 2002

Living Room

I love my living room,
its warm wood-
paneled walls, high
open-beamed ceiling.
But I don't exactly
live in this room.
I *sit* in it. *Sitting room*
sounds stuffy,
but our ancestors
had it right.
I also *look* at tv and
listen to the stereo.
So the iving room should
be called *looking room*
or *listening room.*
As for my bedroom, ahhh!
There is my living room.

May 6, 2002

To a Poem

Rounding a curve,
sounding a word
from a line in my mind
on my morning walk,
and people on the way
might say...*there goes*
that crazy lady,
talking to herself.

Crazy lady or poet...
who's going to know?
To tell you the truth,
I'm a little bit of both,
a precarious balance
on a typical day.
Lean to the right
and I'm saying words
that rhyme.
List to the left and I laugh
out loud at nothing.
our name the same,
Which is the crazy lady?
Which is the poet?
Who can say?
Both of us sign
our name the same,

and on any given day,
if the combination clicks
for a mix of magic,
we might sign our name
to a poem.

May 7, 2002

there is a certain

satisfaction in
symmetry a beauty
of balance
contemplate such calm
you can count on it
for quiet blood through
predictable channels

no ripples no unruly
crimson waves crashing
on shores that shudder

sometimes the circle
of my soul
seeks symmetry
but more often

my impetuous heart
leaps up toward
chaotic encounters

with thunder heads
rising
changing
moving
growing dark

there is a certain
exhilaration in
turbulence
a thrill in thunder

May 26, 2002

A tiny pine cone

from a brawny pine
in my path. I kick
it out of the way,

then lean to pick it up,
hold it upside down
in my hand and study

its swirling pattern of
stiff brown overlapping
woody scales between

which are the naked
ovules. I have news for you, tiny cone:
You will never be a tree.

I will keep you right here
on my desk. You show
me that perfection exists

for its own sake. Your
mother produced you,
then dropped you from

her arms. *Adiós Niño*
She is done with you.
She claims her ground,

gives shade and shelter
to birds. She's working
on a new batch of cones.

And so it goes, and here
you stay, a reminder of
wonders along my way.

May 26, 2002

The Kneeling Aphrodite

I have a head, two complete arms,
sagging breasts, and kneel with
with a groan, so I could never be
a model for the contemporary
Kneeling Aphrodite, a marble statue
dating from the Hellenistic Age,
third century B.C. which personifies
the graceful sensuousness of the

female form. A beautiful young girl
with a perfect body is immortalized
in stone and on display at the Louvre
centuries after her death. She could
not have imagined such immortality.
Can anyone? Not me! Who would
ask me to pose? I do what I can to
improve my body, but pear shape is

still a pear shape, thick or thin. So I
wouldn't even dream of living on as
a statue and someone pointing to me,
saying, *Look at her beautiful form*,
but I confess I tremble at the thought
of someone in the future saying,
Listen to the beautiful words she wrote,
and I quote.....

June 4, 2002

Changing Seasons

Long slender ovals
of dusty dark green
make way for lighter
brighter leaves
at the reach of limbs,
pristine, eager for
their time in the sun.

While the dark ones,
some now rimmed
with yellow,
prepare for fall,
relinquish moisture,
curl up edges.
Leaves do not protest
a change of season.

They quietly turn
to honey gold and flame,
float to earth in one
last flamboyant fling.

Each content
in its own season,
secure in its own beauty,
the falling star
and the ingenue,
shiny side up.

June 22, 2002

Adiós Santa Ana

he was born into fiery
desert winds torching
the Southern California coast
hottest Santa Ana on record

this male child
first born of my daughter
my first grandchild
and the first week of his life
in an upstairs apartment

heat rising like
a hot air balloon
colorful as tongues
of flame an effort
to breathe no cross
ventilation

we wear next to nothing
he she and me
the baby in a diaper
sucking on his mother's
in sleeveless t's and shorts
me washing clothes

dampness increases
and folds of our skin
he she and me
he nuzzling his
mother's neck

she rinsing him with
tepid water in a
kitchen sink
me washing clothes

folding sorting sipping
iced tea stirring
up a little breeze
with a pleated paper fan

then we all lay back
listless too hot to talk
too hot to cry
we close our eyes
he she and me
and so we sleep

each sweltering day
melting into the next
in a turgid flow of
lethargy until a breeze

from the sea like
ice cream truck bells
jingling coming
down the block
on a summer afternoon

heat breaks cracks open
coolness spilling out
and the sleeping beauties
he she and me are
awakened by an ocean kiss

the baby howls
my daughter laughs
I sigh and say goodbye

adiós Santa Ana

June 29, 2002

Out in the Rain with No Umbrella

I am a poet
you are a rapper
I write poetry
and so do you
you and me
we don't see
life the same way
but both of us say
our own truth...
you in your youth
me in my old age
we're not on the same page
so if we don't see
through the same eyes
it's no surprise
but we have
the same name...Poet

and we've both known joy
known pain
both been out in the rain
with no umbrella

I haven't walked in your shoes
but I've paid my own dues
and just because
I don't spill my guts
you gotta be nuts
if you think I'm immune
to the siren tune
of drugs and booze
I didn't choose addiction
but not very many
get through without
knowing what that trip
is all about
and I've been blind
writing words
in my mind

until the time
I could pick up a pen
and see the ink again

and don't ever think
I haven't cried
over a kid
tubes coming
out of his side
in a hospital bed
and lost my mate
of many years
shed some tears

as for childhood
we're not going there
but I learned early on
life isn't fair
it will keep
for another time
another rhyme
over which to weep

so we've both known joy
known pain
both been out in the rain
with no umbrella

I'm not a rapper
I don't write slam
and I don't give a damn
if you think my stuff
is fluff.

there's soul in my words
and that's tough enough

and what about you
it's true
I'd never known
your woes
If you didn't share
your life
your strife
we each have a voice
and a choice
of words to be heard

we've both known joy
known pain
both been out in the rain
with no umbrella

and we have survived
to write about it
no doubt about it
me you
it's what we do
we are Poets

July 5, 2002

Dick and Jane in Pain

Dick. See Dick.
See Dick run.
See Dick pull a gun.

Jane. See Jane.
See Jane get laid.
See Jane get paid.

Spot. See Spot.
See Spot beg.
See Spot lift a leg.

Baby. See Baby.
See Baby cry.
See Baby cry and cry.

Mommy. See Mommy.
See Mommy shoot up.
See Mommy die.

Daddy. Never see Daddy.
Daddy gets high,
Daddy goes bye.

July 15, 2002

The Game Room

I remember a dress she wore. Light powder blue
with white polka dots. She looked pretty in
blue. Matched her eyes. Oh! How they sparkled
when she smiled at us. She came to visit on
her day off from work as a live-in maid for

rich folks. We watched and waited, ran to her,
talked loud so she'd hear us, repeated ourselves,
my sister Gayle, my brother Billy and me,
Sunday afternoons. 1 to 3. Time enough to
walk to a drug store, one with a soda fountain.

We sat in a booth and ordered. Strawberry sundae
for my sister. Pineapple for me. Bright yellow syrup,
chunky tidbits of pineapple over vanilla ice cream.
Whipped cream topped with shiny plump red cherry.
Mmm, loved those cherries! Still do. Ice cream too.

I learned early on that sundaes can be Band-Aids
for anything that hurts: scraped knee, lonely heart,
scolding, disappointment. I can't remember what
Billy ordered. Sometimes he came with, walking on
the other side of the street. Sometimes he sat in

another booth, still mad at her for leaving us at the
Childrens Home. Me? I was just happy to see her and
hold her hand as we walked. When it was wintertime,
the icy bleak cold of Chicago, she wore a long black
coat with a soft furry collar. We visited with her in

the Game Room, played Chinese Checkers, cards.
Go Fish. Hearts. Often she was the only mom. Kids
clustered round her as if she were the village storyteller.
But they didn't want a story. They wanted a piece of
a mom. I could almost hear them shouting, *Dibs!*

Excited to get to stroke her silky sleek legs, feel
the soft furry collar of her wool coat. I staked my claim:
*She's **my** mom. Mine! Don't get so close. Stop crowding!*
At bedtime, my sleepy little sister asks, *Who **was**
that lady in the pretty clothes? Golly!* I knew for sure

she was our mother, even if I didn't remember ever
living with her, (and couldn't recall my father at all).
I take after her. I like pretty clothes too, and people say,
You have your mother's eyes. I hope I have her style,
playing the cards she was dealt without folding,
smiling, bluffing, wearing a pretty dress. She wasn't
dealt a good hand but she stayed in the game

August, 2002

Running on Empty

Just when you think
You've got it made,
The monthly bills
Have all been paid.
Car insurance, cable, trash.
And there's bit of extra cash.
Maybe dinner and a movie?
Feelin' flush. Feelin' groovy.
When all of a sudden,
An ache in a tooth.
A visit to the dentist,
The moment of truth.
An x-ray shows
A problem in a root.
Just when you thought
You had it made. Oh shoot!
Sort of like last month...
I'd paid the bills,
Then got a sore throat
And needed some pills.
The pills cost a bundle,
Every last penny.
Money for a movie?
Zip Zero Not any.
And if it isn't an ache,
It's a knock in the car.
If you don't get it fixed,
You won't get very far.
If you DO get it fixed,
There's no place to go,
Because you can't buy gas
When you're out of dough!

August 21, 2002

Until Now

Friendly waves
from floppy fronds
of baby palms in
a parkway planter.
By myself on
my morning walk,
though
I am not alone.
Lemon yellow lilies
stretch and yawn,
blink at the dawn,
smile at me.
Ruby red geraniums
crowding the pot, call
out a greeting,
Roses,
sunrise in their petals,
merely nod in royal manner.
Cerise bougainvillea
cascades over
a garden wall,
falls on rusty orange
blossomed bushes.

No color clash
in nature.
Heavenly fashion
philosophy:
(now my own)
ANYTHING GOES
Round the bend
and home again.
A lighter spirit
A lesson learned.
First things first.
Shed the drab
bluejean shorts
and anonymous
white tee shirt
Put on my paisley capris
and purple tank top.
Pull out the shocking
pink feather boa,
purchased at a yard sale
on wild impulse,
and never worn
until now.

September 21, 2002

The Price Paid

A young girl
in a battered boat,
afraid to fly red flags,
afraid to make waves,
afraid to sail into
angry gales. Not wanting
to drown before
discovering dry land.
She dropped anchor,
safe in a harbor of
compliance and
stayed there, moored
to moderation.
Older now, she will say
compliance has served
her well. No frown lines,
no worry wrinkles.
A beautiful face. It's true
she has lacked passion.
That was the price paid
for protection. And
she has stayed afloat,
even if she never did
discover herself.

September 26, 2002

The Fog Enfolds

The fog enfolds me like a shawl
of light-weight yarn, loosely woven,
fluffy mohair or angora, shadow gray.
I seek seclusion, don't want to share
myself with anyone else so soon after.
The fog shelters, enfolds my feelings.
I want the explosion of fireworks still
ringing around me to linger, and the fog
enfolds, surrounds the sound, holds
close the afterglow.

September 29, 2002

Comparative Pricing
(for Bridget and Mer)

Three ladies lean
to look at a painting on
the wall of an art museum.
The plaque to the side reads
Egg of Unknown Origin
It is surreal.
The fee to view the exhibit
is five dollars.

Three ladies lean
to look at a diamond dew
adorning a spider web
by the side of the road
in front of the art museum.
It is real.
There is no fee for viewing.

Three ladies lean
over organic lunches,
speaking of spider webs
and diamonds and eggs,
Frida and firewords and fog,
Bridget says, *This is the best
Cobb Salad I ever ate.
I am a bridge.*
Mer says *Where are my
mashed potatoes? I must
remember to photograph
the dipping sauce.*
Trish says, *Me Me Me*
It is surreal.

The food is delicious
and inexpensive, but
there's no way to pay
for a priceless day.

October 3, 2002

The End of Things

Half-life in the half-light
of fine dust filtered down
from innocent clouds,

billowy castles and clowns
float over broken promises,
carrying poisonous particles,

and sunsets stream across
the horizon in a glow
never seen until now when

eyes dim, can no longer see.
So it didn't end with a blast
heard round the world, but

with half-life in the half-light
at the end of things.

October 4, 2002

Summers at Moonlight Beach

the sea the sand the sea the tang
the wind the salt the sting the sand
the kelp and flies sand in eyes
mothers and kids trek across sand
laden like llamas stake out a spot
drop coolers snacks towels and mats
shovels buckets broad brimmed hats

beach umbrella low beach chair
boogie boards sand in hair
sand in eyes seagulls' cries
pebbles shells fishy smells
suntan lotion sun burn
anxious mothers peer and turn
this way that way look at the surf
where are they

anxious mothers frown
heads in the surf bob up and down
voices on the wind call out names
heads in the surf all look the same
where are they

sand in the car in clothes in toes
sand in eyes and ears and nose
towels hung out to dry in the sun
terry cloth flags of summer fun
hungry kids with sandy feet
check out the fridge what to eat

what to wolf down right away
reach for favorite PB&J
satisfied bellies sleepy heads
say good night and fall in beds
dive like dolphins into sleep
dreamless in the swirling deep

wake up in the morning then
head on out to the beach again

October 7, 2002

The Sound Tunnel

Constant rumble tumble
of a power mower grumble
back and forth outside my
window. My lawn is large.
Front yard and back yard
Back and forth back and forth.
The guy pushing the mower
does an excellent job, rows
straight as a ruler. I'm not
complaining. Not exactly.

Yesterday a loud continuous
roar at the condos next door.
Fifteen units and five of them
getting carpets cleaned.
Imagine you're on a plane,
revving up for the take-off.
ALL AFTERNOON.
Now my yard man has switched
to weed whacker,
higher pitched than the mower.
Twice as annoying.

And this morning the street in
front of my house was blocked
off with NO PARKING signs.
Major remodeling construction
at the school across the street.
I have become acquainted with
the construction crew.
The guys are friendly. Cute too.
They call me by name. *Hi Trish!*
Break time is 10:00 A. M. when
the Lunch Wagon comes cruising
down the street, its horn blaring.
Today I saw my first
Concrete Cutting Company truck.
Wow Baby!

I feel like a construction virgin.
It's sort of exciting, dangerous
and really really loud,
Naps are a thing of the past,
but I can still write a poem.

October 9, 2002

Gauguin / Paul and Me in Tahiti

We shed clothes and lie naked in
the hot sand. The blazing sun paints
us mahogany. When we need fluid,

we split a coconut, sip its milky
liquid. We feel famished and bite
into succulent papayas, mangoes,

peel bananas and feast. We seek
shade in leafy palm glades.
Passion vines coil and bind us.

Vivid blossoms give this island
a flamboyance which Paul depicts
on canvases. They will hang

in museums someday. People will
pay money to look at them,
sense the heat, feel the smooth

tan skin of his Tahitian women,
study Paul's flat planes of beauty.
But money means nothing

to us now. We have an abundance
of all that we need. It has been
a long time since Paul tossed in

stocks and bonds, choosing a life
of painting palms and island scenes.
Still, it would be nice to see

the Champs Elysee once again,
but the passage is expensive and
I don't have a thing to put on.

October 21, 2002

Avalanche

I am no longer intimate with snow,
which once long ago called me out to play,
told me what to wear: mittens, scarf,
stocking cap, boots, seduced me with wet
kisses on my tongue when I was young,

slapped me in the face with the help
of Charlie Ross shaping icy ammunition
sent flying like love letters to the target
of his affection, and made my cheeks sting.
It was a boy thing. I knew he loved me.

We squealed with delight, feasting on
the sight of the first swirling flakes silently
arriving in time for Thanksgiving, icing our
hillside with layers of white, a topping more
delicious than whipped cream on pumpkin pie.

Trudging over scrunchy snow to a hill in
the park, we pulled our sleds up to the top,
and raced down, tumbling into blinding banks
at the bottom. With rosy noses, cheeks and
lips, we were Cupie dolls in winter woolens,

snow angels. Charlie Ross pulled my sled
back up to the top of the hill, and we slid
down together, me in back, holding tight,
our screams careening in front of us,
one peaceful winter a long time ago.

Recently I heard he died in a war, one of
the wars between now and then. I don't know
which one or when, and now an avalanche
of bullets and blood threatens to bury my
image of Charlie Ross, shining on the hill,

a snow angel still. Questions I can't stop,
tumble out, blot the hillside: *Was it snowing
when he died? The snow stained crimson
where he lay? Were tears frozen on his face?
Was he screaming? Did anyone hear him?*

Novemeber 2, 2002

Canyon Concert

The canyon sings.
A stream
at the bottom
yodels over stones,
accompanied by
a chorus of frogs
croaking low notes.
Bees swarming
round honeysuckle,
join in with
sonorous hum.
Leaves of cottonwoods
nod approval,
whisper in harmony.
A raucous crow
caws its applause.

November 7, 2002

Thanksgiving Day 2002

A cloudy sky intensifies color
of pink camellias
on a glossy dark green shrub,
red graffiti on cracked concrete,
blue morning glories scrambling
down a leafy blanket draped
over a brick wall topped
by razor wire, almost hidden
in foliage and flowers.
A skinny man with a scraggly beard,
wearing a dirty jacket,
sifts through trash,
retrieves a Hostess Twinkie,
half-eaten, from
a bin made pretty with painted tiles.

November 22, 2002

Dresses in a Shop Window on Coast Hwy 101 in Encinitas

trendy kicky
flippy trippy
fluttery rufflely
feminine ware
strippy strappy
barely there
size 2 or maybe 3
put a one in front
and you have me
fllibberty gibbet
I'm double digit
much too hippy
not very trippy
but topsy-turvy
I like being curvy
and my pocketbook knows
I like buying clothes
so where's a
double digit shop
I'll be there
hippety-hop

2002

Wonder

Gather together dry leaves for a bed,
A pillow of sweet smelling grass for my head.
I'll lay in your arms. We'll look at the sky.
And wonder why. And wonder why.

We'll rest in the hush of a warm interlude,
Dreaming that cares of life can't intrude,
And wish for tomorrow another now.
And wonder how. And wonder how.

I'll lean to caress the smile on your face,
While in my mind I'll picture a place,
Some shadowy room for us to share.
And wonder where. And wonder where.

Your lips will tell secrets I've waited for.
Your luminous eyes will be promising me more.
I'll move to your touch in a leafy glen.
And wonder when. And wonder when.

Gather together dry leaves for a bed.
A pillow of sweet smelling grass for my head.
I'll lay in your arms. We'll look at the sky.
And wonder why. And wonder why.

2002

2003

THE TRISH DUGGER COLLECTION OF POETRY

Temple of Early Morning

I open my eyes and stretch to break
out of the cocoon of night. I rise
to enter the Early Morning Temple.
It is still dark,
quiet as fluttering wings
of butterflies.
I light my light and don a vestment,
long velour robe, soft as fairy fur,
black as the early morning sky.
I see a single star, goodbye kiss
of night when I go outside
to pick up the morning missal
called a newspaper.
I press Mr. Coffee's ON button
and he breaks the silence
with a sputter. Soon the aroma
of coffee brewing mingles with
the scent of predawn, mix of
moldy mist and trace of tang.
I am a priestess
in this Early Morning Temple.
Priestess and
Princess. I own this kingdom
in which the temple is located.
When the sun arrives I will
relinquish my authority.
But in the meantime,
in silence I sip coffee
and search for my horoscope.
What does the day have
in store for me? Can it bring
more pleasure than the present?

January 13, 2003

Feelin' Good

Two nights in a row
of continuous sleep, followed
by a cup of hot coffee, strong
enough to lower my voice,
combine to spark my plugs.
I can do anything, be anyone,
go anywhere, but first a walk
to inspect the neighborhood.
Ah HA!
Four rolled-up newspapers in
plastic sleeves on a wide black
asphalt driveway.
Mmmm.
People gone four days?
Four tenants not yet up?
Two tenants, each receiving
two different newspapers and
not yet up? Newspaper carrier
with four left-over newspapers
tossed here?
Something to ponder
on my way back home and now to
start my long-proposed rhymed
autobiography. Then I will check
out the Flying Trapeze school,
maybe take a turn on a swing,
after which I will
join a fitness center,
pay bills, polish shoes, and
plant purple petunias in my garden.
For lunch I will have
greens with low-fat vinaigrette
dressing and AFTER lunch.........
a long nap is a strong possibility.

January 15, 2003

Upon Reading Out of My Head
by Harry Griswold

The book is slim,
its pages slick,
the poems concise,
their layers thick.
The photos provoke,
their images stark,
textured surfaces
light and dark.
The ink shiny black
of each patient word
which waits to be read,
longs to be heard,
spaced on a line,
the lines in a group.
He calls them poems,
not alphabet soup.
Twenty seven poems
have silently wept
inside the closed book
while the owner slept.
Waiting to be read,
longing to be heard,
finely crafted poems,
every patient word.
Then one slow day,
she picked up a book,
fanned its pages,
took a second look,
read for a while,
lost track of time.
Twenty seven poems,
not a single rhyme.
She finished reading
and said with a smile,
Well done, Harry!
I like your style.

February 3, 2003

Who Knows

Would I have done
differently had I known
he would be gone
shortly after dawn
of the following day?
Who knows?

An answering smile instead
of a shrug concerning
the possibility that I might
iron his favorite shirt
not recently worn because
it was wrinkled? Who knows?

And *really*, who wears shirts
that require ironing anymore?
Which I pointed out to him.
Well, as he replied, he did.

Arrhythmia...musical word.
Flowing sound over vowels.
He walked outside
in chilly morn
before the sun could warm

the ground
where he dropped,
cold as his skin had become
by the time
the ambulance arrived.

We selected clothes
for his body in the coffin,
a suit he had not worn
since he retired,
with that favorite shirt
which I finally ironed...
at least I like to think so.

It was years ago,
and though
the clay pallor of his skin,
icy to my touch,
engulfs me like a tidal wave
from time to time,
details of coffin clothes
are lost, and I doubt
there is anyone who knows.

February 14, 2003

Pleasures of Poetry Workshops.

Just as ennui threatens to wrap
its weary arms around me, saved
by the school bell! I have missed

my writing buddies who make me
laugh, have even missed their
penchant for punching holes in

my poems. I sigh for assignments,
pine for prompts, yearn for afternoons
of assonance, mysterious metaphor.

I bought a brand new spiral notebook
in bright primary green. It seems to
need a fat blue pencil kids used to

write with in primary grades, but
guess what? I also have a new pen,
a Mont Blanc. It was a Christmas

present, though I rarely write with it,
keep it in a secret pocket of my purse
for fear of losing it. I will inaugurate

it today for my first workshop, and
if I don't write any better with
a Mont Blanc than I do with a Bic,

I can blame it on the cheap bright
green spiral notebook. If I only had
a leather bound journal with bond

paper, who knows what magical
images I would pen! But I'll never
go shopping for one. I might find it,

only to lose the illusion that when
I finally get the right tools together,
I will be able to pen a perfect poem

March 11, 2003

TV Digest

She is on a diet,
eats a dinner
of cottage cheese
and fruit
while watching TV.
*Christians Debate
War* on CNN.
She quickly changes
the channel.
She is as hungry
as a lion,
but she cannot
stomach Christians
on the warpath.

March 12, 2003

Then and Now

The rumpled cushions sighed
where he sat and the house
had a vital humming vibration
when my husband was alive.
Newspapers rustled as they fell
to the floor. His electric razor
buzzed around his face.
He whistled as he dressed.
Morning coffee cups clinked
against plates of toast and jam.

Our afternoon tea was a ritual.
Hot water in the kettle screamed
its readiness and was poured over
Earl Grey tea leaves in a white
porcelain teapot. China cups
and saucers clattered on a tray.
Perhaps a piece of banana bread
or poppyseed. Later the rattle
of gathering up the tea things.

His step was solid as he left
on that final day. The front door
shuddered in its closing and
although I was inside, I imagine
he fell with a thud. If I had been
standing next to him, I know
I would have heard thunder.
As it was, I heard the siren
of an ambulance summoned
by a stranger with a cell phone.
Now the cushions are plump,
puffy quiet, pillows stay where
they are tossed at artful angles
in the corners of the couch.
Now I make tea with a tea bag,
sip it from a pottery mug
and the teapot holds fresh roses.
One by one their petals fade
and fall silently to the table,
while the house resounds
with the roar of his absence.

March 16, 2003

On Seeing Half Dome and El Capitan for the First Time

If I had not been invited
to go on my son's family trip,
if we had not come to Yosemite,
not gotten out of the van
at a viewpoint overlooking the valley,

not gazed at Half Dome and El Capitan,
they would have waited several lifetimes,
throughout all my reincarnations, being
shaped by geological periods, movement
and melting of glaciers, upheavals of earth,

waiting for me to realize them at last.
Of course I'd seen photographs, lifeless, flat,
the borders of prints straining to expand,
to encompass miles of mountain and valley.
I'd expected to feel tiny in the presence

of majesty, but no, I'm popping with power.
I witness to make them real, and record
their magnificence in my marvelous mind.
They're awesome, beyond big. I'm a speck,
but I see, I think, I feel and I say...WOW!

March 27, 2003

April Foolish

I can't afford to lose April.
I don't have that many left,
but war news invades
my heart and threatens to
vanquish it along with my
spring fever. So I focus
on flowers, rainbow fields,
the cheerful children of
Mother Earth and April.

I need to feel giddy,
loll around in lilies
fall
in
freesias
and in love. I want
to smell roses and
after shave lotion.

He loves me.
He loves me not.
He loves me!
Daisies don't lie.
He will
forget-me-not.
April is mine again!
The fever's back.
I must take to my bed
of tulips.

April 1, 2003

Clothes

unbuttoned,
unzipped,
unhooked,
unfastened,
fall to the floor
around the feet
of a man and
woman
now nude
in a pool
of clothes
removed to
release a flood
of passion.
Waves of desire
splash over them.
The tide of
a churning sea
rises to their thighs.
Clothes on the floor
silently echo
cries of surprise.
It's new!
It's always new!
All else recedes,
except for lust,
unrestrained by
clothes.

April 17, 2003

Adjustments

She has a studio apartment with
a sleeping loft and a skinny
built-in ladder, rungs hardly a
foot-hold for a size seven shoe.

Her latest couch is a leather love seat,
clearly not for lovers. No hide-a-bed
for stay-over guests. Hardwood floors.
No more cushy carpet to sink into.
Clearly her days of spontaneous

fucks are over, which is just as well
because her back is no longer limber.
She who once turned heads, is now
retired and camera-shy. She who once
had lovers, has two French poodles for

affection, walks them three times
a day between medical appointments
and trips to the museums. She has
many friends in the building which
has a darling doorman. Life is good.

She owns the apartment, is grateful
she can walk, and her memories are
a warm furry blanket as she lies
in her cozy one-person sleeping loft
into which she still can climb.

May 18, 2003

Light at the Edge of Dark

Light dances at the edge of dark,
dipping her in and out of doubt,

teasing her with shadows
while she waits for eye surgery

in a hospital bed. The wait is
longer than the light ray that lures

her like a lover to uncover her legs
and thighs, allowing her to absorb

more for remembering, in case light
takes off without a goodbye kiss,

and it comes to this ..... *Memory*.
She's sleepy as day closes, but keeps

her eyelids open, willing her eyes wide,
while light glides over the edge.

May 24, 2003

Light / Sight

Light from a window
at the opposite end

of her hospital bed
brightens the room

while she waits for
eye surgery. The wait

is longer than a ray
from the sun, time

to absorb and store
light in her memory.

Day closes, light fades.
She becomes sleepy,

but keeps her needy eyes
open to receive the last

diamond drops of light,
willing her eyelids wide.

May 24, 2003

An Ordinary Day

You wanna hear a poem? I wanna say a poem!
Hey! It's not sweet like honey in the comb
It's all about the guts of an ordinary day.
Getting through drudge getting through sludge
all about traffic jams and bills piling up
what gets you through? Words do it for me
they get me wired   in the zone   I wanna grab
those words and make them my own
words boppin up and down in the air
like ping pong balls in a game booth at a fair
bouncing on a blank page rolling around
in a pattern and a rhythm and a saucy sound
ping pong balls with words instead of numbers
but they gotta have a hook to make them stay
to sparkle in your head and not get away
bippity bop they gotta have pop
that doesn't stop cripsy words, crunchy words,
sweet meaty munchy words fuzzy buzzy
wooley words like bees humming in the sun
words glowing like butter on a hot honey bun
words with pizzazz adding jazz to your tango
words for an ordinary day
but what if the ordinary day is crappy?
On an ordinary day,
Joey learns she has leukemia and
Nancy dies of cancer. Billy goes bankrupt
Bob flunks out. Debby flips out.
Sarah has a slip
Marie trips and throws out a hip
Lous gets laid off Rosa
gets laid she's only 13
a woman hits a kid on a bike
she's not seen coming
I confess ain't no kinda words gonna

fix this mess You feel like hell and want
to go down to the sea and yell
LIFE SUCKS But I got news for you Baby.
The ocean doesn't give a flying fuck.
It just says Look at ME Look to ME
I go on ETERNALLY
my tide comes in my tide goes out
ETERNALLY all YOU gotta do is breathe in
breathe out for one micro mini day
and by the way did you see the sunset
last night big orange ball floating on
a tutti frutti horizon then poof gone?
did you see pelicans gliding over
my glistening surface and
swooping down for lunch?
and did you hear the swoosh swoosh
of my lapping waves? Kinda cool huh?
Now what were you complaining about/
and you say Oh shit... I forget...
And on the same ordinary day a kid
wins a spelling bee and hits the headlines,
Nana goes to her grandchild's piano recital
and another kid makes the final out in a
Little League game Maureen finds out
she doesn't need surgery after all
Roberto gets a raise and
Dave gets a 30 day token
and a man leans and whispers
in his lady's ear
the sweetest words ever spoken...
I love you
thus the ordinary day has become
as it always does...extraordinary

June 9, 2003

The Last Phone Booth

she could recall dialed up a faint
ringing desire. Downtown. Lunch
hour. People hurrying past. Cars
bunched up at traffic signals. Horns
blaring. Noisy commotion outside,
and inside the phone booth, a quiet
hum of him standing so close to her.
She had given him a lift to town and

gone along on his errand. He needed
to make a phone call and pulled her
into the phone booth with him, making
her breathless. It was a tight squeeze.
The scent of his aftershave swirled
around them. His hand stroked the
small of her back, reaching down and
under her sweater. She was standing

so close to him. He let go of the phone.
It dropped and dangled at the end
of a long coiled silver metal cord. They
were standing so close to each other.
Then a knock on the phone booth
window, and the bud about to blossom
was clipped at the stem. Snip Snip.
She married someone else. He moved

away. Years later at a reunion, they met.
He said, *Remember the phone booth?*
She said, *You were wearing Old Spice.*
He said, *You were wearing a blue sweater.*
Their smiles said everything else, and
they went looking for a phone booth, but
couldn't find one. They settled for a bed,
resumed what they had barely begun in

the last phone booth worth remembering.

June 19, 2003

Due to the Graphic Nature of

my thoughts when talking with him,
I do not speak my mind.
Our conversation about his product
is yada yada yada. His jeans are tight.
He says, *Do you want the small one
or the big one?* while I'm wondering
if what they say about big hands is
true. I answer, *Oh, the big one!
Definitely!* He rings me up and bags
the bottle of vitamins. Health food
store employees are so uh healthy,
and due to the graphic nature
of the way he places my change, coin
by coin, in the palm of my hand,
I'm a return customer.

June 22, 2003

Night Sounds

A night of deep dreamland sleep
is a one-bathroom-trip night,
as opposed to a couple of trips
or more. I hear night sounds
when I arise to pee, throwing
back the covers, stumbling to
the john. Night sounds
are the same as day sounds,
but as night is shrouded in
darkness, night sounds are
shrouded in mystery or fear.
A car engine starting up by day
is not a matter for speculation.
But ah! In the middle of the night...
A lover leaving? A liquor store run?
An emergency trip to the hospital
or fast-food drive-thru around
the corner? A worker on his way
to a graveyard shift? A robber
making a getaway? It's enough
to keep me from going back to sleep.
My bladder is empty, but my brain
is spilling over with solutions to
The Case of Mysterious Night Sounds.

June 29, 2003

Last Day of the Month

on the first day of the week,
one day before the beginning
of the second half of the year
in the third year
of the twenty-first century,
more concisely, June thirtieth,
two thousand and three percisely,

and my pen skimming across
a faint blue line is on the scent.
My thoughts tumble and words
scamper along on a page,
scurrying to pounce on a poem
like rats on a piece of cheese.
Alas! It's Swiss, mostly howls,
held together by gummy strands.
Oh, for a chunk of cheddar!

Something to sink your teeth into.
You can keep your processed
American, but it's too late for me.
My apple pie has gone bye bye.
Anyone for sponge cake?
Then buy your own damn Twinkie
if you have any spare change.
My pockets are empty,
my cupboard bare. No cheese
in sight. Was it ever there?

June 30, 2003

Marine Mathematics

If the price of a seahorse
is seven matching pearls,
and oysters are ninety
sand dollars a dozen,
how many oysters
would three hundred
sand dollars buy, and

how many sand dollars
would it take
for a bucket of clams?
How many seahorses
would gallop
to the clambake and
who would cook
the croaker?
Who gets to wear
the pearl choker?

July 2003

War of Choice

If we have to have a war,
which seems to be the case,
I'd go for an old time war.
Say one that lasts a couple of
months with fewer casualties
than the heat wave of France
in the summer of 2003...say
like the Spanish American War.

We could liberate a large island
from a foreign power and pick up
some tropical islands of our own
to boot. We could start the war
off by having a Commodore called
Dewey destroy the entire Spanish
fleet of 10 ships (is that an *armada*?)
without the loss of an American life.

Our troops could make a landing
in a place called Daiquiri. Olé!
Sounds like a fun spot for an invasion.
And have lots of good press about
blacks and whites fighting shoulder
to shoulder for the American good,
plus a regiment called the Rough Riders.

Who the hell wouldn't want to be
a Rough Rider under Col. Leonard Wood,
(Let's name an army fort after him)
and Lt. Col. Theodore Roosevelt?
(Let's name a toy bear after him) Hey!
Let's elect him president of the USA.

My grandpa was a veteran of the
Spanish American War which lasted
from April to August,1898. It was long
enough to give him a lifetime of tales
to tell. More than long enough for any war.

July 2003

X + Y = Z

If a man is an X
and a woman is a Y
and they meet and mix
at a Motel 6
and eventually
have a little Z
then X plus Y equals Z.

If X plus Y plus Z
move to a town by the sea
called RSVP
which stands for
Rancho Santa Villa Pico,
where they are known
as D for Dude,
BB for Big Boobs,
and SRK for
Spoiled Rotten Kid
by the BA (for Bad Ass)
across the avenida,
do they have a chance
for happiness?

L M N O.
The BA spells
catastrophe
for the little family.

You see ...
BA has eyes for BB.
One day BA plus BB
drive away in an SUV
minus D minus SRK.

If X + Y + Z + D + BB
+ SRK + BA + RSVP =
alphabet soup,
does X - Y = sushi?

July 2003

Waiting for the Sun

Morning mist merries
heavy hanging arms
of ancient evergreens
with a bridal veil,
an aura of innocent
readiness. We all await
our sun to lift the veil
and lavish our limbs
with radiant embraces,
loose laughter
from our somber insides
and gladden us again.

July 1, 2003

Victoria

There once was a girl called Victoria
Who wanted to get laid in Astoria,
So she drove to Oregon
Where she got it on,
And was in a constant state of euphoria.

It's a long way to travel for a fuck,
But she wasn't having much luck
On the coast of Southern Cal.
So to boost her morale
She went looking for an Oregon buck.

She returned (with a smile on her face)
because she missed her California place.
Oregonians freely fuck,
But she doesn't want a Duck.
She wants a certain Hottie in her face.

He doesn't call, doesn't write. It's the pits.
Victoria is having tantrums and fits.
Whatever she's doing,
She'd rather be screwing.
She's coming apart by pieces and bits.

She's feeling lonesome and not very strong.
Is Prince Charming ever gonna come along?
Be ready with a smile.
It make take a while.
In the meantime sing your own glorious song.

July 3, 2003

Something to Wear

A gauzy black blouse
for a special occasion
resides in my closet
in case he calls and says,
Would you like to?
I'd reply,
That would be lovely.
But the blouse is dusty,
has shoulder creases
from a hanger.
Maybe I'll buy a new one
since the gauzy black
is now a tad tight.
Maybe he'll call tonight.

July 13, 2003

The Too Tired Too Broke Blues

Feel like fallin' asleep on the floor.
I'm too tired to wash dirty jeans.
Gotta go to the grocery store,
But too broke to buy rice and beans.

Wish my bills would fly out the door.
I'm too tired to wash dirty jeans.
My back's givin' out, arms are sore.
Too broke to buy rice and beans.

Wanted kids and I got myself four.
I'm too tired to wash dirty jeans.
My man don't come home no more.
Too broke to buy rice and beans.

Kids are cryin', *Ain't no clean clothes.*
I'm too tired to wash dirty jeans.
Ain't easy being poor, God knows.
Too broke to buy rice and beans

July 13, 2003

Fashion Makeover

Sadness suits you
too well,
sits securely
on your shoulders
like a gown
of muted gray
that became
your bridal garment
when you married
the blues.
It's time to get
a divorce
and go shopping
for a dynamite dress.

July 17, 2003

Perennials

Her well of emptiness
overflows with tears
that streak her drawn
and pale cheeks.
He who placed roses on
her face has gone away,
and she cannot consider
a day when roses may
bloom again. Let her
grieve as she must,
and trust that bare
roots of happiness
are patient and hardy.

July 28, 2003

Insight

A tear drop
can be a lens
for an eye
without a contact
or an implant,
which I discovered
on a sad day
when I saw
through a tear
with sudden clarity
and sharp focus
what I had not
previously seen
through
my scarred window.

I'm not sure
what this means.
Perhaps in sadness
of loss, we gain
insight into gifts
not previously valued
or recognized.
A neighbor
down the street
we had not met,
bearing a fresh baked
loaf of bread,
for example, and the grass,
the green grass
which needs cutting,
grass that grows so fast
and always needs cutting.

August 10, 2003

Private Label

Fresh fruity words and rind
of lines ferment in my mind
until I pour poetic essence
into a stemmed glass of
verse. Rosy liquid slowly
spills, swirling a curve
of crystal imagery.
Fluid syllables
flow and when
the glass is
full and
glowing,
the
poem
robust
and
throaty
with a
bite,
I sip
and
sip and become drunk
on my own vintage verse.

August 30, 2003

September 15th

What separates this day
from the one before
and the one to come
is the *now* of it.
The breeze is cool
on my neck.
A leaf catches
in my hair.
There is movement.
Branches bend.
Birds are busy
with bird business.
This day is alive
with now.
and now is everything.

September 15, 2003

Lemonade and Marmalade

apple butter and homemade biscuits
fried chicken and corn on the cob
boiled spuds with rivers of butter
grandma churned it in a tub
stacks of flap jacks with molasses
slabs of bacon lacey edged eggs
sunny side up and over easy
dancing in a skillet side by side
cherry cobbler and apple pies
watermelon days buttermilk skies
summers down on the farm were great
we ate and ate and ate and ate

September 19, 2003

Rules of Marriage
(after Hal Sirotitz's "Mother said" poems)

Dad never missed Sunday morning mass
at Our Stupid Lady of the Bloody Heart,
(as my mother called his church), where
he met a pretty widow with big bosoms
who needed his help around her house
on Sundays. He said he was just being
a good Samaritan. Mother always said,
don't let yourself fall in love with
a catholic or a jew. Marriage is hard
enough without that kettle of kippers.
I broke it off with Sol Fleischmann, who
became a doctor and takes his family
to resorts for vacations, and I married
Tom, a tv tech, who spends Sundays
on the couch, drinking beer and
watching football on a 54 inch tv screen.
while the kids skate in the cul-de-sac.
I read romance novels in bed and
cry at sad and happy endings.
Mother should have included protestants.

September 19, 2003

Clothes Crazy

The fabric breathes which seemed a good quality
when she bought the yardage to make a suit.
Now, of course, she knows better.
Hurrying to catch a bus, she heard her skirt
gasping, slowed down, apologized and was
startled to hear her jacket snicker. Later as
she looked at a cartoon, the jacket laughed
out loud, and she made the connection.
it breathes therefore it's alive.
She undressed at night, put her suit in the closet,
and shut the door tight. She could rip it up,
but that would be murder. She decided to research
Humane Societies for unwanted breathing garments.
She went to sleep with the bedclothes pulled up over
her ears, thanking her Higher Power for sheets
that don't breathe. She had a nightmare about
disorder in a local thrift shop drop-off bin.

September 20, 2003

Life in Black and White

We divvied up
the black and white
snapshots when she died.

White borders, scalloped edges,
found loose in a shoe box
stashed under her bed.

A pretty girl with bare feet
standing on the running board
of a model T (we guessed).

Smiling wide and waving high.
This must have been her, we said,
Same big eyes, (though not so

sad as those that were familiar
to us). Short bob, dress with a
flirty skirt. *Look at her figure!*

*Who would have thought she was
such a babe. And this guy could
have been our dad...*the slight man,

dark hair slicked back, leaning
against the hood. She could have
told us he was a looker, but she

would never talk about him. The
snapshots of him were few but we
each got one or two of the man.

September 25, 2003

Barbie Joins a Poetry Workshop

Barbie decides to explore
her creativity, thinks poetry
might be a fun hobby and
joins a poetry workshop.
Her first concern,
what do poets wear?
Barbie checks out
a local poetry reading,
takes notes on apparel.
Please God, not sweats.
Her spangle tights
and beaded turtleneck
will probably work.
Next a supply list for workshop:
Dictionary. Look up s i m i l e..
Maybe *smile* misspelled?
Hot pink pen with glitter gel ink.
Light blue or pink notebook.
Barbie writes her first
assigned poem, ignoring
no-rhyming instruction,
as in: try to avoid blah blah blah.
She's like totally jazzed with it..
Ken thinks it is a masterpiece:

There once was a hot dude called Ken.
Barbie knew he was the one for her when
He kissed her with tongue.
And Ken's so well hung!
They've been together since then.

They are keeping it a secret from Mattel
Who would not think the situation swell,
And the Christian Right
Which is so uptight,
And would say they are going to hell.

Ken and Barbie are perfect together.
They are happy in all sorts of weather.
And everybody knows
They have hip clothes,
Like matching outfits in black leather.

Barbie dropped out after the 2nd session.
Poets think they are so sensitive, but
they don't know shit about accessorizing!
Plus ...they didn't like Barbie's poem.
They said it "needs work".
Well, fuck them! Ken loves it!

September 30, 2003

Crayola Introduces 4 Colors to Celebrate 100 Years

I am Burnt Sienna,
one of the five colors
dumped by Crayola to
make room for stellar
replacements. We were
deemed redundant or
(horrors) unattractive.

How humiliating!
However, I was given
a reprieve, spared
by online vote, but
Mulberry, Magic Mint,
Blizzard Blue and
Teal too are gone.

Frankly, I believe
it's a makeover move
for a hip new image to
stem the Magic Marker
menace. The new kids
on the block are Mango,
Tango, Jazzberry Jam,
Inchworm *(what kind
of color is that?)* and
Wild Blue Yonder.

They are comers,
the rising stars.
All I can say is,
Wild Blue Yonder
better look out
for Tailspin Fizzle!
I'm Burnt Sienna.
I will miss my
fellow four.
Color me
sad.

October 11, 2003

Separate Ways

A nice Christian man and single!
They met at St. Paul's.
Sat side by side in a crowded pew,
shared a prayer book which led
to the altar. He was manna from

heaven and she was ravenous.
It all happened so fast, she said,
and she should have paid more
attention to how little he put in
the offering plate, but loneliness

has foggy vision, and she told
me it was too late when she saw
that his wide open smile belied
a tightly closed wallet. And he
had no friends! She felt cheated

to learn that a chilly heart lurked
behind his brotherly love hug.
Now he walks through the house
turning off lights. He pays the
electric bill. She talks long distance

on the phone for hours. She pays
AT&T. They have separate rooms,
bank accounts and cars, eat at
different times, and when passing
in the hall, they draw in so as

not to touch each other. He sits
in his bedroom at night, watches
TV, downs a few beers. She sips
Vin Rosé in hers, reads romance
novels, sews lace on pillow cases.

A *For Sale* sign at the curb reads
*By Appointment Only. Priced for
Quick Sale.* They will split the
assets and move out. They have
already gone their separate ways.

October 19, 2003

Vision

A crinkled horizon seen by
scarred eyes through dusty

louvered windows slanted
open is a wobbely and

striated view limited to those
with skewed vision. Is there

anyone who sees with
unblemished eyes a landscape

free of the cuts and bruises
of life's rumble tumble?

Give him to me. I will hold
him on my lap and rock him.

We will both close our eyes
in peace for a brief reprieve.

October 26, 2003

Boredom

Boredom yawns and shrugs,
takes up too much space
on my couch, wears shapeless
sweat suits, hangs out a lot.

I want to kick her butt off
the couch. Maybe she needs
a check-up...iron poor blood
or something. I yell at her,

Get the hell off my couch!
Go out and play. But I think
Boredom is partially deaf.
She answers. *Huh?* I say,

Look...do what you do best.
Veg all day. I'm gonna boogie.
Boredom rolls over, falls with
a thud, gets up and shouts,

Wait for me! Wait for me!

November 4, 2003

Grandma

She wore black laced oxfords
with two inch rundown heels
from dawn until dark,
and a faded calico bib apron
over her cotton shirtwaist dress

which I had seen her press
with flat irons heated on a wood
burning stove in the farmhouse
kitchen. Her hair, variegated gray,
was pulled back in a tight bun.

I never saw her barefoot,
hair loose around her shoulders,
but I have seen this little lady
grabbing chickens in the farm yard,
twirling them around

until their necks snapped,
scalding them in boiling water,
plucking and whacking them
apart with a butcher knife,
then frying them for the harvest crew
I couldn't make it back to
grandma's funeral,
but I picture her in a coffin,
gray hair in a bun.
She's wearing a faded
red calico apron over
a blue gingham dress,

and those black laced oxfords
with two inch rundown heels,
a Kentucky hill country girl
crossing over, finally free
to run barefoot again,
her hair flying in the wind.

November 4, 2003

The Search for My Lost Found Poems

Almost every poet has what we call,
found poems. Alas, I lost my my own
Found Poems with interlocked rhythms.
As light flows in you can see for miles
the approaching trees and the bright
lotus held high over your childhood...
so curious, so hungry as it happened
every day in San Francisco where

I met a man who said he bought
a boat called Monterey. I asked him
if I could come aboard and please,
would he set a course for Bodega Bay
which has the sound of a rolling tide,
and seemed a likely location for the
notsom flotsom of lost *Found Poems*.

I imagined them floating along side
a dock near a damp tavern where
sailors wait for fog to lift, much like the one
where the man and I sat while he
considered my request, looking at me
with measuring eyes. *And what can you do for me?*
I smiled and replied, *Recite poetry*
for your entertainment while you
handle the wheel. He thought it over.

Do you know the Ancient Mariner?
Oh sure! I lied, I'd read it in school,
a long poem about an old sailor.
Looking for a white whale? I could
make it up as I went along, throw
in a couple of dirty limericks which
I figured he'd enjoy, judging from
his lusty laugh and a backward
glance or two at the busty barmaid.

However, by now, my lost
Found Poems could be washed up
on the rocky coast of Mendocino or
bobbing along the Russian River,
because the man had a different
sort of entertainment in mind.

Well, I'm a versatile performer
and don't object to a roll in the hay,
or a fuck on the focsle, but if

the man sails a boat the way he drops
his anchor, he will go to a salty grave.

I debarked before we set sail, still
searching for my lost *Found Poems*.
I'm hitching a ride up Highway 101
with a guy in alligator boots and
a cowboy hat driving a brand new
tan Jeep Laredo. There's more than
one way to get to Bodega Bay.

November 11, 2003

Friday, November 21, 2003

Robert Frost: A Metaphor is
saying it without saying it

I am writing in a brand new
scarlet red spiral bound
notebook, 5 subject, 80 sheets,
10.5 x 8 inches, wide rule,
and these first lines may be
the most detailed and vivid
description this notebook will
contain. I love new notebooks.

They call me to write. They are
the starting gun of a race to
get it all down in ink before
the finish line, to try to
say it all without saying it:
A billowy gilt-edged cloud
surrounds everyone's sun as
it sets, and lingers in the words.

November 21, 2003

How It Begins How It Ends

A woman picks up a pen
from the table at her side
and starts to write.
A poem? A journal entry?
A letter? You don't know,
but you know it begins
with scribbling about a man
because because
that's how it always begins.

He left. He came. Before
she did. He makes her
laugh. He done her wrong.
He never brings her flowers.
He buys her flowers at
the supermarket.
He picks daisies for her
from her yard.
Buys her dinner...pizza.

He takes her breath away.
He takes his clothes away.
She can't live without him.
But she knows she will.
That's how the poem,
the letter, the journal entry
ends, because because
that's how it *always* ends.

December 8, 2003

Almost There

I am his nana and he
will be ten years old
next week. His party
this coming Saturday
is a sleep over,
brought cupcakes for his
class today to celebrate.
His dad and he pick up
cupcakes at a bakery
and call me on a cell
on their way to school.
I congratulate him,
wish him fun and say,
Wow!
You're almost ten.
He replies, *Yeah,*
I'm almost in college!
I think to myself,
Hey kid, slow down!
The faster you go,
the closer I get to being
almost in the grave.

December 10, 2003

Ode to a Sonnet
(Dancing at the Double Dactyl)

The Sonnet and the Ballad,
a charming couplet,
rhymed in each other's arms,
flowing to the rhythm
of free verse, took a time-out,
close cuddling on a tiny haiku,
then slow danced to a sestina,
while an Ode, his long stanzas
swaying to a villanelle variation,
watched and waited, his eye
on the Sonnet, the way she
threw back her head, laughing
at a limerick. He was entranced
by her lyrical loveliness,
alluring alliteration and yes,
her assonance.
Although strangely at a loss
for words, he longed to recite her.
She was poetry in motion
and his reason for being.

December 28, 2003

Fashion Chic

I am
wearing
earrings,
peony pink
Austrian
crystal
chandelier,
dangling
down to here,
a smidgen
short of my
shoulders.
They
complement
the dress
I recently wore
before you
pulled it up
and over
my head,
tossed it
on the bed.
Peony pink Austrian
crystal chandelier
earrings are very hip
with almost any dress,
and way cool with
no dress at all.

2003

He's the One

If he drives at night
With good eye sight,
He's the one for me.

If I don't like how he fucks,
I'd just say, Oh shucks!
But he's the one for me.

It would be very nice
If he took me to paradise,
But he's the one for me.

If he takes me to the mall,
I'd say that all in all,
He's the one for me.

2003

Perhaps

Give me a piece of paper
and a pen. Let me sit
on the couch and write.

Bring me a cup of tea
and a bite to eat. Don't
expect chit chat. If you

talk to me, I won't reply.
I will be yonder
in the meadow of my mind

where wild thoughts grow
and elusive words blow
across a plain of perhaps.

If I nod off and drop
the pen, don't wake me.
I will be dreaming of

a poem, perhaps written
by me, perhaps about you.
Yes, of course about you.

2003

2004

Too Many Light Blue Lines on a Page
Friday January 9 (2004)

Too many light blue lines on a page,
and I have nothing to say. They are
patient and wait in an orderly way
for my words to take their place on
the line, not calling or shouting,
though they seem to be silently
screaming, *We're not asking for
emeralds or pearls. Just give us
gravel and rocks. We don't demand
diamonds.* I say, *OK OK But you
know you're asking for crap*, and
picking up a pen, I start to write.
Some say it's a gift, to create a poem.
At times like this when the words
resist, I say it's a curse.
Hey! Wait! I'm saved! My pen's
running dry just as I have come
to the end of a page and a poem.
Perfect timing is also creative.

January 9, 2004

Southern California Surprise

ten ta tive
pit pit pit pit
can it be
rain on the roof
picks up a beat
pit pat pit pat
now staccato
pitta pat pitta pat
syncopated drums
come pounding
ta tum ta tum
fantastic
rain on the roof
almost forgot
the sound
of rain on the roof
pound
of rain on the roof
stampede
of drops on the roof
water gushing
rushing to puddle
rain was not predicted
so you can never tell
when a dry spell
will be over don't stop
hoping hear that riot
of rain on the roof
let's float a boat
get down in it
paddle in a puddle
get soaked in it
splash splash
laugh laugh
pitta pat pittta pat

January 20, 2004

Before the Pill

I walked places alone at night you
wouldn't now - too dangerous
Cut across the park in the dark
and looked away if I saw legs entwined
behind bushes in spring and summer,
not winters when the snow-covered
ground drove lovers indoors,
when dirty ice edged the path,
my breath making puffs of steam
in front of my face, hands deep
in my pockets.
Summers my feet would burn from
working a split shift at the diner,
tips piling up in a box in my top
dresser drawer, coins to cover
El train fare to college in the loop,
but in-between semesters, ahhhh,
in-between semesters no homework
and the diner next door to
a residential YMCA,
lots of good-looking guys from out of town
transferred to Chicago, hungry for more
than burgers and fries. They flirted,
said I was cute in my apron tied tight
around my waist. They laughed and
wondered out loud what I looked liked
underneath it the mustard-stained uniform
which finally got grass-stained.
It was summer and I was young and
had hungers too, but I kept
my panties on because mom
always said it only takes once,
which I found out is true, not
on the grass, but in the back seat
of a beat-up powder blue
Buick Le Sabre with a fast-talking.
fast-driving, fast-coming bad boy
with a buzz cut, who flashed bills
and bought beers all around, and

one too many beers will make you
forget everything mother ever said.
That was before the pill...things
change but some things never change.
Still plenty of Bad Boys around and
god knows, they still turn me on..

January 28, 2004

Hazardous to Healthy Relationship

Baby, when I say "Stop",
goddammit.....you STOP!
If you want to learn how
to drive, don't let your
main man teach you.
Take a taxi. Take a bus.
Take a train. Walk.
It takes two to tango,
but run away from
the driving lesson or
risk divorce. He can
teach you how to move
your hips, part your lips,
screw whatever. He can
show you how to handle
a hammer, nail a board,
tie a lure, but for sure,
if you want a relationship
to survive, don't let him
teach you how to drive.

February 10, 2004

Fate of the Fuchsia in an Arid Area

The patient pink
fuchsia droops
from a moss-lined
wire basket.

It hangs by my
front door and
waits for a drink
of water. Rain

or a garden hose.
I fear for its fate
considering

the unreliability
of rain not to
mention my own.

February 22, 2004

Famous Walls

Great Wall of China

Vietnam War Memorial Wall.

Wailing Wall. The Berlin Wall.

The West Bank Wall.

Wall between You and Me.

No trumpets can tumble it.

Built with hurtful deed upon

hurtful deed. Grown tall by lies

and indifference. Cemented

with barbed words. Invisible.

Protective. Indestructible.

Wall that divides and separates us.

Wall at which we remember and

mourn for the time when there was

no Wall between You and Me.

February 24, 2004

Final Respects

Elden from Kentucky,
Grandpa's cousin,
showed up drunk again
in the middle of the night.
Only this time,
with Grandpa passed on,
no one else would let him in.

Grandma said,
Enough is enough.
Cousin Elden
shouted that he'd
come to pay his final
respects to Grandpa.
Aunt Dorothy yelled,
*Then take your jug
on out to the cemetery.*

Which he did, and
was found passed out on
the grave of William Jones.
The wrong William Jones!
Not so surprising since

it was a common name,
and Cousin Elden
could hardly see straight,

much less read an inscription
on a grave stone
in the middle of the night
or even in daylight,
for that matter.

We all figured it never
made no mind to
Cousin Elden anyway,
as most of the time he
was pretty well snockered,

and was even famous
for the various places
where he had passed out,
including the creek
at the end of Richards Street,
not to mention the grave
of the wrong William Jones.

February 28, 2004

The House at the End of Elizabeth Court

The ghost of the murdered
man lurks behind lace
curtains in a murky round
window of the cupola.
Kids on the street shriek at
the sight of the spooky
specter. His pretty young
wife ran off with a suave
blond baritone who gave
a boffo performance as
romantic lead in a show
called, The Merry Widow.
It ran for two weeks and
the pretty young wife did
not miss a performance.
Ladies swooned at the sound
of his voice, fluttered around
his tall handsome physique
like jeweled butterflies round
a dogwood tree in full bloom.
The murdered man was short,
stout, bald and rich. His safe
was discovered to be missing,
as well as his pretty young wife
by police in their investigation.
Sometimes I think I dreamed up
the house at the end of
of Elizabeth Court because I need it.
Three stories, gray frame with
white trim, gables, wide veranda
and a stained glass window to
the side of the mustard yellow
front door through which I
never stepped, but my memory
owns the house at the end of
Elizabeth Court. I am sure of
its sun room with a white wicker
love seat where no one sits.

I can see its spacious parlor,
and dark red Persian carpet.

I have rested on a celadon
green satin brocade settee,
lounged on a sapphire blue
chaise in an upstairs sitting
room reached by ascending
a staircase with mahogany
banister and balustrades.
I wander through honeyed
light of quiet halls, perceive
the sweet scent of creamy
gardenias. I have made a pact
with the ghost. He is confined
to the cupola and I climb
into a four poster bed with pale
peach comforter and canopy.
I am Sleeping Beauty.
My Prince will wake me
with a kiss. Now that
I live in an area of the West
where streets have exotic
sounding names like
Via de la Sopa del Lago Frio
and Calle de los Fritos con Chile,
the house at the end of
Elizabeth Court is the place
I escape to when I need
a break from chores and bills
and insufficient funds, but
funny how a fairy tale can
take a wrong turn and get
twisted. Like last time a big
brown bear woke me. This
time there's a fucking' pea
under the mattress, and I am
watching out for seven little

men, but eventually my Prince
will wake me with a kiss. We
will live happily ever after. I will
keep trying to get it right, though
I draw the line at kissing frogs.

March 3, 2004

On Memorizing My New Baby

I hold my new baby
in my arms. Gaze at
him, fingers and toes.
Count them. Yes!
The correct amount.
I fondle my new baby,
feel his smooth soft
skin, study the shape
of his shoulders.
Look at the length of
his limbs, listen to
his sounds and smile.
You ask how I can know
him by heart. How can
I not? I have created him
word by word, line by line.
He is indelibly inscribed
in my heart, in my mind.

March 5, 2004

March Morning

Crows caw caw
in early dawn.
Dogs pull their
masters along
on morning runs.
My coffee cup is
empty so I rise
for a refill and
go outside to
pick up the Trib.
I sniff a hint of
Spring arriving.
An old guy in
a baseball cap
across the way
winks and smiles,
tests his pitching
arm, warming up
for the game he
has been sitting
out, but *now*
maybe, just maybe.

March 7, 2004

Days of Wine and Desserts

The defenseless
teaspoon drops
out of sight
down the garbage
disposal and gets
the bejesus
knocked out of it
until its clackety
clack clamor
impels a finger to
flip the off-switch.
It is retrieved,
still useful,
though scarred
with jagged edges,
not suitable
for company.
Careless hands toss
it into the back of
the silverware drawer.
It will be summoned
only if all the shiny
pretty ones are
unavailable.
Once I was polished
with a patina
and placed beside
the dessert
at dinner parties.
Oh, those days of
Cherries Jubilee!

March 9, 2004

Sestina for Bill

I used to play Solitaire filling empty hours,
kept myself busy knitting scarves. I would sew
and crochet until the day I met a poet called Bill.
He took me dancing, out to dinner and read
his poetry to me. He was not a man of means,
but we walked hand in hand on country roads.

I am strong. Bill claimed he liked a lady who rowed
her own boat. We sang a love song we said was ours,
he with his deep voice, gentle manner, kind mien,
his warm hazel eyes shining down on me, and also
Bill wrote me loving notes and he would bring red
roses, but I started to notice he never paid the bill

at the diner. It was me. He no longer fit the bill
for Prince Charming when he walked out and rode
off for no rhyme or reason last week. I reread
the many sentimental notes and cried for hours.
All his pretty words didn't make that so and so
less of a scoundrel for leaving. I felt demeaned.

This poet plunged into my placid lagoon of mean
temperature and rocked my row boat, did Bill.
I had been floating in slow serene circles. He was so
hot that my ice floe started to melt and erode.
A tidal wave, he washed away my cool blue hours,
splashed me with purple, shocking pink, passion red.

A letter was delivered which I have not read.
I stared at the envelope as if in a trance, I mean
mesmerized. I was silent, didn't move for hours.
This charmer in blue jeans and a cap with a bill
who had walked with me down a country road,
what could he possibly say to erase my hurt? So...
I will pick up my knitting and I'll start to sew.
Time heals all wounds are wise words I've read,
and I'm secretly glad I danced down that road,
danced off my shoes, stockings too. We did a mean
tango. Someday I'll smile when I think about Bill.
Maybe soon. I find it tiresome to cry for hours.

I'm so much better off than before, by all means,
in a cedar chest dried red roses, poems written by Bill,
in my heart country roads and a love song that's ours.

March 12, 2004

Like Billy

Is the path to
every outhouse
always through
a chicken yard?
Chickens puck
puck as I pick
my way around
chicken shit.
I'm in a hurry to
pee. I can't take
it out and aim
a stream behind
a tree like Billy.
I love vacations on
grandpa's farm,
the barn and cows,
sweet smelling hay.
I play in the loft.
I don't miss the city
except for the indoor
facility. Outhouses
are stinky so I
hold my nose since
I can't hold my pee.
Chamber pots at
night are almost as
bad. Sometimes I
want to be like Billy.

March 15, 2004

3 Line Poems

Ride a sea tortoise to where ocean meets shore.
Seek shade beneath an avocado tree. Daydream
of warm water swirls, of peace and pearls.

The sea turtle dreamed of life on land where he
could rest beneath an avocado tree, while the tree
envied his watery world of mermaids and pearls.

2 down, 7 across, c a r a p a c e fits, but what the hell is it?
Look it up! Domed shell of sea tortoise. 4 down, 9 across,
tree bearing dark green fruit, inside creamy. Easy! Avocado tree!

March 17, 2004

You Could Have Put Me on Your Speed Dial

You say that you will call. You never do.
Enough of weepy waiting by the phone,
I'm off to celebrate my last boohoo.

I thought we were much more than just a few
strip poker games in our personal fun zone.
You say that you will call. You never do.

Words come easy when you want to screw,
And easier to forget. I should have known.
I'm off to celebrate my last boohoo.

I wonder where you are, don't have a clue.
Perhaps beneath a rock, a slimy stone?
You say that you will call. You never do.

I've cried for fucking hours over you.
It's party time! Break out Dom Perignon.
I'm off to celebrate my last boohoo.

We have had our final rendezvous.
I am done with waiting here all alone.
You say that you will call. You never do.
I'm off to celebrate my last boohoo.

March 19, 2004

Do Not Go Backless into That Cold Night
(apology to Dylan Thomas)

Do not go backless into that cold night.
You need a cover-up at close of day.
Cough, cough into your handkerchief of white.

Though fashion gurus know that bare is right,
The scantily clad models, sick are they.
Do not go backless into that cold night.

The shivering strapless girls in colors bight
Dance on cruise ships sailing in the bay.
Cough, cough into their handkerchiefs of white.

Passengers to Minneapolis on a flight
Land in winter with its frigid way.
Do not go backless into that cold night.

Chicks in mini skirts are a lovely sight,
And if they weren't so cold they would be gay,
Cough, cough into their handkerchiefs of white.

And you, a model of unusual height
Curse the cold and for a coat you pray.
Do not go backless into that cold night.
Cough, cough into your handkerchief of white.

March 22, 2004

To the Slaughter House Workshop
(for Harry Griswold)

Gather up books,
crack down tables,
fold chairs.
Leave the room bare
as we found it, spare
as our poems have
become. Take
handouts, words of
writing advice with
us as we go out
the door, stepping
on amputated
lines bleeding on
the floor. Secretly
I retrieve a few,
rescue some
of the severed
words to use
in a *damn good*

poem Harry has
assigned for next
week's slaughter
house workshop.

March 23, 2004

You Skipped Across

the still deep pond
of my heart, rippling
its calm surface
and sank
to the bottom,
buried in the sands
of my affections.
There you remain.
When I am alone,
I sift the grains of sand,
feel the weight
of a skipping stone,
still warm
from your hand,
and I am not alone.

March 25, 2004

A Taste of Trish

is a trifle tart.
She flirts with fun,
plays with words
that linger. Her
fingers beckon
you to enter
the place where
she lives inside
her poems. Go
on in. She says
she won't bite,
but watch out,
she just might.

March 27, 2004

Moving Through the Blues

The pebble is worshiped
in parts of Africa as I discovered
on the third day of our journey.
A hairy man fresh out of the jungle
jumped with powerful feet into
our path. Everyone around me
plunged into serious thought of
danger, but fingering the sacred
speckled brown pebble, a bequest
from a dusky gypsy for a larger than
usual tip, and intoning the blues
that move through twelve measures,
helped me to realize how much
the trip had allowed me to switch
identity. I told the others not to
jump to conclusions because I was
wearing a pin striped shirt with
a Scooby-Doo tie. There's a space
for someone else to roost inside
of everyone, and the newly revealed

me was polished enough for dinner
at a three star restaurant. If you
wait on the shore somewhere
upstream and hesitate, you will
find your nails rustling into
the places they join. You will end
up aging in Youngstown. What is
it like living where the secret flows,
one who knows the power of
the sacred pebble? The gold fish
was dead this morning, and now
close to dusk, I am taken by
the colors of everyday clouds.
If I deviate from the way I usually
do things, a big hole smolders in
the dusk through which I move
measure by measure, humming
the blues, fingering
the speckled brown pebble.

March 29, 2004

Cockatiel Crisis

Empty bird cage!
Grab Max the cat
who arcs his back
at Rocky's shrill
whistle, peers at
him, sizes him up,
hissing. *Who left
the door open?* Slam.
Bang. Too late now.
Kids scatter, dive
outdoors, scan the sky
for a cockatiel on
the lam. Dad thunders,
Who let Rocky out again?
Quick! Check out Angel.
Cool...secure in cage.
Cul-de-sac kids
scramble up trees
to catch a flash of
Rocky. Dad calms
down, brainstorms,
captures Angel's call
on a pocket recorder,
carries it outside,
cranks up the sound.
Rocky takes the bait,
pops up on a branch,
Dad props a ladder
against the tree,
climbs up, grabs
the break-out bird.
Kids clap, cheer,
Way to go, Dad!
Mom pecks his cheek,
coo coos, *My hero!*
Dad preens,
puffs out his chest,
whistles a catchy tune.

April 2, 2004

Tables and Potables

Do I ever put
a pot of coffee
on the coffee table?
Nope.
Not even a cup.
I put my feet
on the coffee table,
dump magazines,
stack books,
drop newspapers,
but coffee?
Never!
Coffee goes
on the end table,
odds and ends
on the coffee table.
It's not hard
to get it right.
Hot chocolate
and tea are
also end table
items. Scotch,
however, is
an either-or
potable and
preferably
put on both.

April 3, 2004

Kings and Things

A king-sized bed holds court
in my bedroom, adorned
by rosy print comforter
and puffy pillows.
Each morning I pay homage,
lean over, bow to smooth

its sheets, barely disturbed
by solitary sleep. My hands
caress its coverlet, a width
too far to reach across,
so I move from side to side,
plump pillows, straighten

bed clothes, as I go back and forth
in a daily ritual. Do I spend
a third of my life in this big boat
that floats on dreams?
It would be a third *plus* if I had a lover.
And it wouldn't be so neat, rather,

rumpled by eager hands tossing
aside bed covers, jumbled by erotic
tumbling. I'd leave it so...a messy bed
telling a lusty tale of sex in the sack.
His majesty could care less about
wrinkled sheets. He'd enjoy the show.

April 18, 2004

one line

one word
one sign
one world
the word
is love
the sign
is peace
the line
can reach
from you
to me
then we
will sing
one song
of love
the world
will hear
one voice
for peace
one line
one word
one sign
one world

April 18, 2004

Seals Versus Swimmers

Those who want the seals to go
from the Children's Pool in La Jolla
annoy a segment of citizens who
say the seals should stay.
Swimmers and Seals, Arabs and
Jews, Bosnians and Serbs, Doves
and Hawks shove and squawk.
Suggestions, discussions, proposals,
reports. It's a difficult solution.
The seals have reclaimed the beach.
Teach your children to not go into
the water and to beware of seals
that do not cooperate by confining
themselves to floating rafts.
The seals think people are daft,
and tides come in and tides go out.
Seals bask and people shout.

April 20, 2004

No Sad Song

No willow weeps
in my backyard.
No dark shadow

crosses my heart.
You went away
and the silence

of your absence
is strung with
beads of sunlight,

with creamy
lustrous pearls,
words whispered

in my ear, your
lips soft on my
face as you were

leaving. The air,
heavy with musky
spring, hums with

echoes of lyrical
sighs and sweet
refrains we sang

with one voice.
I cannot be sad.
Your presence

remains and you
will return, never
having been gone.

April 24, 2004

Friendship

Flowers in my garden are faithful.
I do not tend soil around their roots,
yet they come and go as seasons
segue from spring to summer to fall.

Perennial posies persist
through dry spells,
pop up again to say,
Hi! We were here all along
through sleeping.

Wanton wild blossoms scatter
all over the yard,
beyond brick borders
of assigned beds,
shower me with cheerful faces
like wet kisses
from an adorable puppy.

I want to sprinkle them with my words,
write them a love letter or a poem.
Darlings, I've been meaning
to write and say how happy I am
you stopped by for a while
to color my life with your smiles.

April 27, 2004

Girl Talk

We sip spiked punch on the porch
in late afternoon heat,
look at leafy branches
reaching to snag a bird on the wing.
We speak of things ok, men.

About how we both want to snag one,
and as long as we're dreaming,
make him a hottie with a big package
who brings us little packages
with shiny trinkets inside and roses
ok, carnations.

Make him sensitive and creative,
a Virgo. Well Scorpio, Leo,
Libra whatever
as long as he can get it up.

Actually, we can help out there.
And a beer belly is not unacceptable.
We don't want to settle for less
than our soul mate, but the playing
field narrows as time runs out,
and we may be willing to compromise.

We know he exists, likely dreaming
of *his* soul mate: big tits, big hair,
big lips, swivel hips who does
the Kegel crunch, cooks Thai naked
and tangos and oh yes, loves football.

May 4, 2004

Met a Guy in San Francisco

Drives a cab. Took me
from the airport to
my hotel. He's in a band.
Had a gig that night.
Gave me his number.
I called him to pick me up
when I left. He brought
me his CD. Plays accordion.
Hmmm. Well, whatever.
Lebanese dance music.
I'm not into that scene,
but if his music is
anything like his driving
and his smile, I'm his
#1 fan. Met another
guy down by the wharf
selling harbor cruises.
DJ by night. Poet too.
Freestyle rap. Cool.
We traded poems and
numbers. San Francisco
is like that. Or maybe
it's me. I'm going back
first chance. Elias will
pick me up and maybe
teach me the Lebanese
dance. Chaz and I will
rap by the wharf. I've got
it wired. It'll be a blast.

May 5, 2004

Sunny Saturday Morning

Bam! Sunshine
right out of
the black box
of night.
No coastal haze
that may burn
off by ten, then
again maybe not.
It's an in-your-face
sunny day. Hooray!
Don't know which
way to turn first.
Better head for
the beach. find
a place to park.
Stake out a spot.
Drop towel, mat,
beach chair where
the sand is free of
kelp and pebbles.
Or maybe I'll shop
at Seaside Bazaar,
or hike the trail
along the bluff.
Enough of writing
away the day. This
is one of those times
I wish I would run
out of paper and ink.
I wouldn't have to
think, the decision
made for me. Hey!
Sudden inspiration…
I have a wastebasket!

May 8, 2004

Laughter Matters

Laughter matters.
Giggles and chuckles
carry the weight of
day on their shoulders.
Smiles smooth and
ease our way through
a maze of labors.

When sadness casts
its shadowy spell,
and our tears flood
the ground around
our feet, a smile and
hug from one who
cares can evaporate
the sorry lake.

Laughter waves
its magic wand and
Presto Change-o!
Tears are gone.
The air is filled with
ho ho notes that
chase away the blues,
Laughter matters.

May 10, 2004

Moonlight Express

Flowing hair in moonlight,
white diamonds in the sand,
rhinestones on her hand.

She was dancing flamenco
with a Spaniard from Granada.
Guitars were on the strand.

Purple jacarandas brushed
smoky shadows on mantillas
and sombreros. Melodious

velvet voices serenaded fiery
dancers that castanet night.
They tossed off their shoes,

the dance became a dervish.
Twirling. Twirling. The moon
lowered, kissed their shoulders,

close enough to bite into its
juicy lunar treats, taste its
sultry nectar. The ocean

roared approval and applauded,
Ole´. A tidal wave gathered
them up and swept them away.

under a canopy of midnight

They rode the crest to Bali
under a canopy of midnight
blue and the magical moon,

landed on a tropical beach,
coughed up seaweed and stars,
then made their way past tiki

lights and totems to a table
laden with coconuts and dates.
They drank and ate till sated,

and it was good. Smiling young
maidens in grass skirts chanted
in an island tongue as they led

the entranced couple to a lanai
covered with bamboo and palm
leaves. They entered into a garden

of delights, it was better than
good, slow dancing to a timeless
tune under a conspiring moon.

May 10, 2004

Stayin' Alive in Diners and Dives

Scotty, a fry cook missing the tips
of two fingers of his left hand
sliced country fries in-between calls
to his bookie and swigs of whiskey
from a bottle hidden behind pots.

He was putting up orders faster than
I could slap them down in front
of the breakfast crowd at the diner.
Fifteen stools at a horseshoe counter
stuffed with rumps of hungry bears,
and Rosie didn't show again,
didn't even call in sick.

Only reason the boss didn't fire
her ass outta there was because
she let him feel her up,
sitting on his lap in his private office
with the door locked. I know.
I'd been there too,
only he didn't get nowhere
with me even though
I needed the job real bad.

He needed me too. Who else
would work a split shift and stay late
if Rosie was sick, which was a lot?
That day was a frenzy of skillets sizzling,
empty coffee cups clamoring, *More! More!*
Jumping like hot grease at the edges
of eggs over easy, I grabbed a pot and
started to pour when somebody asked
for a spoon. That spoon broke
the dam holding back a flood of tears!
I ripped off my apron, went out back,
sat on the cellar steps, had a smoke
and headed on home.
Nobody ever said a word about it.

Didn't dare. The boss tiptoed
around me for a while,
but didn't fire me. Seemed like
I was stuck there forever,
up to my knees in melted cheese,
buried under burgers and shakes
and chicken fried steaks,
until the day Tony, a big tipper
who was sweet on me,
popped the question
over peach cobbler.

That called for free a la mode!
I untied my apron, tied the knot
with Tony, and I was outta there
faster than you can say,
Hold the mayo!
Rosie got knocked up,
and went back to the farm.
The boss was busted for
income tax evasion and did time.
Federal.

Last I heard, he was working
as a bouncer in a dive on Kedzie,
west side of Chicago.
Scotty's horse finally came in,
and he bought the diner.

Nobody ever found out who ratted
on the boss.
My money is on his wife…
should say ex-wife,
who owns a dive on Kedzie,
west side of Chicago.

May 10, 2004

Weather Report

There is no fall
in my heart,
no winter.
You may see
a fading flower,
dried leaf
or trace of snow.
My outside
does not match
my inside where
Spring prevails
and knows
no equinox.

May 16, 2004

All Things Considered

My things are scattered
about the house,
here and there without
care to confine
themselves to assigned
spots, books
on bookshelves,
pencils and pens in
a cup on the desk,
magazines in a rack,
scarves on a hook
in the closet.
They seem to say
We will lie wherever we like.
Long ago my things
were contained
in a single brown paper bag.
I carried it myself to
The Children's Home
where it was
emptied into a couple of drawers ...
panties, socks, red polka dot sunsuit,
Patsy Ann doll, little blue purse.
Years later in the solitary splendor
of my foster home bedroom,
quarters for a queen compared to
a stark dormitory with iron beds,
my things had a whole dresser.
They knew to stay there, to not
venture into other parts of the house
belonging to *them* who took me in.
How do things know when it's safe
to spread out and take over a place?
First shoes left by a chair, socks
dropped in the hall. Paper clips.
tooth picks litter end table. and
everything stays where it strays.

May 17, 2004

Breakdown City

The dishwasher broke
down, so I laid in
a stack of paper plates.

The clothes drier
went out, so I strung
up a line in the yard.

The tv picture tube
blew up, so I started
to read books.

The car engine stalls
and a tire's going flat,
so I'm hoofing it.

Money would fix it all,
but I don't have a fix
on how to get the cash.

Why do I feel younger?
I've returned to my youth
when I wasn't entangled

by conveniences. Have you
ever wondered if you could
go back? There's a way.

May 18, 2004

All That Jazz

Licks, riffs and grooves
of my daily life I improvise.
Does anyone have it down?
I make it up as I go along,
trying to blend with side men
jamming.
Truth told, I don't know shit
about jazz or life.
Somebody hands you a horn.
You blow and hope the notes float.
Is it music? Hell, yes! Fingers snap,
hands clap, heads nod if you're hot.
If you're not in the groove,
and ain't got rhythm,
the joint clears out
and it gets lonely,
but you go on playing,
because when the music stops,
a CLOSED sign goes up on the door
and blue notes fade into
an empty cold gray space
called *Silence*.

May 21, 2004

May 24, 2004

I put on the day,
reach up and pull
it over my head.
Silky lining slides
down my hips,
fits like a dream.
Each seam slips
round my curves.
This day was meant
for me, hint of naughty
in decollete´,
its fabric splashed
with laughing flowers.
Tousled heads scatter
petals among pleats.
Irresistible sweet scent
of mist kisses my skin.
Shoes? No shoes.
This is a day for bare feet.
I'm going to play, dressed
for fun, ready to run
barefoot in the sun.
Don't let your day
hang in the closet.
It wants wearing.

May 24, 2004

Cold Scolding from My Refrigerator

I quit making ice
and you cried,
craving cold crunch
between your cruel teeth.
You were careless, Love,
in not renewing
my maintenance agreement.
You bragged about
what a fabulous bargain
I had been, then took me
for granted.
The price of neglect is high.
Take heed.
I could leave you for good.
Beware the repair bill.
The ice maker man cometh.

May 26, 2004

The Chirpers and I Are Early Risers.

I flip the coffee maker switch,
go outside to fetch the newspaper.

We sit on our respective perches.
Mine's a couch, their's a branch.

I pick at an almond croissant.
The chirpers prefer juicy worms.

After a bite or two, we take wing
to join our respective flocks.

Mine gathers at the Plaza where we
meet to walk. The chirpers line up

on a telephone wire. Later we fly off,
alert to a flash or sparkle, glint

of glitter in the grass, shiny word
or two for a poem, string for a nest.

May 31, 2004

Sleeping Secrets

Not all her secrets lie
in a little church cemetery
across the road from the farm
where she was raised.

Some remain in the riddle
of a few brand new shirts,
men's size large, on a shelf
behind her bedroom closet door.

They too are tight-lipped, no slip
of the tongue about my father,
the man I never knew,
the man missing in family photos.

Secrets also hide in the spare room
closet where out-of-season woolens
are stored, and guarantees
for appliances, long since trashed,
are stuffed in an old hat box.

Secrets nestle in dresses
on padded satin hangers,
lacy dresses sprinkled with sequins,
price tags still attached,
dangling like answers to questions
I never had the chance to ask her.

Her secrets sigh with relief and
snuggle down into a deep sleep.

June 1, 2004

The Sweetest Cake

The sweetest layer cake ever tasted,
velvety yellow with fudge frosting,
beckoned from a deli case in downtown
Chicago. We bought it, Joey and me.

Split the cost and traded off carrying
the cake box through streets crowded
with sailors on leave, in a time of unreal
peace between Hiroshima and Korea.

We brushed shoulders with guys in uniform,
hoping to catch the eye of one who might
glance twice. Teenagers, Joey and me,
hungry for sweets and a taste of danger.

We swiped a knife from a Walgreens'
lunch counter, a fork from a 5 & Dime.
And giddy from our crime spree, we found
a park bench near the lakefront and

feasted on yellow cake with fudge frosting.
Tummies stuffed, we lay in the grass,
looked up at a cloudless sky, vowed to
follow our dreams and be friends forever.

Pineapple Upside-Down, Chocolate Mousse,
Black Forest, Angel Food. You name it.
Never a cake so sweet as that velvety yellow
with fudge frosting, or a day so delicious.

June 4, 2004

The Widow

She talks on the phone:
yakety yakety blah blah blah...

Would you believe...?
Barb's cancer is back.
It's the pits. More chemo.
No shit! Check out
the Dollar Store.
Batteries two bits.
Norm had a stroke.
Can't talk, can't walk.
Forget Blockbuster.
Library has videos,
buck a week.
Flo had to put him in
Villa Serena. Goes there
twice a day to feed him.
Says the food tastes
like crap. He doesn't
complain, but she does,
wishes that he could.

The clock tick tocks as she talks:
yakety yakety blah blah blah.
No one to remind her of how long
she's been on the phone.
No one calling, *Come to bed, Baby,*
and warm my bones.
The telephone wires are hot.
Her bed is cold.

June 12, 2004

I Can't Stop Writing the Poem

to fold the clothes. No matter who waits
or relies on me, I'm still a writing woman.
I'll always order take-out.
He folds his own shirts. Expecting that
from me can stop our tenderness.
He won't take me away
from the poem. I'll never get back
to *woman's work*. Now and ever
there's a notebook, a hungry notebook
in my hands, and somewhere a maid
standing next to a phone
listening to it ring,
ready to answer our call.

June 13, 2004

The Caper Solution

Dump your capers
in a strainer and rinse
with cold water before
tossing them in a salad
or ...lemon chicken?

Nobody ever told me!
Then one day I saw
my daughter-in-law
rinse her capers, and
I'm thinking, *Hmmm.*
I guess cooking school,
Cordon Bleu, teaches
a thing or two.

When I was her age,
I didn't know capers
existed: tiny pickled
flower buds of a spiny
trailing shrub of the
Mediterranean region,
in pricey little jars next
to pickles in Vons.

Pickle relish I knew,
put it in my tuna salad.
But since my David's
Betsy introduced me
to capers, my tuna
salad has pizzazz.

I've never rinsed my
capers, so I wonder,
could it be the brine
that makes mine
the tuna of the town?
It's probably just as well
I don't ask, don't tell.

June 14, 2004

Another Kind of Quiet

Last weekend was a kind of quiet
you know God said, *Shhh.*
Birds swallowed their chirps,
flew on silent wings.
The street was still. No rustle of leaf.
Trees stood mute as hooded monks.

Thick air hovered over unspoken words,
ready to smother them
before they could be uttered.
The quiet was heavy with unborn sound.
Last weekend you were not here.

This weekend is a kind of quiet
frothy with hum and buzz. Breezes stir
the wisteria. Nearby a flutter of flight.
Smooth music from across the way:
What a marvelous night for a moon dance.
The quiet is scattered by tire crunch,
car door thump, footsteps, my heartbeat.

The air is lighter than souffle´,
the quiet alive with floating phrases
hushed by kisses, whispers trailing
into sighs, a melody of murmurs.
This weekend you are here.

June 19, 2004

A Last Poem

Every poet writes one, unaware.
Suppose this were mine.
As I see my hand writing words
on the page, I thank God
I got a manicure yesterday.
I should break out my Mont Blanc pen
that I never use for fear of losing it.
Surely it's the appropriate pen.
And I'll pop on my pave´ diamond ring.
I want to do the last poem thing right.
There's no bond paper around.
This battered notebook will have to do.
I have chosen this poem
from the 10,000 I could have written.
But get this it doesn't know
it's my last poem.
It speaks of beginnings.
It doesn't know. It speaks of hope,
love yet to be discovered.
It tells of joy in sunrises,
goes on about promises of life.
It ends with plans for tomorrow.
It's part one of a series poem.

June 20, 2004

Before Words,

a smile in greeting,
an embrace. Before words,
a gasp of joy, sigh of pleasure,
hum at tender touch.
Long since the advent of words,
still a smile in greeting,
an embrace, a gasp of joy, a sigh,
hum at tender touch.
Still meetings with no need for words.
Your tongue has a language all its own.
It is fluent in silent speak.
Talk to me now with your tongue.

July 22, 2004

Saturday Morning Sounds

Sputter of coffee maker,
slap of paper on pavement,
siss siss of lawn sprinkler.
Dogs bark in the distance.
Click. The fridge motor kicks in.

I miss your scuffle of slippers,
your sleepy Good morning mumble,
yawn, sinus snort, stream
of piss in the toilet bowl.
Intimate sounds more familiar
than my own heartbeat.

At first I lingered in listening,
held myself quiet to better receive
waves of your sound.
Where there was only silence,
I filled it with loud music.

There is a place where despair
dissipates, but you don't know
you're there until the sound of
your own humming fills the air.

July 31, 2004

Like in a Fitzgerald Novel

They both smoked Lucky Strikes.
She used a long cigarette holder,
carved ivory, wore a floaty gown
of chartreuse chiffon, a mink jacket.
Diamonds dangled from her ears.
Her scent was Shalimar perfume.
She reeked of reckless extravagance.

It was another country club affair
and sure, I'd stay all night
as always, sleep in the extra bed
in their little girl's room.

They both looked swank like in
a Fitzgerald novel, he in his classy
black tuxedo. I could imagine
a ballroom swirling with a bunch of
swells, backless dresses, clinking
cocktail glasses and cigarette smoke.

Kiss kiss the kid, then out the door they went.
One bedtime story. O.K. maybe two
if you don't whine. Did you brush your teeth?
Nighty night, to the kid Tuck her in upstairs,

then bounce down to scrounge for
cigarettes, booty for the babysitter.
Bottles of amber liquid beckoned
from a built-in bar of the rec room,
a couple more on a shelf behind books.
This Side of Paradise. Tender Is the Night.

They would come home tipsy
and fall into bed. I would have had
my own fantasy cocktail party
in which I was rich and irresistible,
and likewise, fallen tipsy into bed.

That's how the nights ended.
That's how the nightmare began.
Like in a Fitzgerald novel.

August 7, 2004

Fishing for the One That Got Away

She is excited, feels a pull,
hears the splash
of a combination of words,
compelling sounds,
hodge podge of hanky panky,
loose lettuce lattice work
of crusty criss cross crafting.
Sometimes a sparkling word
jumps out of the word pool
and flops on her shore,
but more often she has to fish
tug the words with a tight fist,
grab their tails,
plop them together on a line
where they wiggle
like slippery silvery sardines
until they settle for the scaling.
The pond is deep and teeming
with an elusive prize catch.
Trolling for words takes time
She doesn't mind.
She'll spend her whole life
fishing for a line that flashes
koi in sunlight.

August 9, 2004

High Tea and Headlines

She tugs her sweater close
to hug her shoulders
against the morning chill,
woolly afghan on her knees.

A crease of a frown
reveals her faint unease,
as she reads about militiamen
hunkered down among
mausoleums and tombs.

She sips green tea, eats
crusty toast spread with butter
and quince jelly.
The Shiites are not cooperating.
Rebels hold firm.

She is surprised to hear
a distant rumble of thunder,
a curiosity in Southern California
where it seldom rains.

It strikes her that if she were in Iraq
and heard the same shuddering sound,
she would quickly hunker down.

Turning to the obituaries,
a practice of her Medicare days,
she scans the page. No notice
of a familiar name passed away.
Four more fallen Marines.

Another crease of a frown
as she turns to Section D,
to Horoscopes
and Household Hints,
takes another sip of tea.

August 13, 2004

Haiku Havoc

Haiku is a thing of my past.
I tried my hand at it once,
entered a haiku contest
which led to haiku havoc.

It happens I have a knack
for haiku, however I was to find
haiku taking over my mind,
invading every thought, appearing
in my dreams. Seventeen syllables,

five, seven, and five in three lines...
seems harmless, but beware,
haiku hides behind poems
that are taking shape, invading
their space. I call the condition,
"Creeping Haiku-ism".

Once you are in the haiku place,
escape is highly unlikely.
Out of desperation, I emailed
a friend the following message:

Help! Stuck in Haiku.
Not a city in Japan
but a form of verse.

He replied, *Trish, you*
can stop writing haiku now.
A blessed release!

Haiku days are gone.
I have moved on to sonnets.
Goodbye obsession.

August 21, 2004

Cool Cute Surfer Dude

Will he die of embarrassment
if I tell him he is cute?
My lanky eleven year old grandson,
hair hanging in heartbreaker brown eyes,
pushing my grocery cart to the car?
Finally I say, *I don't know if it's cool to tell*
a surfer dude he's cute, but I tell all my
friends that my grandson is a cool cute
surfer dude. He smiles and says, Hey,
Nana, *do you still have that Eminem CD?*
When I reply, *Yes*, he asks if he can
borrow it to burn a copy for himself.
I say, *Sure, dude.* I guess he thinks I'm
cool too. Maybe even kind of cute.

August 29, 2004

The Weeping Goddess

The sound of her trickling tears
in the fountain
relieves my fever, slows my pulse.

As I gaze at her weeping stone face,
stillness like a bright white wave
flows through me,
quiets my crazed appetite.

I could lift my arms
and fly halfway to Africa,
but I am content to lie here

on a garden lounge,
surrounded by trailing vines
in a leafy green haven,
floating in a sea
of unfamiliar peace.

I am released, for now,
from temporary remedies
of momentary madness.

August 29, 2004

Mist and Memory

I look up, surprised to see mist
enveloping oleanders, cedar trees,
fences, the ruby red bougainvillea

muted to a blur. No hint of fog
when I picked up the paper at the curb
after dawn. It must have slipped in

while I was looking down, frowning
at headlines, having toast and coffee.
It arrived unannounced in the same

subtle way thoughts of you
saunter into my mind any old time
as if they had range rights.

A car glides along the road, headlights
glowing in the mist which will lift
and clear, disappear to wherever it hides.

But the mist of my mind where I find
the glow of your face, remains.

September 1, 2004

Big Black Birds

with big black wings
flap flap flap
from the ficus to my rooftop,
and thump thump thump
all over the roof
until they flap flap flap
back to the catalpa.
When did the big black birds
figure out they own this place
and take possession?
They don't have permission
to roost in my trees,
but they fly back and forth,
with no concern for me.
Their constant flap flap flap
and raucous caw caw caw
are driving me berserk.
I can't even watch tv in peace.
I'm thinking of taking off
and flying to a place of no birds.
Where the hell would *that* be?
Heaven?

September 12, 2004

Replacements

The Belle of Portugal, blush pink
climbing rose sprawls
along the rail fence,
its woody branches reaching
up into the cedar,
and a pink camellia grown
as tall as the apple tree,
still here after all these years.
Me too.
But the Cecil Bruner on a trellis
and an ornamental peach tree,
a passion flower vine and
the orchids, all long gone.
You too.
I haven't planted anything new.
You were the gardener.
The roses on the dining room
table are fake. They don't fade,
don't die, look almost real.
It's easy with flowers.
A rose dies, and that's sad,
but you don't mourn.
It can be replaced.
You plant new or go artificial.
People are the problem.
I always thought your stem
was sturdier than mine,
your branches more durable.

September 12, 2004

Autumn Adagio

Days of early dark.
Lengthening shadows
of late afternoon.
Autumn in its maze
of golden haze hallways
leading to drizzly
moisture laden mornings.
Trees release yellow, red
and brown leaves
announcing the dance.
Bare branches flaunt
spiny nakedness.
Sodden leaves color
the ground beneath
once emerald canopies.
Spring's passed, summer too.
Winter now gathering fast.
Celebrate the season,
this autumn, this fall.
Embrace its bravado.
Dance to its flaming adagio.
Twist
and
turn.
Twist
and
turn.

September 15, 2004

Road to Paradise

She crossed California by night,
and finally arrived at her destination,
a thousand towns away from streets
arched with oaks back home. It was
midnight black so she couldn't see

any orange groves along the road,
but the orange blossoms...had to be
orange blossoms! A sweet exotic scent
that gave her a buzz on even before
her first gin rocks at a beach front bar.

The road over mountains and vast drab
stretches of desert had been dusty, dry.
She stopped for coffee, grabbed burgers,
short naps, gassed up, checked maps,
and pressed on to a fresh start out west.

In paradise at last, with ocean breezes
on her face and the sound of breaking
waves, possibilities sizzled like sparklers.
She could begin again, could even believe
she was beautiful. Wow! What a concept...

beautiful *and sober*! But the acrid glare
of the next day's sun exposed bruises
and boils, dry rot and mold. She was stuck
with the same lumpy body, same monster
thirst, another strange man in her bed.

Her past had come with her to California.
The only way to shake it was by walking one
day at a time along a road she'd stumbled
upon once before. She may try that way again.
There's nowhere else to go. She's on empty.

September 17, 2004

Forbidden Fruit Jam

I took a taste of raspberry jam
when her back was turned,
dipped my finger in the jar,
looking over my shoulder.
Nobody saw it
so I didn't get in trouble.
Two things I learned
when I was young...
Make sure the coast
is clear before you dip,
and forbidden fruit-jam is
sweetest. Its taste stays
longest on the tongue,
long enough to put a smile
on an old lady's lips.

September 21, 2004

A Poem A Day

Yesterday's poem has gone to bed,
snug in its syntax,
having reached the end of its lines.

Today's poem yawns and stretches
its legs, sits on the edge
of the bed, words swirling in its head,

spinning variegated threads of thought
to weave in a web of images
spreading across a page in inky design.

Tomorrow's poem may be today's delight
in a summer morning,
a poem born from the womb of tonight.

September 22, 2004

Life & Death & Bills & Stuff

Her husband's ashes weigh 13 pounds,
including the box made to hold them.

The mahogany box 6 x 9 x 8 inches tall
probably weighs three pounds in all,

That gives the ashes ten, more or less.
It's a lot heavier to lift than she would

have guessed. You think *ashes to ashes
and dust to dust* and imagine fine silt

sifting through fingers. Weightless.
But imagine a 13 pound frozen turkey.

Drop that sucker on your foot and you've
got a broken foot, or broken toe at least.

He said he didn't want to be scattered
at sea, maybe under a tree in the yard.

She decided to keep him close by where he
could continue to keep an eye on his stuff.

So her husband's ashes in the mahogany
box are at home on top of a filing cabinet

where they monitor bills and receipts, watch
as she tries to reconcile bank statements,

as if guiding her in the stuff he used to do.
If he were alive she'd bristle at his vetoes,

but still, she wishes she could hear him say,
Better watch the phone bill next month, Baby.

September 24, 2004

The Beast in Me

Lions with patina on their manes
molded from molten metal,
stand steadfast on ageless legs
with the fixed regal bearing

of bronze beasts. Through blizzard
and downpour, wicked winds
and unruly sun, they reign in front
of the Chicago Art Institute,

one on each side of the entrance,
their silent roars suspended
in midair as they guard Chicago's
pride on Michigan Avenue.

Dare to ascend the broad stone
stairs between them, and venture
into the lair of wild brush strokes
and color, explore savage sculpture.

I did and saw Kandinsky's canvases,
Rodin, Degas, Matisse, Seurat's
Sunday in the Park. *Ohhh!* and *Ahhh!*
were not enough. I roared.

October 14, 2004

All the News That's Fit to Print

Deacon graduated from high school
when he was three. How many kids
can claim the same? Granted he was
twenty-one in dog years, but for a dog
to graduate at all got his picture

in the newspaper. He was photogenic.
Part collie, part golden retriever,
probably the most popular member
of the senior class. Up on the stage
with the principal, Deacon wagged

his tail like a flag at a holiday parade.
The audience clapped and cheered
for him like for no other graduate,
including his master, my son David.
The principal announced both names,

but handed out only one diploma.
Not a problem for Deacon or David.
They were having fun following in
the footsteps of Mary and her little lamb,
continuing a rule-breaking tradition.

We in his family knew Deacon was smarter
and more accomplished than any other
dog on the planet, but now it was in print
for all to read. You believe everything
you read in the newspaper, don't you?

October 17, 2004

Canyon Cat, Feral and Free,

slinked away from the man's
hand offering a bowl of food,

approached the bowl when
the man turned his back,

waited at the edge of the yard,
watched as the man weeded,

prowled in bushes out of reach
until a pouring rain, then he

turned to the open door
of the garage and skooted inside,

crept on top of a rag rug, slept,
let the man touch him,

purred when the man picked him up,
set him on a stool, brushed him,

owned by none, friend to only one,
a man he allowed to stroke him,

ran away when the old man died,
slinked back into the canyon.

October 18, 2004

Giddyup

Desire paws the ground,
prances around my hips,

rubs up against my legs,
swishes its tail in my face.

Desire won't settle down
until my man bridles it

and rides that wild pony
to the end of the trail

where we lie in the pasture
of each other's arms, wet

with sweat and all the sweet
streams we galloped through.

Desire, tuckered out, settles
down, grazes, nuzzles my neck,

sleeps. So do we. Later we wake
at the sound of a whinny, then

my man slaps that wild pony's
rump and we giddyup! Again.

October 25, 2004

Love Conjugated

I love
I loved
I have loved
I had loved
I will love
I will have loved
I am loving

you love
you loved
you have loved
you had loved
you will love
you will have loved
you are loving

we fuck
we fucked
we have fucked
we had fucked
we will fuck
we will have fucked
we love fucking

October 25, 2004

What Is Love, My Love?

Love is a transitive verb.
Lose it as a noun. Don't
use what you can't define.

I love you, peanut butter,
jazz guitar, walks in the rain,
film noir, fucks in the afternoon,
falling stars, salsa fresca
on tacos, iced tea and you.

Not an all-inclusive list,
or necessarily in that order,
but you are always first

and last, my love.

October 25, 2004

Farmers Who

Those who sow seed,
daisies and corn,
zinnias and wheat,
who till the soil
and wait for shoots
to appear, who fear
late frost and pray
for rain, they believe
in crops, have faith
in the cycle of life
from roots to ripe
to reaping. They wear
the harness of acres
passed down. They are
familiar with hard work,
heartbreak and harvest
following furrows made
by their fathers.
They plant and scan
the sky for signs, eat
their spuds and beans
and meat. At night
they never count sheep,
dream of sleeping
past dawn. They get up
in the dark and farm.

October 31, 2004

My First Admiral

Say you have a baby
at a large navy hospital
on a major navy base
with admirals aboard
and lots of gold braid.

And say your maternity
stay includes the first
Saturday of the month.
Guess what's in store for
you? Admiral's Inspection!

You will be told to neatly
fold clothes in the bedside
chest. Don't forget to
stagger drawers open
as you stagger with sore ass

to remove personal belongings
from the bathroom.
Sit up in bed or in a chair.
Your choice. Robe on,
of course. Corpsmen will

bring babies to mothers
from the nursery for feeding
after the admiral makes
rounds. Nurses and corpsmen
will scurry through halls,

in and out of rooms.
Loud speakers will be heard
announcing the admiral's
progress. *Admiral on fourth deck,*
coming down to third.

The admiral will be impressive
in uniform and white gloves.
He will poke his head in your
room and smile. You can
relax. You pass. Babies in

the nursery never cooperate.
They cry continuously,
but they always pass, else
there would be the first
Mothers' Mutiny in history.

My first admiral didn't tell me
my first baby was perfect,
which I already knew, but
he did say I was looking good.
I guess he was worth his salt.

And later on in life when
you are feeling low, burdened
with dejection, it might give
a mental lift to recall that you
passed Admiral's Inspection.

November 1, 2004

Pity the Poor Farmer

with five daughters and only one son,
and he the youngest.
The girls comb his golden curls,
feed him tidbits of blackberry jam
on biscuits.
He's too tiny to help with the chores!
the girls cry out to their father.
The girls milk cows, slop pigs, gather eggs.
The farmer's wife holds the darling boy
on her lap, strokes his rosy cheeks,
gives him the kisses
that the farmer misses plowing the lower forty.

November 1, 2004

The Gold Miner

Wearing my yellow slicker
and walking in the rain,
I brave the slippery steep
slope up from the beach.

I reach the top and
turn around to wave
at the sea and sand.
My legs tingle. My heart
beats like it's going fifty
over speed bumps,

and from high on the bluff
I see a stunning rainbow
arc across the sky.
I search my mind for words
to describe it, to say

in a new way how the rainbow
sparks my spirit, starts it
spinning cartwheels and try
to put those words into lines
of a poem, my pot of gold.

I scribble the day away,
ignore chores, skip lunch,
drink too much coffee,
filling the trash with scraps,
hands slicker yellow with

the dust of hours spent
mining for gold, the pot far
from full. I fall asleep and
dream of a little man
called Rumplestiltskin.

November 8, 2004

At Miracles Coffee House
in Cardiff by the Sea

The fat belly of a bronze sun
sits low in the bent arm
of a pine tree leaning
over a cerulean blue tile table
on the coffee house patio.
We face the sun, Victoria and I,
trolling for words to describe
this place that harbors surreal
in cerise bougainvillea sprays
within reach of the beach,
where walks on the sand spawn
desires to be wild as waves
at high tide, to risk everything
for a honey syrup summer
of molten gold moons,
bronze fat-bellied suns.

2004

This Is Just to Say

(1)

I have lost
your love letters
that were on a shelf
in the closet

and which were
tied in a bundle
with red ribbon

Forgive me
I think they
were thrown out
with your clothes

(2)

I have found
the gin bottle
that was behind

your tackle box
and which
you were probably
hiding from me

Forgive me
if I am passed out
it went down so good
and I was so bored

(3)

I did not receive
the valentine
that you probably

didn't consider
sending and which I
knew not to expect
but I did

Forgive me
I used your
credit card to send
myself roses

(4)

I have put
the birthday dinner
that you requested
and for which you

are late in the fridge
five minutes
in the microwave
should do it

Forgive me
for being pissed off
and leaving

(5)

I have used
the Nordstrom
credit card that

I promised not to
but which was so
tempting and
my old clothes are

so last season
Forgive me
if I expect you
to forgive me

(6)

I have written
another
This Is Just to Say
poem that sounds

similar to the rest
and which have
become tiresome
so much depends

upon a few words
Forgive me
if I just say
Fuck it

2004

2005

FLOWER POWER

Do flowers have power?
You best your sweet aster they do!
Flowers helped to put Encinitas on
the map. Flowers are the feather in
the city's cap.
Imagine a winter of love surrounded
by (speaking alphabetically)
alluring alstromerias and various
beguiling begonias bewitching
bromeliads...cutie-pie carnations
come-hitcher camellias in Cardiff by
the Sea darling dahlias and dazzling
daisies and now I have come to E
but the only thing that comes to me
is ECKE...exciting exotic enticing
ECKE poinsettias velvety scarlet
rosy pink and white infinite
varieties, I could recite all night but
Chianti Red and Enduring Pink are
the latest of the great varieties I
think...now on to fascinating
fuchsias and frivolous freesias
frolicking in funky Leucadia
glorious glads and groovy geraniums
heavenly hibiscus happening in
Leucadia...merry minx marigolds
mixing it up with naughty
nasturtiums & uh oh! Naked ladies
followed by Oh! Oh! Oh! The big O
...orchids in Olivenhain
provocative poppies and passionate
petunias pucker up in Queen Anne's
lace...racy ranunculas in your face
and a rose is a rose is a rose
and everyone knows it grows in
Encinitas it's picked packed and

shipped in Encinitas...
seductive snapdragons
sexy sweet peas
sensuous sunflowers if you please
totally tantalizing tulips tripping
through Leucadia
utterly euphoric euphorbia
volumptuous verbena and
vivacious vincas
W for wildly wonderful wisteria
I'm skipping X
thank you very much
not to bore you
with Latin names and such
y is for yummy yarrow
and at the end of my list...
zesty zinnias that you can't resist.

Any and all of these flowers make
a beautiful bouquet and
this winter of love...spring, summer
autumn too, there's no better way
to say...*I love you...*

Symbols of Encinitas on the city's
official seal include a sun setting
over the ocean beyond a bluff,
a seagull flying above...to the left,
a horse and of course,
a flower on the right.
What a fantabulous sight!
Roses to you Encinitas.
Love and kisses. Good night.

January 20, 2005

No Leftovers

There are no stacks of fabric scraps
in the back of my linen closet.
No cotton squares, no patches
of calico. No odds and ends
of denim, no lengths of wool.
No pieces of you.

I give away remnants or throw them
in the trash, and get past the past.
No going back to make
something new from scraps.

Oh sure, some make crazy quilts.
Not me. I go shopping for a bolt
of fabric to play with, to make
something new. No remnants.
No scraps. No traces of your face.
I erase reminders, get past the past.

Old clothes too, for that matter.
Nothing sadder than an old dress
that no longer fits...too tight,
doesn't feel right.
Don't hide it out of sight.
Buy a new one. Get past the past.
Nothing lasts forever.

February 3, 2005

etc. etc. etc.

I've been assigned to pay attention
to images, to her many many images,
to details, endless tedious details.
Elizabeth Bishop is a yawn.

A nap calls to me. I will snooze under
my part acrylic, part wool cozy afghan,
its bumpy stitches of thick fuzzy yarn,
variegated black and charcoal gray,

with lavender flecks, purple patches
and touches of turquoise in a pattern
of linear ridges like furrows in a field
of newly planted beans, precise rows

closely spaced across its 48 by 60 inches.
Soft and cuddly as a mohair teddy bear,
knitted on size 13 circular steel needles
that flash like icicles in sunlight

and glide like butter on a hot griddle.
Elizabeth Bishop's poetry leaves me cold,
but this admirable afghan, crafted
by my hands, as carefully constructed

as a fine poem created by a poet's mind,
this afghan will warm me as I dream
of writing poetry good enough to endure
and appear in anthologies after I'm gone.

Like Elizabeth Bishop.

February 7, 2005

Ashes in the Dust

It's early this year. Ash Wednesday.
I scan a wall calendar hanging
on the sagging broom closet door.

I remind myself to send valentine's
to my grandchildren. My finger moves
across the row of little squares

as if reading braille. It slows and stops
on February ninth. I am surprised
to see that today is Ash Wednesday.

I close my eyes and I'm back at St. Mary's,
kneeling at the altar rail, Father Foley's
pot belly at my eye level as he presses

his thumb on my forehead, depositing
a spot of ashes. How old was I?
My boobs were round enough to make

me blush when Billy Borden looked
at my chest, and I felt a tingling when he
walked along with me. Coolest acolyte

in the parish. That was then. Today I'm
passing on mass. I've lost faith in sermons
and saints, though I do believe in God.

I see Him in a child smiling at a caterpillar,
leaning to feel its fuzzy back, fascinated
as it wiggles its tiny trek across the sidewalk.

And I pray in places other than church.
Walking past a liquor store...dear God,
continue to keep me safe from the booze

I've craved since I was underage and it was
watered wine that gave me such a fine glow.
At Nordstrom...dear God, please, let it fit.

It's on sale for half-price and irresistible.
At the beach...thank you, God, for blessings
from waves of grace and cloud-laced sky.

I'm passing on mass today. I will walk
a path with God by the vast bluegreen sea,
having left behind ashes and wine.

February 9, 2005

American Gothic

Loud resounding lament:
Oh No! moaned Loryna.
Not another broken ankle!
She had tripped
on the bumpy cement
in the parking lot of
Mable's 24 Hour Waffle Shop.

Loryna leaned to rub her leg.
Stiletto heels were a mistake,
though sober, it might not
have happened. When was
the last time she was sober?

Oh yeah, briefly, at half past
her first drink of the evening,
when the night sky was
a somber black umbrella
scattered with lackluster stars.

Three drinks later it was polished
to a shiny black canopy crowded
with constellations colliding and
comets careening like in Van Gogh's Starry
Night. Bet Vincent had
a buzz on when he painted that one.

Loryna quivered from chill air
on her bare arms. Where was
Oliver when she needed him?
Earlier when she was nude
descending a staircase,
he could not disguise his ardor.

But as shadows lengthened,
as his birthday party
escalated into near mele,
Oliver disappeared
into the bopping crowd
with a loud blonde
in a low-cut blouse,

Life had come to this...
down on the ground
on the wrong side of town.
She saw a tower of regrets
and canceled liquor store checks.
Loryna started to cry,
salty tears stinging her cheeks,
when she heard a screech.

Round the curve swerved Oliver
in his jalopy.. He came to a stop
in the parking lot, hopped out
and picked her up. They staggered
into the waffle shop together.

Nighthawks like Oliver and Loryna
are grateful for Mable's.
Hot coffee would sober them up,
brace them to face stormy weather.
Loryna leaned into Oliver.
He smelled of lime cologne and home.
Maybe sober could be O.K.

February 11, 2005

Hey Good Lookin'! What's Cookin'?

Three Italian meatballs
and grilled veggies from a deli.
Three minutes max
in the microwave.
I eat alone watching tv.
Don't cook much.
Scramble an egg or two.

But if Ernest Hemingway
were my house guest,
I'd be stirring up osso bucco
and paella con whatever.
I'd say, *Papa, smoke*
that cigar out on the porch.

We'd have amigos over
every night, drink Cuba Libres,
swap fishing stories.
I'd fall off the wagon, get sloppy
and come right out with it...
So you won the Nobel Prize.
But that don't make me
one of your fans

Papa's such a grizzly bear of a man.
I'd have to give him my bedroom
with the king size bed.
God knows I wouldn't want to
sleep with him. The beard.

The snoring. The little dick.
C'mon all that
blustery macho bravura!

But Lordy! I'd love his belly laugh
and party spirit. I'm off to dig
a pit in the yard. Going to roast a pig.

Papa'd want a fiesta to celebrate
my new poem.
Olé! Gotta hand it to him.
He'd like my poetry,
say it's as hot as my
chili con carne that he'd
put away by the pot full.

If Papa were my house guest,
I'd shop a lot more than
I used to: rum, wine, chips,
tequila, limes, dips.
I'd lay down the law about
picking up after himself
and not smoking in bed.

He'd start talking about
going on safari,
so I'm learning to shoot.
But bullfights?
Ay Caramba! Corrida? Nunca!
Pendejo baboso.

I don't know how long
Papa'd stay, but the place
would be a graveyard
without him. Hey!
Maybe F. Scott would drop in.
Fitzgerald, you know.
Sophisticated. Handsome.
My martini kind of guy.
We'd get along famously.
I wonder what he likes to eat.
I already know
what he likes to drink.

I might discretely advertise:
Trish's B & B for Famous Authors.
Spirits Welcome.
Liquid & Otherwise
One can only hope John Steinbeck
would see it and check in,
stay a while
Between you and me,
he's my favorite.
Ah, what I wouldn't do to
get tight with Steinbeck.
And I bet he'd like deli food!!

February 11, 2005

You Do What You Gotta Do

Sober clouds lament weight
of immanent rain within.
Shadows handle dramatic effects.
Eager trees toss their leaves
across cement paths in the park.
Bare branches seem to quiver
in stormy weather and bend low.

I pick up a brush and blend,
then rub my eyes.
The strong odor of oils
on my palette begins to smell,
but I'm almost done.

One more dab of ocher
at the top,
a stroke of burnt sienna
in the corner.
Finally my signature
and date, 11-29-68.

Autumn Afternoon in Central Park.

I hope it sells so I can
get back to abstracts.
Tourists are suckers
for Central Park and
the rent is overdue.

February 12, 2005

The Recipe

Maria's face glows
as she goes on about orzo.
Orzo cooked in a separate pot,
then added to the stock
for Italian Wedding Soup.

Maria's hands wave in the air
as she praises the density of orzo.
It's pasta, she explains, but looks
like rice and retains its texture
through reheating which is nice,

because she makes a lot...a pot,
a vat, a cauldron it seems,
with all the chopping and slicing,
dicing and mincing, and
stirring of the simmering soup.

Her eyes flash as she expresses
her passion for fresh basil.
We've been walking and talking,
Maria and me. Sometimes it's
she who listens as I recite lines

of poetry boiling in my mind.
Other times I'm mesmerized
by her steamy affair with squash
and plums, sauces and soups.
Her eyes glisten as I listen

to her rhapsody of recipes,
until we come to a bend
in the road where we part.
I hurry home to stir a poem
stewing on my front burner.

And if I'm as good on the page
as Maria is at the stove,
when you've read my poem,
you will look up and say,
Any more in the pot?

February 16, 2005

Traveling Through

Hitched a ride
on a ballpoint pen.
Wrote my way
out of a town
called Dispair
in a lonely state

of mind.
Followed faint
blue lines down
spiral binder
highway through
stickery brush

and wild flowers,
scary canyons.
Reached impossibly
happy peaks.
Crossed bridges
over flowing phrases.

Fished and caught
a few keepers.
When the ink
runs dry, let it be
in a green field
of possibility.

I will put down
the pen
that saved me
and gave me
a rollicking ride.
The trip of a lifetime!

February 22, 2005

Shall We Dance?

A messy morning.
Pewter gray sky spits
rain on sloppy ground.
I knock over my cup,
spill coffee,
drop muffin crumbs
down my front.

The newspaper sprawls
across the couch,
falls onto the carpet.
The easy chair is stacked
with old magazines
and catalogs for the trash.

The easy chair
where my Mr. Neat
once sat to read the paper,
sip tea, work the crossword.
So neat he ironed
his own pants,
steam-pressed crisp creases.

I pull mine from the dryer
and put them on rumpled.
I don't even know
where I stowed the iron
after he died.

Hat tree, foot stool,
shoeshine box, recliner
all disappeared over time
as I redecorated,
though his whistling
still drifts in my ears,
and now and then I get

a whiff of cordovan brown.
I see him around every corner.
We are dancing. Laughing
and dancing. We get down,
rock 'n roll, do the twist.

But I've decided
to look for the iron.
It's time to redecorate me,
press my pants
and polish my steps,
get ready to dance again.

February 25, 2005

Are you still dancing with the devil?

Christ! Trick questions at seven A.M.
after a multiple gin rocks night.
Once more I've displayed a talent
for twirling a dervish.
I do, *Finger to the nose.*
Walk a straight line, ma'am,
better than morning- after third degree.
And the matter of the missing shoes?
Somewhere in the night a pair
of sandals were flung off my feet
to better dance on the sand
beyond the beach front bar.
Moonlight on waves called to me
louder than you did,
drowning out your *Come home,*
Honey. Come home.
I'm too tired to lift my head to barf.
Must I explain the part
where the cop
made me leave the car parked
on the road and called a cab
to take me home?
You know the part
when I woke you up for a ten
to pay the cabbie.
Were you faking sleep?
It's hard to tell what's real.
We're so good at pretending.

March 6, 2005

The Significance of a Secondary Color

He drank a bottle of orange wine in the course of this day.
Essence of orange seeped into the swell of morning sky,
an orange sun rising over smoldering blackened hills,
orange fingers of flame grasping for more virgin green.
Noonday heat was like looking through orange cellophane.
It colored a street corner where a barefoot boy begged
for coins to buy an orange popsicle from the ice cream truck.
The neighborhood was covered by an invisible orange tent
of heavy sweetness from a candy factory where a woman,
sallow-skin, gray hair tucked in a net, packed 25 pound boxes
of sugar-coated orange slices all the long orange day, fingers
calloused, cut by waxed-papered liners, sanded by coarse sugar.
Underpaid laborers picked tangerines in groves under orange skies.
Evening. Sinking sun trailed an orange scarf across the horizon.
The moon came up, immense orange globe hung low over a house
where a weeping girl, wild orange hair piled high on her head,
cursed orange blossoms that had turned to bittersweet
when her man threw the empty bottle and lurched out, slamming
the front door. He stumbled into the car and sped off.
Sirens screamed in the damaged night. Orange cones marked
a stretch where a car overturned, and a man's body
lay broken and smashed in the road because
he drank a bottle of orange wine in the course of this day.

March 12, 2005

After They Lost The Farm

Grandpa in long sleeved shirt
and black suspenders sat
on the porch swing, while

Grandma in a calico dress
and feed-sack apron stood
at the sink peeling potatoes.

The two in the same room
only during meal time,
sitting at the round table,
boarders between them,

but no words between them.
They had nothing more to say
to each other after they lost
the farm and moved to town.

Grandpa, stooped and limping,
no longer able to plow,
now Grandma on sturdy legs
made beds and cooked

for boarders. Grandpa cried
when the cows were sold.
Grandma cried when he died.
I wondered why.

March 15, 2005

Choo Choo

The pushy freight train
of thought
shoved its way
along a poetry track,
connected more words
at each stop,
picked up steam,
then stalled on a siding.
The engineer
out to lunch,
his destination certain,
has no timetable.
A good thing,
what with washouts
and derailments.
He will know
when he pulls into the
right station.
There will be a poem
flagging him down.

March 15, 2005

Obituary

If you read the obituaries,
you may have noted that
Peter Duncan
passed away in his sleep.
That's the cleaned up account.
Fact is, he had a fatal heart attack
while fucking Trudy Newcomb,
his neighbor's flirty-eyed wife.

The tragedy is he was gone
before Trudy came.
Sophie, Peter's widow,
selected an economy coffin
from the mortuary brochure.
The memorial service was brief.
The dry-eyed widow wore red.

The dead have their own page
in the newspaper. Section B
at the back. When Sophie learned
the paper charges for obituaries,
dollars per inch, she declared,
Three inches tops for that no-good
two-timing bastard.

Did Sophie ever have a word of
praise for Peter? Indeed, Sophie
was heard to say repeatedly,
Peter was good about keeping up
with his life insurance premiums.

One month after Peter Duncan
passed away in his sleep,
Sophie booked a Caribbean cruise.
Trudy enrolled in a CPR course.

March 18, 2005

High as a Kite

lollipop purple tulips
flip flop in the breeze
bold blue delphiniums

burst into bloom
and rubber-ducky yellow
daffodils pop up in beds

and Nana's breaking out
in pink polka dots
on a short flirty skirt

with a lacy top.
Spring's kite is flying high
on a silver string

of hope, swaying in
sweet pea-scented vapors.
Everybody's out to lunch

and getting drunk
on dandelion wine.
Everybody's got a crush

on somebody.
Dreamy eyes all over
the place. Silly smiles

on everyone's face.
Love bugs are biting.
and it's so exciting

twirling around up high,
tied to the tail
of a kite in the sky.

March 21, 2005

Nobody Had a Camera or a Car

when Skip was a kid.
Nobody he knew.

His best friend, Teddy,
was called to matron's

office and introduced to
a lady in a silky blue dress

and white straw hat.
She pointed a little black box

at Teddy, told him to smile.
He did and she clicked,

then patted him on the head,
Teddy told Skip she smelled

like day-old cinnamon buns
that the Children's Home got

for free from Pedersen's Bakery.
Next week Teddy was gone.

Adopted out. That day
Skip told Billy he didn't trust

cameras or cars either.
Said his daddy drove off

in a big black sedan
and never came back.

Then Skip tripped Billy
and slugged him with his right,

got sent to bed for being bad.
Skip crawled in bed, pulled

the sheet over his head.
Nobody's gonna see *him* cry.

March 27, 2005

Painted Lady Puzzle

Painted ladies are migrating,
dipping and diving
on fluttering wings, finding
their way from Mexico
to a cooler place up north.

How many make it?
I've never read an estimate
Does anyone take a count?
Guess it's one of those
eternally unsolved puzzles...

Like missing socks.
How do they disappear
in the dryer?
Six pairs tossed in.
Five and a half pulled out.

Does the ocean boil
when the sun gets red-hot,
plops into the brine?
When did I lose my youth?
Why did you leave?

March 30, 2005

Downstairs People Come Up

for our Friday afternoon programs,
pushed to the front in wheelchairs
by aides, Marjean and Coralee.
Vernon, a volunteer, plays guitar.
We clap hands to the beat and sing.
I'm a Yankee Doodle Dandy.

Sunny Vista keeps us hopping.
Hula dancers. Bingo. Sing-alongs.
I miss Dan. He always used to find
a seat next to me. Smiling. Joking.
Broke his hip. Got moved downstairs
and I haven't seen him since.

Marjean says they keep
the downstairs door locked.
Precaution. They don't want
downstairs people wandering off.
Like the time a crazy lady
with wild hair... I get mine done...

anyways, this crazy lady burst
into the lounge, yelling for Stan...
whoever *he* is. Marjean grabbed
her fast and dragged her away.
They'd have to carry me
to ever get *me* to go downstairs.

Come to think of it...
that's what Dan said.

April 2, 2005

In My Current Fantasy

We drive along the sand
in a silver Jag.
Ripe watermelon time.
Sunset. Your hand
on the wheel,
mine on your thigh.
I shiver. Cruising.
with you so close,
your tangy lime scent,
desire in your eyes.
High tide dashes
at the road. We park at
a Fish N' Chips shack.
Sip wine on the patio,
watch for the green flash,
sing low, off-key,
Red Sails in the Sunset.
We laugh, touch,
dine like bears straight
from a winter cave, gnaw
bones, suck marrow,
get drunk and sated,
collapse in afterglow
that rivals moonlight
on red tide

April 10, 2005

Sluts Have All the Fun

She tosses out
a flamingo pink
ball point pen,
while reaching for
a lime green.

The more she writes,
the closer to the end
of the pen's life.
She lifts them by
the handful at a bank.

Cheap neon-colored
give-aways,
flaunting the name
of Fidelity
Savings & Loan.

Her precious Montblanc,
black princess of pens,
will never run out of ink.
It's pocketed in a special
place for safe-keeping.

It rarely feels the heat
of her thumb and index finger,
burning zeal of a spill
of words, excited scrawl
of scribbles.

Pity the poor princess.
All dressed up and
no place to go. Cheap
sluts in trashy rags
have all the fun.

April 12, 2005

To Be Continued

The violet neon night crackles
with jazzy saxophone riffs,
smells like velvety white magnolias,
raw pine lumber and shell fish
in a sultry gulf coast mix.

A tortoise shell comb adorns
the platinum blonde hair
of a woman with melon breasts
wearing a strapless scarlet dress.
She sways to a torch tune,

tears streaking her makeup,
painting a sad clown face.
She slips into slurred lyrics:
Someday he'll come along,
the man I love. and he'll be...

Christ! Too many drinks
and she thinks
she's a nightclub singer.
I cringe, remembering
another night, another song
long ago.

I want to touch her hand
and tell her it's going to be ok
as long as she keeps singing,
doesn't lose her voice, her way.

But she'll just flip me off
and tell me to shut the fuck up.
I know because I wrote the book.
It's a work in progress. I am
the first chapter and the second.

Actually it's a work in progress.
It's true I'm coming close to the end
but the excitement is not over.
You'll be pleased to know I'm
saving the best for last and I'll
be sure to create a happy ending
I'm a sucker for happy endings.

April 16, 2005

Wet Paint

stops me from sitting
on my favorite bench
to watch ducks glide
on a pond in the park.

A dark green smudge
on the tip of my finger
reveals that the paint
is still wet, tacky.

I couldn't resist.
Like when I see a sign
at the beach that reads
Dangerous Rip Tide,

I have a sudden urge
to feel the tug of a rip.
What is it that makes
us want to cross over

the line of a posted
No Trespassing?
The flag of desire is
marked *Forbidden.*

My life is spiced by
times I crossed the line,
leapt off a railroad
trestle into a lagoon

and survived,
excited to be alive,
shaky and wet,
but with no regret.

April 22, 2005

It's All Relative

I want to be a bad girl,
slap that mean kid,
captain of B Team.
He always picks me
last for his side, says
I'm slow, too fat.

I want to get sent to
my room by my dad,
telling me not to
come out until I'm
ready to apologize.
It won't ever happen.

I don't have a room.
Don't have a dad.
But if I did, I'd grab
my cat, a tabby,
stomp to my room,
slam the door, flop

on my bed, cover up
with my very own quilt
made by my very own
grandma, hug my cat
and cry myself to sleep.
I'd be in heaven.

April 24, 2005

Slam

Hi...I'm Nana
known to some as Naughty Nana
naughty but VERY nice
in truth I'm a two-timing bitch
caught in a tryst with an audience
while getting it on with words
and worse...in a torrid love affair
with verse...
kind of a kinky threesome
the French call it ménage à trois
oh those French! They make
cheese sound sexy and seductive...
voulez vous fromage?
I call it deep dish apple pie a la mode
HOT deep dish apple pie a la mode
French vanilla ice cream dripping
down my chin...me with a grin...
mmm...crust to lust for...filled with
succulent sweet spicy apple slices
to die for...
ice cream buttery rich
which brings me back to the stage...
here I am at the La Paloma...
home of the Full Moon Poetry Slam
Hot Damn! Slam land in Encinitas
and you...the audience...
belong to me for three whole minutes
not much time to make you mine
but I'm gonna get down and
turn you on...I know what you like
and how you like it...I know words
I know how to hold your attention

not to mention your...well
we're not going there

I'm aware of your hearty party
appetite for sexual innuendo
and I do intend to please you

but it's not just a score
I'm going for...the most points
in the joint to anoint a winner
oh no...much more...
much more than a score.

I'm a poet and I want you
to know it

and if one of my lines
stays in your mind
for reflection...
I've made a connection
It's YOU I adore
what I come here for...
you and the words
and although tonight
you're horny and hot
for what I've got...
I need to know before I go
to it and do it...
Will you respect me
in the morning?

May 1, 2005

I Wonder

I wonder the color of his ashes.
Some shade of gray or black,
like the color of the day he died,
or the color of gloom
in every room with him gone.
His ashes are heavier
than I would have guessed,
at rest in the mahogany box
with an embossed cross
on the top. But what color?

May 7, 2005

Fridays

I wish I could say
we go to Julio's
on Fridays...
do the cantina thing...
cerveza, tortilla chips,
guacamole,
mariachis. Olé!
Eat fajitas. Clink
glasses...salud!
The whole enchalada.

But we don't do
a fucking thing
on Fridays.
All week long
we look forward to
going to Julio's
on Friday and
by Friday afternoon,
we can barely drag
our bones home
from the office.
Flop on the couch,
put up our feet,
stare at a blank tv.
Too tired to look
for the remote.

Who the hell
goes to Julio's
on Fridays?
Teens on speed?
We're past that scene.
Guess we'll have to
wait until we're retired
to go to Julio's
on Fridays.

May 9, 2005

It's What You Make It

Puffs of whipped cream
from a squirt can
mound up in the bottom
of my coffee cup.
It's a Sunday morning
kind of treat and this is
only Thursday.

I like mixing it up,
wear hot Saturday night
dangle earrings
on my Monday morning walk,
holiday rhinestone bangles
on my wrist as I reach
for a can of tuna
in the Canned Meats
aisle at Von's.

And underneath my jeans,
a lacy scarlet thong,
excellent accessory
for a torrid tryst.
You never know,
at least I like to think so.

Makes a walk down Dairy
an adventure,
a stroll through Soups
an escapade from
the same old same old.

I'm a diva in Deli,
a super star in Spices
a biker in Bakery.
I'm a Lettuce Head Hunter
on a Supermarket Safari.

May 12, 2005

Worst Case Scenario

Ten years ago I was trying
to lose ten pounds, my novel
was stuck on page eight and
Mr. Right nowhere in sight.

Ten years ago my visa was
maxed out, car in the shop
for body work and my body
crashed on the couch.

Ten years ago I was out of
cigarettes. It was raining,
my ceiling leaked
and the rent was overdue.

Ten years ago I cried.
Could things get any worse?
Indeed...I could be
ten years older.

May 16, 2005

Listening to the Radio

Pillow under my head,
drone of an announcer's
voice drifts over from
my husband's side of the bed.
Game tied up, one man on,
two out in bottom of the ninth.
It's a double header,
so there's no
bunching up tonight.
I moaned,
*You love baseball more
than you love me.*
But he didn't hear past
the cheers for a homer.
After my husband was
called up to the Big Ballpark
in the sky, it was just me
and the radio, still tuned
to the same station.
I tried to turn the dial,
but a heart string
stopped my hand.
Bases loaded,
pinch hitter at bat,
reliever on the mound,
full count, and I swear
the empty side of the bed,
where sheets remain
cool and smooth,
rumples a tad.

May 26, 2005

Medium Point. Black Ink

Not blue. Never blue.
Wide rule lined paper.
Can she write a poem
with fine point and blue ink
on narrow lined paper?

We will never know.
She'd rather use
a #2 pencil than blue ink
from a fine point.

It's one of those weird
writer things. Like clothes.
She knows she writes
better in a black robe
over a silky red nightgown.

And bare feet. Two cups of coffee
and she's off on a writing
safari. Two martinis work better,
but two were never enough,
and after three, it's slippery
steep slope where a poem
stumbles and falls on its ass.

So it's coffee and a black robe
over a silky red nightgown,
and a medium point pen with
black ink on wide rule
lined paper. And bare feet.

June 6, 2005

The Glory of the New Computer

She has arrived. She's gotta G5.
Don't mess with her.
She's gotta 10.4 processor.
That's the fact, Jack.
She's gotta new iMac.
It's a sexy machine, lean and mean
with a great big 20" flat screen.
It's a Tiger. Hear it roar!
It's better than the macs before.
It's so quiet. You oughta try it.
You'll wanna buy it.
You think you're fine with a system 9.
Well, think again. You need a system 10.
It's so easy, Honey.
You don't need money.
It's practically free. See ....
all you gotta do is sign on the dotted line.
0% interest for tons of time.
Yes indeed. She's got high speed internet.
The girl's all set and yet .....
Just the other day I heard the girl say,
FUCK! It won't start up.
Just my luck to get an apple
that's a lemon.
I'm screwed. Now what do I do?
Where's that toll-free number
for the dumb and dumber?
She's frantic and ranting as she looks
and moans when an automatic voice
gives her a choice of options.
She yells, *Help*,
feels like she's tangled in kelp,
drowning in a sea of tears,
her worst fear realized ...
There Is NOBODY Out There.

But story goes on and on.
Yes, there's more. It's such a bore.

She finally gets through, says,
What do I do? She gets to know
every Tom, Dick and Joe
on the Help line.
She knows them all. *Hi there, Paul.*
How are things in the Philippines?

SBC DSL ... swell. AOL makes her wanna yell.
And screw Yahoo. She can't get through
on anything if her computer doesn't power up.
She wants to throw up when her kid says,
Grow up, Mom

and don't burn your return policy.

You might need it as she did.
I kid you not, and now she's got
a NEW new computer.
All she had to do was say,
Things ain't goin' my way.
The store arranged a simple exchange.
Then another install and all in all,
she's operational. Sensational!

And the best advice she ever got was NOT
from a technician. A wise friend said,
Try going back to bed.
Which actually helped by clearing her head.

And when she awoke, the words she spoke
were, and I quote, *Fiddle dee dee!*
I'll think about that tomorrow.
(words borrowed from Scarlett O'Hara
in Gone with the Wind)
The End

June 15, 2005

June 18, 2005

The moment when he said, P*erhaps you can't*
handle it. Maybe you had better stop,
was precisely when she shed her pants,
when she was almost bare and steamy hot.
And there would always be a scarlet A
emblazoned on her memory of that day.

June 18, 2005

Insert Me Like a Comma

into your life line.
Dash me Dash me Dash me
across your page.
Place your parentheses
around my phrases.
Apostrophe me
into your contraction.
Hyphen me in-between
your double-word nouns.
Put my exclamation mark
after your expletive.
You need me
to punctuate you
and I want you
period.

July 1, 2005

Cheerio Spagettio Oreo Blues

**I got the Cheerio Spagettio Oreo Blues...
oh brother!
summer vacation is bad news for mother**
kids out of school don't know what to do
mom, I'm bored good Lord!
2nd day of summer vacation
and I've already used up my ration
of patience read a book cut the grass
quit sittin' on your ass watchin' tv
leavin' dirty plates in the kitchen sink
do you think I'm your maid?
I'm not gettin' paid
**I got the Cheerio Spagettio Oreo Blues...
oh brother!**
kids out of school don't know what to do
I can tell them what get off of your butts
make your beds that's what I said
pick up your clothes quit pickin' your nose
straighten up this place
take that frown off your face
take out the trash quit sittin' on your ass
I got the Cheerio Spagettio Oreo Blues
kids out of school don't know what to do
chores aren't cool kids want to play
all day every day
mom mom you don't understand
we NEED to go to Disneyland
mom mom kids beseech take us to the beach
take us to the mall buy us all more stuff
we don't have enough stuff CD's iPods DVD's
mom mom please please
**I got the Cheerio Spagettio Oreo Blues
and a doozy of a headache a mega migraine**
do I have to explain? Pardon me while I referee
the latest bout I hear a shout
mom mom he socked me in the eye
she starts to cry he replies she was starin' at me
you don't care it's not fair
and on and on to eternity

I got the Cheerio Spagettio Oreo Blues
I'm goin' crazy lazy kids layin' back eatin' snacks
I'm runnin' outa food outa energy too
I'll tell you what I gotta do
because I'm going out of my mind
unless I find a private place my own space
where I can hide
gonna crawl inside the dryer
spin round and round
and never get found
**I got the Cheerio Spagettio Oreo Blues...
oh brother!
summer vacation is bad news for mother**

July 7, 2005

It Was As If

you never existed.
No more tangy lime scent.
No remembrance
of your solid broad shoulders

and long legs sprawled over
mine. No tune we danced to
playing in my mind, and I'm
surprised by a feeling of peace

as my heart beats steady, slow.
I don't know what turn I took to
reach this place. I no longer see
your face everywhere I look.

And the fever has passed.
At last I breathe evenly, deep.
I sleep without dreaming,
and wake hungry for fresh fruit.

July 11, 2005

The House Yawns

The girls are gone.
Layers of quiet
are piled high
to the ceiling
in every room.
Scattered sandals
and half-empty
coffee cups on
end tables
have vanished.
Order has taken over.
I miss the soft chaos
of pillows and blankets
covering the floor,
donuts half eaten.
towels draped
on door knobs.
A whirlwind of girls
and grandkids hurling
hugs and kisses,
chatter and laughter
to the rafters.
We yawn, the house
and I. It's our nap time.
We will dream the girls
come back to wake us,
then shake us up again.

July 28, 2005

Coming Home

We turn our faces to each other
as you speak creamy bon bons.
Your voice can persuade
stubborn stones to scramble
into the core of a fiery volcano.
Over the roadblock of reason
we tumble.
Wild roses know our secrets,
scatter petals in our path.
Dragonflies dip and dart.
Somewhere thunder.
My heart? We move in
eloquent unison.
Our sighs murmur sonnets,
kisses whisper bliss.
Hot honey lava heals
the sting of my need.
Here at the peak
where we ache to stay,
I have forgotten the place
calling me home.

August 8, 2005

That Summer of Love

a housewife cruising up the coast
picked up a hitchhiker in
faded jeans and bright tie dyed tee
Sun-streaked hair to his shoulders.
Head band. Backpack.
Dusty tan leather sandals.
Carried a sign: San Francisco.

Everybody on the road was
headed to Haight Ashbury,
Everybody but the housewife
putting three squares daily,
well, maybe two, on the table
for her tribe between time-outs
with hippie artists, Pied Pipers

to the flower child inside her,
passing around the pipe and a jug
of red, haze of incense in the air.
So she picked up a hitchhiker
in jeans and sandals. She too,
in jeans and tee shirt, barefoot,
her bra abandoned, scent of
patchouli oil on her tan skin.

The hiker paradise in his eyes,
a wide smile inviting her into the sky
with fireworks. How do I know this?
Honey, I filled half a journal
with lines of ecstasy on the beach.
We were all there, mellowing out
in psychedelic glow. Tripping.
Some of us survived to sigh about it,

and some to write about it.

August 13, 2005

Antarctica

Nothing colder than an I.C.U.
Cold bright lights. Cold white

sheets soon to be stripped from
a cold narrow bed. The doctor's

voice frigid, *He's gone.* Avalanche.
I've lost my equator. I'm freezing,

numb, buried deep in snow.
We were supposed to sail away

together into the sun. Now he's
gone, and I'm adrift on a ice floe.

August 14, 2005

Skipping Stones

It takes a keen
eye to pick the
right skipping
stone. Smooth.
Flat. Its weight
in your palm
not too light.
Like men.
You pick right
and he skips
across your
surface with
enchanting
ripples. Your
heart skips
beats before
he sinks into
your pool of
memories.
Some make
a big splash
and are gone
with a thud.
Others keep
on skipping
across your
dreams.

August 15, 2005

Weather Report

The fog feels like rain,
The garden needs sun,
mourns a loss of intrigue
between light and shadow.

A chilly gray blanket
enfolds my soul.
I long for July's heat,
a sky swollen
with golden promise.

I want to run once again
on the beach in the sun
salt air kissing my skin,
and my feet welcome
the embrace of sand.

August 20, 2005

Night Sounds

Windows open wide.
Hot summer night.

Dark.
Cicadas screech.

Crack of gunshot
down the block.

Then quiet.
Did somebody die?

Can't get back
to sleep.

Now a siren
stabs the silence.

Might as well get up.
Turn on the tv.

August 27, 2005

Katrina

A raging beast howls and leaps
through the breach,
surges to devour the city.
Behold! That which was foretold
has come to pass ...
the last sad day for thousands,
and more in despair,
the devastated who waited for
help from a sleeping giant
so slow to wake.

September 4, 2005

Pucci Gucci Donatella Versace
Mount Suribachi camouflage green
dressmaker dummies in frozen poses with
featureless faces wear in style high fashion
gowns of passionate brown and burgundy
brocade with laces cuffs ruffles and petticoats
accordion pleats draped and shaped by pricey
designers scattering sequins and zig zagging
pinking shears cutting across imported
raw silk pastel tinted taffeta wide wale
corduroy with saddle-stitched seams
Snow White and her entourage
seven cute little men in
vintage Disney make
an appearance while
Cinderella twirls
in a yellow dirndl skirt
a retro look that doesn't work
flighty parrots on fashion show
runways flirty birds in bright feathers
scarlet macaws strut and squawk
parakeets and cockatiels in latest spring
greens & blues for the cruise set preen & flap
wings a nymphet sings on a stage & tables are
laden with dozens of donuts maple glazed crumb
and banana nut muffins chocolate chip cookies and
cinnamon buns but the big bowls of donut holes have
disappeared along with Cinderella in size 9 spectator
pumps yummy treats are ignored by paddle flat models and
swizzle stick starlets though scurrying rats have a razzle dazzle
blast nibbling sweets after packing Cinderella off to the castle in a cab
having reneged on the coachmen gig insisting silly suits with lacy bibs
are a fashion faux pas but the nitty gritty is that Donna Karan saw Calvin Klein
smashing the pumpkin declaring Darling it's so totally last season pathetically
passé
and this
year's
fashion
night
mare
it's
gotta
go

In Vogue
September 16, 2005

SUNDAY HEADLINES 9-25-05

FASHION WEEK IN NEW YORK
RITA BATTERS THE GULF COAST

HEMLINES ARE UP
LEVEE DOWN IN NEW ORLEANS

RED-CARPET-READY DESIGNS DAZZLE
RED CROSS STATIONS SWAMPED

FASHION LINES DELIVER DIVA DRESSES
FEMA DELIVERS SURVIVAL SUPPLIES

GARMENTS FOR WEARING TO GALA EVENTS
GARMENTS FOR WADING IN TOXIC WATER

FASHION WEEK IN NEW YORK
RITA BATTERS THE GULF COAST

September 25, 2005

Wood Chippers & A Mother's Guilt

Unruly shrubs
grown tall as trees
have come down
in half a day.
45 years they grew
wild and free.
Like my 4 kids
who grew up in
this old house.
The shrubs,
gnarled branches
twisted and tangled,
are gone.
Like my 4 kids.
But the kids didn't
disappear into
a buzzing
wood chipper.
Though I confess,
in times of stress,
I used to wish...
...well

September 25, 2005

Lullaby on Tracks

Engineers wave,
conductors lift caps
to the kid on the
sidewalk across
from the tracks.
The kid with
skinned knees,
short bob and
bangs, standing
in front of the
Children's Home
where she's lived
long enough
to trust the 8:29
to be on time.
The passing train
is more familiar
than family and
more reliable
than mommy
who comes
to visit her
now and then.
The train whistle
coming through
calls to its friend:
Whoo oo Whoo oo
Her constant
companion is
a moving picture
show, more
exciting than
Saturday afternoon
double features at the
Rialto on Chicago St.
Hobos in boxcars,
uniformed soldiers
in troop trains,
mile-long freights,

cabooses with
red lanterns at the
end of dusty cars
bearing names
of every railroad
line in the USA:
Burlington, L & N,
B & O, Santa Fe,
Northwestern,
names taking
her to places in
her mind. She
says them by
heart, recites
them like nursery
rhymes, falling
asleep to the
only lullaby
she's ever heard.
Chugga Chugga
choo choo
Whoo oo oo
Whoo oo oo

October 7, 2005

So It Has Come to This...

Happiness is a cup
of hot coffee
early in the quiet dawn,
before the spawn of
a *Things to Do* list,
before anybody else is up,
while my hands hug
a cup of high
mountain brew,
before I remember you
are gone and there is
no anybody else.

October 7, 2005

The Vanilla Man

When grandma put on her pretty pink apron
saved for best, I guessed
The Vanilla Man would be stopping by.

A few times a year he'd come through
in his Ford, wearing a suit and carrying
a case filled with vanilla and spices.

A fresh apple pie on the sideboard
and gold-rimmed pie plates set out
also spelled something was up.

Grandpa would eye the prize apple pie,
make as reaching for it, winking at me.
Grandma'd slap his hand and snap, *Later.*

We all knew the first slice would be served
to The Vanilla Man after business was done.
But first he would slowly twist off the cap of

a little dark bottle, lift it to Grandma's face
leaning down, his hand so close to her lips,
enticing her with, *Get a whiff of this, Mattie.*

It used to be *Ma'am* way back in the past.
Grandma'd close her eyes and breathe in,
then sit back and smile. Visions of spice?

I'll take umpteen bottles of that, she'd say.
A baking lady needs a lot of vanilla.
When I was a kid I used to wonder how

grandma knew that Today Is the Day.
Now I know she stored every thing he said
in her head, his return date checked in red.

Nothing like the scent of vanilla to put
spring in your step, roses on your cheeks.
My Vanilla Man is due in two weeks.

October 22, 2005

Repartee and Reverie

Coffee house. Five, six years back.
Ordered coffee of the day. No latte crap.
Guy sitting at a table against the wall.
Black leather jacket. Light blue

dress shirt open at the neck. No tie.
Shades. A stranger. Empty chair
across from him. I sit and sip. He looks
up from his paper, says, *Hi Beautiful!*

I've been waiting for you.
Yeah. Right. Like I wish. In fact,
a lift of his brow questions
what the hell I'm doing in his space.

I'm brash, ask, *You from out of town?*
Chicago, says he. *No shit!* says I.
My hometown. *What high school?*
Fenwick, says he. Catholic boys high.

Did he know the Foley brothers?
Went there too. Lived over on Scoville.
Then the guy asks what I do for fun.
I'm a poet, I reply. On the spot he quotes:

To make a prairie it takes blah blah blah.
Four, five lines. Emily Dickinson.
Then he stands and hands me his card.
Send me some of your stuff. I did.

Never heard back. End of story? Not quite.
I looked up and learned the Dickinson,
still recite it by heart, and often in reverie
I see the stranger sitting there, wearing

a black leather jacket, see him put down
his newspaper and look over at me,
the lift of his brow, and now
I see a prairie, one clover and a bee.

October 24, 2005

Compulsion

I never tasted Sangria
which came out after I sobered up.
Sangria sound of samba nights,
serenades, castanets, passion.
I went for passion a lot. Never lasted
past three drinks, but wow! The glow!
I've narrowed my addictions down to writing.
Laying it all out on the page. It's a way of
giving it away. And by the way, I wonder if
a Cosmopolitan is better than a Martini.
No. Couldn't be. My current drink of choice
is hot coffee. Strong hot coffee. I need it,
really need it, to keep me going because
I can't stop writing.

November 1, 2005

Postpartum Debut

My legs sleek in nylons. Nylons!
My face surprised by glossy plum
lipstick, black mascara. Mascara!

We take off for a night on the town.
Just the two of us, mommy and daddy.
I feel naked without a diaper bag,

baby blanket, bundle on my hip.
and as weightless as tiny flowered
baby's breath, nearly as excited as

when my baby first smiled at me.
But I'm lost outside the nursery.
No clue what to do, how to

talk to grownups. I'm searching
for *Me* inside mommy.
Where is she? I need her now.

She'd know how to act, how to talk.
She had moxie. I'd give
almost anything to get her back.

But not my baby. Not my baby.

November 4, 2005

Monster Manual

A Fed Ex man will deliver
a huge carton to your door.
He will hand you a clip board,
tell you to sign on the dotted line.

You will stare at the carton,
scratch your head and say,
A carton big enough to hold
a dishwasher. Too heavy to lift.

Too big to fit inside your door.
Impossible to ignore.
You will call Fed Ex for a pickup,
be put on endless musical hold.

Thunderous growls and thumps
will erupt from inside the carton.
You will shudder, grab a skillet,
butcher knife, broom, bug spray,

finally be inspired to tape a sign
on the carton. FREE in large letters.
A pickup will stop, two guys get out,
hoist the carton, haul it off.

Do not be lured into thinking
you are rid of your monster.
You will suddenly see its
grotesque leer and bulging eyes

in the hall closet, behind
the shower curtain,
in the back seat of the car,
and it will freak you out.

The best defense is to welcome it in.
Monsters are not without fear.
Embraces disarm all sorts of
beasts, make them disappear.

November 11, 2005

Aubade

I wake at dawn
without an alarm.
I've never been late
at my desk in
all these years.

You, my love,
who married
your child bride,
are retired and
take your time

in rising.
Once it was you
who took your leave,
let me sleep
while I could before

our babies cried out
and got me up.
Now the babies grown
tend to their own.
Soon I too, retire

and we will stay
in each other's arms
until noon
if we so desire,
if there's still a fire.

November 15, 2005

A Little Too Late to Change

I want to go out
in the middle of a line
as my pen falls
from a hand gone limp,

leaving a trail of words
in delicate script
that looks like
lacy black filigree.

Note to self:
Work on penmanship.
Needs improving.

I want to go out
in the middle of a line
as a leather-bound journal
slides off my lap.

Note to self:
Buy leather-bound journal.
Toss spiral notebooks.

I want to go out
in the middle of a line
looking cool and slim,
dressed in hip threads.

Note to self:
Dump sweat pants.
Buy new blue jeans.
Lose 10 pounds.

I want to go out
in the middle of ...

December 19, 2005

All the King's Horses

Sirens cut across coastal fog.
Living close to Hwy 101,
sirens and screech of tires
blitz my ears every day.

But that day flashing red
scarred my heart.
And sent me scrambling.
We have your daughter
in emergency.
My living room tilted.

The drive to the hospital took
an eternity. New craters
of the moon were discovered.
Comets crashed and burned
a hole in the earth's crust.

My daughter's body covered in blood,
her face slashed by broken glass.
A doctor did
what all the king's horses
and all the king's men couldn't do.

Thank you, God. Thank you and
forgive me for staying away from
your table. I had long ago lost
my taste for wafers and wine.

I sensed Him say, *That's O.K.*
My love is not confined
to the communion table.
We can meet
on walks if that works for you.

We both like the weightless still
of early evening, the quiet light of dawn.
Though when I'm out of tune
with life, I harangue
the why of strife long into afternoon.

He doesn't give advice or reasons,
just holds me close so I won't
stumble in the rubble of burned
down buildings, as He will until
the end. Some things you know.

November 22, 2005

Chicago Afternoon July 1934
Corner of Wilson and Dover

Hey Mister! You my daddy?
Buy me an ice cream cone.
You got his smile.
Same soft brown eyes.

I remember even though
mom said to forget it 'cause
you ain't never coming back.
Wait! Stop! A nickel?

The girl, scabby knees,
tattered blue sunsuit
patched in the seat,
pockets the nickel, jingles

loose coins through her fingers,
then leaves. Getting too hot
to work this corner. No shade.
Pavement burns her bare feet.

She lies about their smiles and
the eyes never even come close.
Gold flecks in soft brown. The light
in them when he looked at her.

A girl could spend a lifetime trying
to find the man with those eyes,
moving on up from ice cream cones
to martinis. Still blinded by the light.

December 30, 2005

For Lurlene in a Western State
on the Edge of the Great Divide

she lazy swings in a hammock
sips a tall cool one at her side
wishing her drink was a cowboy
she'd chug a lug that dude knock
his Stetson off his brow and how

soon as she downs her drink
Lurlene rocks her skinny ass
out of the hammock slides
into snake tight jeans and trots
out into the night yowling with

yee haw twang electric strings
this filly will two step her way into
a guy's spread you wanna see
grab her hand be her music
be her band swing her round to
a country tune never cut her loose

she has lines like a spinning riata
and can rope a bucking bronco,
brand a maverick she's got a thing for
roustabouts no doubt her heart is as
large as Wyoming under an expanding
and cloudless sky but whoa partner

first she has to vet you check you out
make sure your boots have pointy toes
none of those dude shoes Nikes or
Adidas she's had her fill of running men
she's ready to do-si-do pack Wyoming
in your back pocket straddle your saddle
and gallop to a rodeo in the Pleiades.

2005

Monet's Waterlilies

I spot a lily pond
out the grimy streaked window
of a second-class railroad car
passing through Giverny countryside
at a clackety-clack rate of speed.
Ah Ha, I surmise.
Exactly as Monet first spied
his precious waterlilies,
became obsessed
with the blurred flowers
and pale pastels
seen by his myopic eyes.
He might have lost his spectacles,
leaning over the aisle
as they slid out of his pocket.
There was no optician
in Giverny, and so...
how fortunate for us.

2005

2006

A Wolf in Priest's Clothing

One on one parochial fun
in the parish parlor following
teen dances in the church hall.

Jitterbuging to the jukebox.
Glenn Miller. In the Mood.
Dorsey. Tuxedo Junction.

A dreamy priest. Dark slick
hair with a widow's peak.
He smells of incense and sweat.

A plain plump girl, thick glasses,
prays he will bless her with
the press of his hand on her back.

He seeks her out from across
the hall. Her Savior. Spins her
around, teaches her the steps.

Soon he will teach her to move
her hips, to use her hands and
lips in dark places. His angel.

January 1, 2006

Fa La La La La

scattered
strands
of silver
tinsel
tor n tis sue paper
in the trash
twisted
red
ribbon
crac ked orna
ments
candle stubs
prayers for peace
in sh re ds
t a t t e r e d
remnants of
the season
to be
jolly

January 6, 2006

The Trade-off

Five pillows don't cut it,
don't take the place
of a man in my bed.
Five pillows. Down-filled,
sateen covered,
600 count Egyptian cotton.
Creme de la creme
of linens.
But they don't breathe,
talk back, bite my ear,
push me away
when I hug too tight.
Nevertheless, I make
a nest of five pillows,
crawl in and cuddle up
to dream of a time
when my man and I
burned up the bed.
Truth be told,
I sleep better now
than I used to.
It's a trade-off

January 15, 2006

The Nature of My Poetry

Victoria says she doesn't write
about trees and twigs and crap like that.
Neither do I, not being a nature poet.
Which leads me to wonder...
what kind of poet am I? But back to

trees and twigs and crap like that.
Actually, I would consider shrubs.
I love the shape my mouth makes
when I say *shrub...SHHH* rushing
through rounded lips at the start,
explosive booming *BAH* at the end.
Exactly the opposite of *bush.*

Bushes and shrubs. Shrubs and
bushes. What a splurge of sound!
A barrage of sound. And how about
bushy shrubs or wow! A *hedge*
of bushy shrubs. I could use that.

A hedge of bushy shrubs
surrounds a forbidden garden
in the delta of a lush exotic land.
An old explorer pokes a pole
in the hedge, searching for a way
to enter this place of tasty treats.
Sweetest of all is stolen fruit,
its juice like honey on the tongue.
Who needs the fountain of youth?
Forbidden fruit makes him young.

Ah ha! *Erotic* Poet. That's what I am.

January 16, 2006

The Nana Chronicle

Three pairs of earrings
for twelve bucks!
Twelve smackeroos,
as Davey used to say.

Want to feel old?

Davey, the grandkid who
beat you at Go Fish
is now cruisin' for repos.
Lookin' to buy at nothing down,
fix up and resell.
Venture capitalist at nineteen.

His cousin, Mimi, is ten
and trendy. She and I enter
Claire's at The Mall.
Claire's, mecca of preteen
accessories. Buy two pair.
Get one free. Such a deal.
What Nana can resist?

Want to feel young?

Your gorgeous glam
fashionista granddaughter
copycats your sparkling
dangle earrings,
and the two of you
go hand in hand, struttin'
down the mall. Stylin'.

January 18, 2006

The Tacky Factor

Artificial philodendron is tacky.
Ask my youngest son.
He will tell you.
My reply?
I'll take tacky. It doesn't die.

My living room is a garden of tacky.
Regal fake red roses
hold court on the coffee table,
their perky, though tacky,
petals will continue to bloom
long after I am gone.

If the same could be said
for my poetry,
I would be happy.
My lines floating
on the wings of time.

Thing is,
tacky poems go
to an early grave.
Many of mine
have died aborning.
Oh my god! So tacky.

Ashes to ashes and dust to dust.

January 21, 2006

We'll Always Have Paris

The Kortuba Mosque in Marrakech, Morocco
can almost glow in the sunset.
So reads a travel column in today's Tribune.
I must go there. It's only a seven hour flight,
nonstop from New York to Casablanca.

Ah Casablanca! When I arrive I want to
have a Daiquiri at Rick's American Cafe´,
stand by the piano and say, *Play it again, Sam.*
Listen to Sam tickle the ivories and sing,
You must remember this. A kiss is still a kiss.

But my bank account is zero, bills piled high.
A trip to Marrakech, Morocco is pie in the sky.
I'm going to rent a DVD, kick back and cruise
to Casablanca on my couch. Who needs
the Kortuba Mosque! I'll always have Bogie.

January 22, 2006

All Those Clothes and Crap

crowded into one walk-in closet.
Like cattle in a cattle car, olives in a jar.
Slacks and sport coats, ties on a rack,
button-down shirts, belts on hooks,
oxfords, Reeboks, flip flops, thongs,
pumps and tennies, sandals, boots,

skirts and blouses, blue jeans, sweats,
a flowered silk dress saved for best.
His on the left. Hers on the right.
Like cattle in a cattle car, olives in a jar.
All those clothes packed in tight.
Rammed and smashed, gasping for air.

Hangers squeeze, wrestle and poke,
groping for places on sagging poles.
Like cattle in a cattle car, olives in a jar.
Shoe boxes stacked on shelves above,
shoes in a few, snapshots in some,
one with love letters from overseas,

service ribbons and captain's bars
jumbled in a rusty tin at the back,
Like cattle in a cattle car, olives in a jar.
I wish I had more room for my things.
Her chronic lament layers the walls
like countless coats of latex paint.

A day will come when all of his clothes
have gone to the Salvation Army.
She'll have lots of room for her things.
Neat and tidy like in her dreams.
Not like cattle in a cattle car, olives in a jar,
but blouses on the left, skirts on the right.

Hangers with spaces in-between,
and the closet will seem as empty
as the hours ahead, empty as her bed.
And she will lament the loss of a time
when all of their clothes snuggled tight
like cattle in a cattle car, olives in a jar.

January 25, 2006

Valentine's Day 2006

Valentine's Day arrives yet again
catching our men off guard.
It's hard for guys no matter how wise.
Valentine's Day is a minefield for men.

It's the same every year.
Puts fear in the heart of Tarzan.
Oh my god! I forgot to get roses.
No one supposes Jane will
forgive and forget.
You can bet Jungle Man
is going to pay for many a day.

So go on out all you guys
and buy a surprise for your sweetie,
or you will be needy in the bedroom.
Outta luck if you wanna fuck.
Trust me on this. A kiss won't cut it.

Roses are red, violets are blue.
If you want to screw,
buy flowers, bon bons, bling bling too.

Listen up, Romeos,
I've been around a while.
I'll tell you how to make
your sweetie smile,
how to make your lady
open her arms to your charms,
part her lips, move her hips.

Violets are blue, roses are red.
Hand over the goodies
and hop into bed.

A final word of advice.
It would be very nice.
if in your haste,
you remember to say:

I love you, Honey.
Happy Valentine's Day

January 26, 2006

Lights Camera Action

My life is a movie. I am the star.
There was an audition and
I got the part. It's a musical.
Well, yeah, you have a point
but my voice will be dubbed.

And I'm perfect for the role...
over-the-hill broad with pizzazz
meets young stud with beard
and scorpio tattoo who plays guitar.
It's love at first sight. Of course,
the guy *is* visually challenged
But they dig each other and hook up.
Well, yeah, that part is fantasy.

He writes a song, strums it in bars,
the song catches on. He makes a demo,
shops it to DJ's on 95.7 FM.
It catches on. Rockets off the charts.
Well, yeah, that part's fiction.
Maybe more like a memoir.
Who gives a shit anyway!
It's INSPIRING.

A Hollywood studio options the story,
signs me up to play myself.
No Honey, not *with* myself.
So that's where it's at right now.
Sort of on the back burner.

Seems they're coming up empty
casting the Young Stud role.
All the hunks on the A list
are making gay cowboy flicks.
No money in hetero.

In the meantime, I'm practicing my lines,
adding a few snappy ones of my own,
making guest appearances
and working on my acceptance speech.
And oh yeah, I'm gonna wear Valentino.
Red Valentino

January 28, 2006

Mom Tells Lola to Get Lost

Kids are on the back seat
playing on the internet,
mom's riding shotgun,
online on her laptop.
And what about the driver?

Dad's at the wheel
linking his car with
a folder on the desktop
of his home computer.

Which is why he missed
the freeway exit.
Which is why he hollers,
Who the hell turned off Lola?

Mom slinks back in her seat.
Lola, the know-it-all-bitch
of the van's guidance system,
is beyond irritating.

Lola tells him to turn
and he turns.
Without argument.
She tells him to stop.
He fucking stops.
Just yesterday mom
heard dad say,

Lola's voice is so
mellow and sweet.
She never yells
or talks back.
I wonder what
she looks like.

January 30, 2006

The Dark Dropped Down

and covered us like a blanket.
Did you know the dark can hold you
close enough to smother?

The lights came on like magic
when my mother dropped a quarter
in the slot of an electric meter box.

There was a night when the dark
dropped down and the quarter jar
on a shelf near the box was empty.

Mommy has to go out for a while,
but I'll be back quick as a wink.
See if you can count to a hundred.

She meant me. Billy was only three.
He couldn't count to a hundred.
Could I? Baby sister cried and cried.

I don't know how far I got. Nor do I
remember my mother coming home,
or the magic of lights coming on.

All I recall is counting counting
counting in the big black dark night,
Billy by my side, his hand in mine.

February 8, 2006

Overheard at a sidewalk cafe:
Are you sure you don't speak French?

He was waving
a croissant in the air
as he spoke,
crumbs on his goatee,
snooty uppercrust
on his tongue.

My reply to him would be:
Oh, yes. Quite sure.
I also don't speak Gaelic,
Swahili or Romanian.
I do speak a smattering
of Spanish.
And how about you?
Are you sure you aren't
an arrogant asshole?

February 10, 2006

Western Union Will Discontinue
All Telegrams Effective 01-27-06
(Headline in Union Tribune)

The last telegram was sent,
I imagine, to say he died.
The uniformed boy
on a rubbled street in Iraq.

I wish the last telegram
had been sent to me by
my lover who left
unexpectedly. Took off
in a huff after a fight over...

what was it?
My refusal to divulge
a secret hidden stash?
Or maybe the drunk who
made a pass, asked me
to dance and I accepted.

I wish the last telegram
had read: *Miss you madly.*
Will soon be back,
instead of shrapnel words
about a soldier boy in Iraq.

Or could it be the last telegram
was sent by the president of
Western Union to his grandson?
A message that went:

This is the last telegram. Save it.
Some day it will be worth a mint.

February 19, 2006

The Last Resort

A tree has fallen across train tracks
deep in a Pacific Northwest forest.
A passenger train stops where
Sacagawea, raven-haired daughter of
a Shoshone chief, led Lewis & Clark
through trees like these close as
cloves in a pomander ball.

City folk who don't know pine from
juniper, spruce from fir, sprout frowns
at an announcement over the loudspeaker:
There will be a delay of an hour or more.
Shadows merge as day plays hide and
seek with twilight, settles into evening.

A bearded man in black and tan plaid
flannel shirt and jeans, fingers
a Buck knife in his pocket, recalls
the earlier announcement:
*In an emergency, passengers will
debark only as the last resort.*

A relief to leave Portland,
his mother with Alzheimer's.
A trial to reach Seattle, his ex high
on supply from her current boyfriend.
Either direction he's screwed.
The last resort sounds like nirvana.

A squinty eyed plump woman,
black hair to her rump, sprawls across
two seats, yawns, confides to
the gray-haired lady on the other side
of the aisle, *I live mostly on
reservations. Travel a lot in my work.
What's this about a last resort?*

The gray-haired lady whispers to
a botoxed blonde facing her,
*Some kind of work! Bet it ain't
trading beads.* She presses her head
to the window, peers at trees.

Used to be evergreens in her yard
when she had a yard Smelled nice
and piney. Clean. Not musty like her
room at Glen Manor. The last resort
would smell like home.

The botoxed blonde tapped her
acrylics on an InStyle magazine.
The upkeep was getting her down.
The last resort, a Pine Needle B & B
with hot tub and cozy pub where locals
go for the natural look? She could
stop shaving her legs, quit Prozac.

The natives are restless in car 109,
ready to declare the last resort,
break out and blaze a trail a la
Sacagawea, set up camp. The man
in jeans reaches for his Buck knife.

February 26, 2006

Time to Lay the Tulips to Rest

though one or two stand tall,
holding on to a trace of dazzle.
A dozen scarlet darkened
to dusty burgundy,
leaning low over the table,
petals wrinkled, weary wide.

I've kept them past their prime,
entranced by every aspect
of their changing lives. From
bright red buds closed tight,
slowly opening to ripe fullness,
revealing velvety yellow pistils,

finally giving way to heavy heads,
limp stems and dropped petals,
each phase in my eye's embrace.
From shy maiden to lush lady
to declining diva. To the end.
Oh, to be somebody's tulip!

February 26, 2006

Blocked In

The block is too big to ignore
or move without a crew and
a forklift. Ink black. Heavy as
a cement tub holding
a ten foot fishtail palm tree.

Large white stenciled letters
on each side of the block spell:
WRITER'S
It sits in the middle of my living room.

A trip to the kitchen
to refill my coffee cup requires
a detour. I have bruises on
my right hip from banging into it,
spilling coffee on the carpet.
Bad words have been uttered.

When occasional friends stop by,
I apologize for the monolith
in the middle of the living room.
Only temporary, I say, wondering

how the hell I'm going to get rid of it.
I hear concern in their voices
when they ask, *Have you seen
a doctor lately?* Same with Lupe,
who quit when I told her to

clean around it, don't bother
dusting the top. She grabbed
her car keys and cell phone,
ran out muttering,
Madre del dios. Loca. Loca.

whose only reply forever and
always always always is:

Write about it. So simple and yet
so impossibly hard, especially
without a pen. Where's my pen?

There it is, hidden in plain sight
on the table. I pick it up like
it's a foreign object, not quite sure
what to do with it.

And there's my notebook!
I grab it, blow dust off the cover
and start to start to
oh fuck! just start to write about it.

About how I don't get any sleep
because I see black blocks
with blinking white labels
behind my closed eyelids.

About how I can't get away
from the monster block.
Its invisible eyes follow me
down the hall, my home
no longer a refuge.

About how the stenciled letters
taunt me, make me feel like
a wannabe writer going nowhere,
a pathetic poetic disgrace
with no place to hide.

I write on and on into the night,
detail dimensions of the block,
get up to double check its height
and stare, stunned. Poof! Gone!

February 26, 2006

Still Life: Sunflowers & Irises

They fling themselves across the canvas,
reaching out of a gilded frame to pull me
from a trance as I stand and stare at
their wild fiery flamenco. I can almost hear
castanets clicking and guitars strumming.
Bold strokes of golden yellow sunflowers,
splashes of lavender irises in heel-tapping,
hand-clapping colors shout, ¡Olé!
They sway, petals flying, denying *Still Life*.

March 10, 2006

All in a Day's Work

My web stretches from branches of
brambles to twigs of a sycamore tree,
its long-fingered green leaves turning
to rust, dust on the ground where
a sleek fat beetle creeps, coming close
to my lunch bucket, orb of my labor.

A kid with a stick hops by, stops
and stares at my web, a spoked
circular grid. He lifts his arm as if
to strike. I scramble on my quick
long legs, glad to have eight, wait
till it's safe, then begin to spin.

March 12, 2006

Salmon Season in Pacific Looking Bleak Once More (San Diego Union-Tribune 03-20-06)

Mom made salmon croquettes
when she came to visit.
She knew a thing or three
about cooking. And men.
Salmon croquettes
were my husband's favorite.

Mom's gone now. Dad too.
My husband 8 years ago,
He was a whistler.
Off-key. Through his teeth.
I still look up and smile
when I hear wind
whistling down the canyon.

Haven't bought a can
of salmon since.
Don't like it.
Probably a good thing
considering
the predicted bleak season.

Cojo and chinook salmon
in their prime, swim up river,
in harm's way of dams
blocking them from their
spawning habitat. They die.
The dead are counted.

March 21, 2006

Left Behind

He forgot his jacket,
gray hooded zip-up,
men's medium,
hanging over the back

of a chair facing
the computer
where he checked
train times.

Gone this morning.
I drove him sunup
to the station.
I'll leave his jacket

hanging there
until he returns.
Don't know when.
He didn't say.

Chilly evenings
I may wear it, slip
my short arms into
long gray sleeves,

wrapped in traces
of woodsy scent.
It will keep me warm
one way or another.

March 23, 2006

The Changing Times

I read old news in The Times each day.
The paper is delivered from a car.
I will be sad when papers are passé´,

(the message that the young convey).
Get real time news on tv from a star.
I read old news in The Times each day.

I scan the pages in a certain way,
back to front which seems to some bizarre.
I will be sad when papers are passé´.

I like the smell of ink, don't mind delayed
body counts of soldiers slain in war.
I read old news in The Times each day.

I turn to horoscopes in Section A,
sipping tea dressed in a silk peignoir.
I will be sad when papers are passé´.

My eyes, though going bad to my dismay,
still read fine print obits although it's hard.
I read old news in The Times each day.
I will be sad when papers are passé´

March 26, 2006

The Missing Man

lurks in every piece
she writes.
He's the empty place
at the side of snapshots...
Mommy Daughter Space.

Hunger creeps onto lines,
sneaks into phrases,
worms its way into words.
What would drive her
had he not gone?

Was there a moment
he hesitated? Would she
have screamed, *Go!*
I need to spend my life
writing down the pain.

April 6, 2006

Spare Parts

We barge out of the womb
with two of them: eyes, ears,

arms, hands, legs, feet.
Only one heart. Not a good

plan. God should know we
need at least a dozen,

a baker's dozen of hearts.
They break like Easter eggs

hidden in the grass,
stepped on and smashed.

My own heart is patched,
bandaged, taped, barely

the same shape it once was
when it beat fast for you.

April 6, 2006

Foster Child

Strange narrow bed
in a dim corner
of a strange room.
Scent of sour sheets.
A child sleeps, dreams
of home. Red brick.

Side porch. Picket fence.
Her closed fist holds
tight a rusty key. It fits
a lock in a front door
with a tarnished
brass knocker.

In strange houses
with strange beds,
polite people tell her,
This is your new home.
She knows better.
Home will always be

where sheets smell
of lilacs and sunlight.
She hides the rusty key,
tries to remember
the name of a street
lined with big leafy trees.

April 9, 2006

Victoria Writes a Poem a Day

and I decide to try it too, wondering where
the words will take me as they pull me along
on the page. Some exotic destination like
Sestina or Pantoun? Been too long waiting for
the uptown bus to get me out of a stuck place.
My pen is on the scent, skims a faint blue line.
Thoughts tumble, words scamper and scurry to
pounce on a poem like rats on a piece of cheese.
My wastebasket's stuffed with crumpled paper balls.
Good thing I have a dumpster. And don't give me shit
about not recycling. I'm already going to hell for
splitting infinitives, plus going down on Denny Dixon
in the stock room behind the xerox on lunch break
back in the days when I had good knees.
C'mon...you KNEW I was bad.
Where will the words take me? Looks like
another trip to the dumpster. O.K. So a poem a day
doesn't work for me. My poems are capricious,
pop up through cracks in asphalt like weeds,
fly in open windows like buzzy bees, hide in shells
on the beach, snooze on my pillow like fat cats.
Try as I might to pounce on a poem, it's the poem
that captures *me* ...when its willing to be tugged &
twisted & shaped on a page & only then.

April 23, 2006

Meanings

You think the clouds are clouds.
They're not. And the doll on
the ground with smashed legs
is not a doll. Its glass eyes
stare up at clouds.
Maybe the doll is the girl
you once were, the clouds
your future. No.
The clouds are white as
angel wings. Not a single
thunderhead in sight.
But the doll is a possible.
Smashed legs may say
you're not going anywhere.
And the doll's glass eyes?
You don't *really* see
he's leaving long before
he goes out the door.

April 28, 2006

Without You

The still is more still,
the dark darker.
Not a leaf stirs.
No stars in the sky.
No sound of surf,
nor seagull cry.
No heartbeat
next to mine.
Who would have
thought cold
could be so cold,
the well so deep?

May 10, 2006

Weathering the Storm

After the wreckage of last night...
rain smashing against windows,
winds pounding low
branches of oaks,
words hurtled like spears,

the spent storm stillness is heavy
with exhausted angers,
the floor littered with barbed words
dropped like bullet shells.

The creek runs high.
Leaves, washed free of dust,
sparkle in sunlight,
and we are still speaking.

May 22, 2006

Duality

My other self lives
in a parallel world
of shadows.

She screams, weeps,
stamps her feet,
pounds her fist, yells.

This self who writes
words on a page,
borrows lines from

the other one who
writhes in the dark.
From time to time,

I lift my pen and say,
*Thanks. I couldn't
do it without you.*

My other self replies,
*I will do your crying.
Try to keep it light.*

May 24, 2006

It's Snowing

so you know
the glass globe
has been turned
upside down.

Two tiny people
in a tiny sleigh.
A tiny church with
a tiny steeple.

A scene of peace
in a flurry of snow.
My own world
turned upside down

is a flurry of ash.
Tell me how
the tiny people
got inside the glass.

May 27, 2006

For Tyree Grant Dugger

When he left he took
the *West* with him.
Used to be a bolo tie
around his neck,
Stetson on his head,
country western on the radio

All gone with his boots.
All traces of dusty trails
erased when I packed up
his Louis Lamour books,
took down the framed
cowboy from the wall.

Goodbye Old Paint.
Forgive the cool jazz and
Matisse prints.
Not your cup of
Sarsaparilla,
but your brand is forever
stamped on my heart.

July 9, 2006

Norma

Her face was a mask
of thick pasty beige,
flesh-colored makeup
to hide...not quite...

a port wine stain
splashed across her face.
One of the older girls
working in the kitchen

at summer camp.
Chopping cabbage for
slaw. Washing dishes,
trading extra desserts

for helping hands.
I was always up for
more chocolate pudding.
Her name was Norma,

her tongue was tart,
dishing out acid remarks
with spaghetti. *Stay in line,
Fatso! Shut your trap, Stupid!*

We'd look away from her face
with its pasty beige mask,
shiny from summer heat
and steam rising from pots.

I can't remember Norma's hair.
Long or short? Brown or blond?
But she was loud, clowned
around and laughed a lot.

If you asked me the color of
her eyes, I couldn't say.
I didn't see beyond her mask.
I looked down. I looked away.

June 9, 2006

The Carlsbad Watershed Network
& The San Elijo Lagoon Conservancy

My canyon hillside is dotted
with little red flags on stakes
marking spots where a crew
planted seedlings...501, I'm told,
starting at the fence on the top,
down to the creek at the bottom.

The creek sings as it trickles out
to sea, happy to be free of
arundo, non-native giant reed
that looks like bamboo and
invades like Mongols, chokes
out all growth in its path,
clogs and dams up the creek.

The Watershed Network's
Invasive Removal Project
includes my canyon. It's news
to me, but welcome as
weighing in 10 pounds lighter
than last I stepped on a scale.
Oh my, Yes! I agree to let
the agency clean up and replant
the canyon at no cost to me.

Ten men in coveralls go to war
against arundo, hacking away
five days straight with machetes
and power saws instead of rifles
and machine guns, filling four
construction dumpsters.

They drove off leaving the hillside
denuded, looking like a slag heap.
Said they'd be back to plant when
the time was right. That's like
your mate saying he'll take you to
Jamaica when he wins the lottery.

But two months later, after three weeks of
drizzle, it seems the time was right.
Last Tuesday a pickup pulled into
my driveway with a crew of men and
a trailer full of plants in flats.
501 of various varieties, I'm told.

I've been thinking a lot about that *ONE*.
500 and ONE. Precise, decisive 500
and *ONE*. No wishy washy number like
about 500 or in the neighborhood of 500.
Someone takes counting seriously.

Can't you see him leaning over,
pointing his index finger, counting
groups of ten all the way up to 500?
He starts to write down the number,
but stops as he spies a seedling
behind the flags. *Oops! Missed one.*

The crew spread out in the canyon
with diagrams and maps showing
where the various plants were to go,
with shovels and flats of seedlings,
and of course, the little red flags.

There's a tender green vine with
a yellow blossom down by the creek.
I think it's the *ONE*. I saw a worker digging
a hole and, placing the vine gently in the

ground, he smiled as
he tamped dirt around its roots.

I bet he's the worker who counted
the plants, all 500 and one of them,
and I bet he made sure to save
a place by the creek for the ONE.

June 12, 2006

dense quiet

of sultry damp
in lazy limp
summer dawn
arms too heavy
to lift and reach
for each other
feet so slow
to walk across
the divide
perhaps in fall
we can come
together
winter will be
too late
what with
blizzards
frozen roads
all that
slippery ice
and snow
snow snow
cold snow

June 27, 2006

Thank God for Cardboard.

Writing my way out of this box
with a cheap Bic might not be
an impossible trick after all.
Hardwood with a grain, burls,
couple of knots, I'd be stuck
without a power saw. My words
can't cut even quarter inch ply.

I'd be trapped into decorating
the interior. Murals of
swaying palms, sunset on
the horizon. I'd imagine up
a pillow...goose down with
blue and white striped ticking,
quilt, snacks. Fritos for
the comfort zone of my box.

Then to sleep, to dream
of escaping the *thing,*
the *thought,* the *experience.*
Just wander off into a maze
of danger...

bloody limbs in debris of
land mines, spiny cactus,
porcupine quills, twisted tongues,
cracked crust, forbidden kisses,
twilight of gin, acid reflux,
deficit spending, migrants
in makeshift shacks, pierced lips,
tar pits, switchblades,
sonic boom, panic attacks,

tick tick tick tick tick tick tock

of alarm clocks and
time bombs, stalled engines,
screech and honk of rage,
needle tracks on arms,
on hems in sweatshops,
finally reach the pukey green
pea soup pond of opacity,
dive in and swim.

July 13, 2006

Truncate

It didn't cost a dime,
this polished gem
added to the trove
in my mind.

He sent it to me in
an email message...
a new word:
t r u n c a t e, *truncate*

I looked it up and now
it's mine to share with
you as I truncate this
note in the middle of

July 15, 2006

Edgy

edgy edge of danger
rim of granite slab
center graham cracker
whirlpool vortex swirling swirling
caught in a rip tide

brain cranium mind
mind over matter
what matters? what
matter? does matter
matter? I don't mind
it's no matter to me

The way you wear your hat,
the way you sip your tea,
oh no, they can't take
that away from me.

I can lose it lost gone bye bye
out of my mind
out of sight out of mind
hindsight better than blind

and when I lose it
I'm lost mine what I say
stay loose

July 18, 2006

After Thumbing Through *Legitimate Dangers*

My cocoon crumbles.
I have shed many skins.
See these big-knuckled
crippled fingers barely able
to cradle a writing tool.

You understand. Of course,
you understand. You understand
everything I say in my familiar
conventional way.

Though I have long longed to
take you on a wild ride that makes
you grab the dash, grip the rail.

But I break no boundaries,
stay within the speed limit.
I never even got a ticket.

Guess it's ingrained, a cellular thing,
the need to drop sweets in a trail
leading to a gingerbreak cottage.

So I salute the new & emerging
who zip you off to uncharted territory
in hybrid vehicles. You may be seduced by
their recent anthology.
Take mine. I'll sell it to you half-price.

July 20, 2006

July 22, Emily

How many poems
did Emily Dickinson write?
Hundreds. Over a thousand.
All those journals
written in longhand. Black ink.

Jesus! No *Spell Check*.
I'm thinking ahead
to when my computer dies
and I don't have the bucks
to buy a new one.

I'll be going back to
longhand too. Black ink.
And back to the dictionary.
So, yeah. I get it...
All those short ones.

Now how to make them
stay in your mind?
Ah ha! I get it...
Short ones that rhyme.

Add a certain slant of light,
or a prairie and a bee.
Live your life as a recluse if
you want to write like Emily.

July 22, 2006

Things I Learn From My Grandson

Take Saturn, for instance, with all its
rings and moons. My grandson Grant,
who is 13, says astronomers are
always discovering a new moon of Saturn.
Seems like a new one every month.

And I think about planet Earth
from which we look up and stargaze,
how we have a new moon every month.
It's the same old moon, only new,
full of promise to wax large enough to

hold all the hope of the world.
Hope for a date to the prom, for peace
in Egypt, hope that the tooth ache
is not a root canal, that the new baby
will have 10 fingers, that the money

will hold out until payday, that the rattle
in the car's rear end is a loose wrench
in the trunk, that the mole is only a mole,
and that a grandson will grow up and
discover another new moon of Saturn.

July 23, 2006

The Last One

no more
not another
ever
the sun will pour
liquid gold
into my clear eyes
tomorrow or
maybe the day after
too many empties
too empty

July 28, 2006

Conflict

The bridge is wet,
surprised by
overnight rain.
Cool air slides
down wide avenues.
My green island
glistens with
beads of moisture
on leaves
reflecting peace.
Images seen on
the silent screen,
remote on mute,
deny Eden.
Somewhere glare
and clash.

July 29, 2006

Born on a Freeway

in a Toyota mini van
stuck in a traffic jam.
Ten pounds. Wow!
That bruiser didn't
just pop out.

Same day
an African Gray parrot
broke out.

Thing is,
the bird was fed,
cage kept clean.
No reason to flee,
but first chance,
the parrot took flight,

adding its doo doo
to serious bird shit
splattered on car
fenders and hoods.

Hey! It's all good.
Keeps the car wash
business afloat.

Thing is,
what would we do
without quick little men,
white rags in hand,
scurrying like ants on

a cinnamon bun crumb,
to polish our chrome
for tips in a can?

August 2006

Origami Crane

A creamy white origami crane
launched by a breeze
floats down from a chest,
lands on a sea foam green rug
by the side of an occupied bed.

He who crafted the origami crane
with its complicated folds, fucks
the woman for whom he made it.

She of simple folds...yawning, wet,
redolent, would have fucked him anyway,
knows his capable fingers *et al.*

The creamy white origami crane,
now wears a rosy pink blush
in its voyeuristic role, soon dashed,
as the woman falls out of bed and
smashes it. *Oh, fuck the crane!*
She came. That's all that matters.

August 22, 2006

My Very Educated Mother
Just Served Us Nine Pickles

Pluto's getting a lot of press.
Mostly negative. Sort of like
a pop star photographed
topless by paparazzi.

Poor Pluto. Done nothing wrong
except to be discovered by
an astronomer so excited
he probably peed in his pants.

Now its planet classification
is being re-examined...size,
shape, orbit. For one thing,
Pluto's orbit around the sun
is tilted. Totally unplanetary.

I am, however, in favor of
keeping the solar stuff as is.
I'm too old to learn a new
memory crutch sentence for
remembering the planets.

Let any change wait until I'm
gone from earth and have
taken my place in the universe
somewhere near Xena,
which may or may not be
a planet. I'll let you know.

August 24, 2006

Just the Way It is

Ice melts and people die.
I spill coffee on
the obituary page.
Can't read it anyway.
Print too light. When
did what's his name die?
His wet kisses sweet.
Now ocean breezes
grace my parched cheek.
I live at the beach.

August 28, 2006

Where Were You
When It Happened?

The rising sun exploded over
blinding white snow banks
that long ago December
afternoon of a Sunday drive
outside of Chicago.

I fingered the plush back seat,
my feet in black patent
Mary Janes barely touching
the floor. Hot air flowed in
waves from a heater up front.

A staccato voice spit words
from a car radio. The man
driving, his name John or
Tom, turned up the volume
while a lady in fur coat and

beads, turned to smile at me.
A rich couple treating a kid from
the orphanage to an outing.
I stopped biting a fingernail
and tried to smile back.

I had never met them before,
nor heard of Pearl Harbor.

August 28, 2006

It's Night & You're Out of Vicadin

When the sun dies in inky seas
and brine boils, one by one
blinking lights come on, lead
the way to coals glowing with
heat of passion spilled from
cauldrons cooking entrails
of sentences spoken in anger.
Random kind words fade into
pallid paper boats making sail
for black caves of silence.
You will remember roars.
You will close your eyes
and see lightning.
There will be no sleep.
Big-chested pain pounds
an indestructible drum.
Your screams cannot be
heard beyond the jagged
reef of your agony.

August 29, 2006

Thanksgiving Day Leftovers

Sister Prisca took the call
when Mom phoned about
my meeting her downtown
at the Bluebird Bus Station.

I had money in my pocket
for the el train fare,
wearing my Sunday best,
although it was Thursday.

I suppose that *meet* at ten
sounds like *leave* at ten,
if you're hard of hearing
like Sister Prisca.

When Mom called again,
it was already too late
to make it to grandma's
in the country by bus

for roast goose and hugs.
I ate dinner at St. Mary's
with the rest of the kids who
had nowhere else to go.

Roast turkey was salted
with tears, but pumpkin pie
and whipped cream tasted
yummy. We got seconds.

September 2, 2006

mom's **wild** ride

i climbed on behind and held tight
to the stranger on a motorcycle my arms
clutched his middle my cheek pressed
flat against his back
whiffs of gas leather musk **jump-started**
my pulse the only time
i ever hitchhiked
my hubby and kids
dropped
fishing gear and stared   i believe the kids even
stopped fighting over who got which rod and reel
shouting as the motorcycle
roared
off to town leaving them in the dust of
our campsite under oaks dripping
mist
near Pismo Beach they were
hoping to catch corbina with worms for bait

i was looking to catch a ride out of humdrum

i hooked it with tight jeans the biker
dropped me off
in front of a shell shop in town a l o n g l o n g
walk back to camp on s h a k e y legs i crashed
on an air mattress in the tent and **woke** with
a start at shrill voices of kids squabbling over cards
i must be **home** that night corbina sizzled
on the camp stove thanks to the catch of the day
and my hubby's kisses sizzled in the tent
thanks to
the one that
got away

September 6, 2006

Housewife's Holiday

She's never been to Brazil,
but she can samba,
never gone to the Copacabana,
but she dances the carioca,
and when she washes clothes,
she goes to Ipanema.

She listens to Jobim and
though she knows she will
never be tall, tan and lovely,
her lively legs lust for a certain
syncopation. The housewife
goes to Rio when she dusts.

She tosses a salad as she
sways to bossa nova, flies to
Rio de Janeiro in her mind,
while she sidesteps advances
from a handsome neighbor
eager to teach her the tango.

September 10, 2006

The Right Fit

She's a hard fit. If a skirt slides
over her hips like hot chocolate
on ice cream, the bodice clings
like casing on a dry salami.

And shoes! Her toes pinch when
her heels sit snugly in pumps.
If she ever finds a well-fitting pair,
she wears them past their prime.

So too, the man whose arms
embraced her with a dream fit
when they first met.
He was a one of a kind design.

She slipped him on and never
took him off. Even when
seams split and the hem ripped,
they could be mended.

September 14, 2006

Even Warblers Left Their Nests and Flew Down to Listen

Uncle Ray sat in the sun on a porch swing
strumming a 6 string guitar. His voice
filled the yard with listeners. Ladies hanging
out wash down the street dropped their
wet sheets back in the basket and ran to sit
at his feet. Neighbors passing by, stopped
and swayed to the tune of, *I'll be down to get
you in a taxi, Honey*. Better than anything
on the radio. He could yodel too.

He had become family when he married my
Aunt Velma and oh, the fun at family picnics!
Corn on the cob. Fried chicken. Cherry cobbler.
Uncle Ray's guitar. Him singing. *Let me call
you sweetheart.* Pitching horsehoes,
Uncle Ray always got the most ringers.

Not much he coudn't do except hold
down a job. Last one was clerking at
Dewey's Hardware. The boss fired him
when he caught his wife giving Uncle Ray
a bonus behind the pliers and screw drivers.

Uncle Ray's 5 sisters, all old maids,
Cora, Bess, Ruth, Amy and Laura lived
in a big white frame house next door to
Uncle Ray's little cabin he'd built to get out
from under lace doilies. But close enough
for them to see their baby brother.

They kept him in ribs and rhubarb pie,
his favorites. And chased off pretty girls
who stayed too late at the party. All except
my Aunt Velma, mom's hubba hubba sister.
She wore blue eye shadow, black mascara,
and dark red lipstick. A fake white gardenia in

her permed hair, narrow hips swaying to
Uncle Ray's rhythms. They got married after

he planted a pumpkin seed in her tummy,
and soon as Baby Ray Jr. was born,
Cora, Bess, Ruth, Amy and Laura swooped
down on him with sweet milky tidbits and
hovered over his crib waiting for him to
open his eyes, squeal and kick his little feet.

Aunt Velma pulled on mesh hose and
kicked up *her* feet while Uncle Ray sat on
the porch swing strumming his guitar,
singing. *Five foot too. Eyes of blue.
Has anybody seen my guitar?*

She went to town and started hanging out
at Delroy's 24 Hour Diner, a truck stop where
her girlfriend, Gert, waitressed making big tips.
And when dottie, working the 5 to 10 shift quit,
Aunt Velma was hired. And met Bucky...

not tall and wiry or good looking like Uncle Ray.
And he couldn't play the guitar or sing.
But Bucky brought her little presents, a bangle
bracelet from Tuscon, turquoise ring from Reno.
And he didn't have any sisters.

I'm the only one she told before she left.
See, Aunt Velma and me got real close
after she started working at Delroy's.
I'd ride my bicycle over to the truck stop
after school and she'd give me chocolate
shakes and french fries for free.

And after I finally met Bucky, she was
always asking, *Isn't he cute? Isn't he nice?*
And I thought, *Well...no and yes.*
She left and I was the only one who
missed her. Not Uncle Ray. Not mom.

Not Baby Ray, although she sent him
picture postcards from Montana and
Colorado. One to me from Hollywood.
Hi Honey. Wish you were here.
The palm trees are fabulous. Give
Baby Ray a kiss. Say Hi to your mom.

But I didn't. I don't talk to mom at all.
Not since I saw her kissing Uncle Ray
on the porch swing. He calls me
his Princess. Who does she think
she is, his Queen of Araby?

September 18, 2006

On Neptune Street

A vintage beach cottage,
gray paint flaking,
holds fast to its bluff top
ocean front spot.

now boxed in by
two-story mansions
smelling of wet paint
and lacquer.

The street is lined
with construction vans
and pickup trucks
parked at the curb
next to luxury cars.

van / van / pickup
Lexus / Mercedes
van / van / pickup / Jag

Music of the street
crescendos
with pounding hammers
and buzzing saws.

The nocturne mood
of the neighborhood
has crossed over
to rock and roll.

For Sale signs stud
high-priced sod.
Crews in hard hats
knock out weathered walls
and frame up contempos.

A shabby old-timer
at the corner of the block
frowns and hunkers down.

September 23, 2006

Worry

I breathe. I worry.
Simple as that.
Starting with
the boogeyman,
and forward to
flunking a test,
losing lunch money,
missing the bus,
missing my period.

Endless fuel to
keep worry fired.
And it burned
with frenzy when
I became a mother.
Of course, I passed
the boogeyman on
to my kids who are

now themselves
parents and expert
worriers. God knows
what knots in *their*
stomachs and lost
sleep over *their* kids!

And still, they have
enough worry left
to include me.
Mom, I'm worried
about your steep
stairs, the brakes
in your car,
slippery bathtub.
I taught them well.

September 26, 2006

Danger Ahead

It's enough to be on the road again.
We drive head-on into the full moon rising,
still low over the road, and it seems as if
we're finally making a getaway. From the pain
in your side. From the scent of another's
gorgeous skin. From I can't remember what.

The enticing full moon in desert night sky
brimming with glittering galaxies pulls us
into the promise of a place where everything
is perfect, though it feels like I've been on
this road before, seen that same sign:
Danger Ahead.

October 10, 2006

Chicago 1945

Miss Lawrence sharpened
five long yellow pencils
with a pocket knife blade
before the school bell rang.
She lined up the five pointy
yellow pencils on her desk,
patted her blond waves
held in place by bobby pins,
cleared her throat, *Ahem,*
and said, *Good morning,*
Class. Miss Lawrence
frowned and glared at Will,
shushing him in mid-whisper.
Fractions and grammar,
social studies and science.
Dismissal a hundred and
twelve yawns away when
droopy heads popped up
at the sound of the bell and
kids shuffled for the door.
Miss Lawrence, elbows on
the desk, leaned down
and pulled bobby pins
from her hair, letting loose
soft waves. She tossed

yellow pencils in a drawer,
their points worn down from
check marks and corrections
on collected papers in neat
piles at the side of her desk
Then she stood, stretched,
and reaching for her purse,
she sang a little tune, *Take*
me out to the ball game.
A ticket for the World Series
was in her purse, Cubbies
against the Tigers. A letter with
an APO return address in her
lingerie drawer under lacy black
panties. She had fingered the
words, *Coming back to you,*
Honey, until the ink was faint.
She'd met him at a USO dance,
insignia flashing, dancing close
to dreamy music, his quicksilver
tongue in her ear. Smiling, she
switched off the light and closed
the door, still believing in happy
endings for a few more days.

October 23, 2006

Little Girl Blue

She leans to test
the bath water
with a manicured
fingertip, turns
the tap to add
a stream of cold,
trails a lotioned
hand through
foamy bubbles,
contemplates
her legs, blue
veins like back
roads on a map
of her decline.
Next she lights
a rose scented
candle, presses
Start on a stereo,
and the sound of
Nina Simon like
a wounded dove,
wraps around her.
She drops a thick
white terry cloth
robe on polished
gray granite tiles,
turns to gaze at her
face in the mirror,
her swollen eyes.
Then she places
a razor blade on
the rim of the pink
porcelain tub, and
slips into water as
the song ends.

November 3, 2006

Then the Letting Go

*After great pain, a formal
feeling comes.....*
Emily Dickinson

I've got to get a handyman
to prop up the fence.

Leans more each year
since my husband pounded

the last nail in once proud posts.
Hire a guy to slap a coat of

white on ragged rails,
the patchy peeling paint.

My feet tingle as I shake
a formal feeling.

Now to find clippers in
this tangle of dusty tools.

The honeysuckle's gone
wild as a neglected child.

I better water the grass.
Maybe plant some pansies.

December 11, 2006

Mother's Day

All day long, every damn day
she lifts laundry from
the washing machine, flings
blue jeans into the drier,
slaps jam on slices of bread,
wipes sticky finger prints off
door knobs, trips over toy trucks
and baby dolls, plastic bats
and building blocks, drinks
cold coffee, eats leftover crusts.
This day is sparked by hugs
from tiny arms wrapped around
her thighs: *I love you, Mommy,*
by excited shrieks from her kid on
a two-wheeler bike: *I did it! I did it!,*
by her husband's sudden hands
on her waist as she leans over
soapsuds in the kitchen sink.
Go sit down, Baby. I'll finish up.
And she postpones running away
for another day.

2006

2007

I Would Have Kissed

his bald head as he
leaned over the table
before I took my own

place, had I known.
I would have poured
his second cup of

coffee, had I known.
As it was, he rose
to do it for himself.

And I would have
told him that I loved
him one last time.

It's just as well.
He would have figured
something was up.

January 22, 2007

Lie, Lying, Lay, Have Lain

Last Sunday I was not old.
Monday on Oprah: *60 is the new 4o.*
Yesterday my daughter turned 55.
So today that makes me... what?
I almost flunked 3rd grade math.
No gold star ever graced my eraser-
smudged arithmetic worksheets.
Story problems were a bugaboo.
That steam engine going 90 miles
an hour still gives me nightmares.
How long will it take for the train
to arrive at a station 82 miles away,
and how many people give a shit?
This is the story. There's no way
my daughter can be a senior citizen.
I don't care what AARP people say.
However, if her advanced age buys
her cheaper movie tickets, great.
She loves to go to the movies. Me too.
My college algebra instructor had
eyes like a leading man. Why else take
advanced math? I'll never forget his
dark thick lashes, intense glances,
velvet mole close to his lips, even if
I can't remember the Pythagorean thing.
When my kids asked me for math help,
I replied, *Ask your Dad!* But grammar?
I can conjugate with the best of them.

February 8, 2007

Fowl Play

A duck in front of a house,
smack dab in the middle of
a path, stood still and stared.
The woman who lived there
had opened the door to go out.

She stopped and stared back.
It was a mallard with a green
head, a purple breast, a male.
She knew mallards. Before her
kids got wings and took flight,

they had mallards, Duke and
Duchess. This drake looked
like Duke. The woman didn't
want to frighten the bird away.
She smiled and started to call

to her husband to come see,
a habit that would be hard to
break. After a while the drake
waddled off towards the street,
then sat in shade at the side of

the door shut and tiptoed to
a window to spy on the bird
sitting solid, owning the spot.
Was the drake her husband?

Had he come back to check on her,
to make sure that she was ok?
He used to say that he wanted to
come back as a peregrine falcon.
Which made her a bit uneasy.

Did she really know him? A *falcon*.
Fierce hunter. Fastest creature
on earth in it's dive, swooping down
on helpless prey. Jeeze! She'd
rather be a sea otter playing off

the coast of San Francisco.
In time their shrubs grew tall as trees,
and family pets were put to sleep.
They made a will, began to speak
of plots and services. Which hymns.

He wanted Streets of Laredo sung,
which turned out to be a No No
at St. Andrew's Episcopal church.

She settled on Amazing Grace.
God isn't perfect. He took her
husband first, and though sending
him back on feathered wings,
He got His birds seriously mixed up.

Or did He? She can talk to a duck,
pet a duck, train a duck. The drake
will stay. It's a lot like a man. Give it
a place in the shade to sit, a little tin
dish for water, a great big one for food.

February 9, 2007

Of Mattresses and Cats

On my morning walk a discarded king size mattress
at the end of a driveway. Faded blue stripes on
dingy white ticking. I search for words befitting
a dear departed mattress. Maybe not so dear?
My mind bounces about on mattresses, those I've known
including a few I would never own up to.
Turning into a winding side street I meet two sleek
Siamese cats adorned by sequined halters
with jeweled leashes held by a lean regal lady
wearing silver sandals, cerise scarf on her head.
They seem to be of some importance. I feel I've wandered
into a fairy tale and soon a poodle in a blue silk suit
with a black bow tie will pop out of the bushes.
I tuck that snippet under my cap, into a mental notebook.

From Summit Avenue I see the ocean sparkling in
sunlight, diamonds dancing on its surface.
Floating above, a flotilla of fluffy white clouds.
I'm dazzled by so much sky and shiny green leaves
washed clean from last night's rain.
Limber men in yellow hardhats climb trees
to trim cracked branches. I scan the scene
for ribbons to weave into a nest of words.
I gather seed to feed my lines like a mother bird.
When I push a poem out of the nest,
mortality rate is high. Weak lines, lame words,
broken wings. But if a poem takes flight, it might also sing.

February 7, 2007

The Reluctant Voyeur

I'd be propped up on a plump pillow
in the middle of a big bed, if I were
her teddy bear with glass button eyes.
I'd see her dressing to greet her lover.
She holds up a gown to the light,
drops it in a heap on the floor,
then slides another with lace trim
from a hanger and shakes her head.
So much fuss for so little wear!

At last, of course, she'll slip into
red satin, the backless gown.
Looking in a mirror, she fingers a spot
on her face and frowns, then smiling,
leans over me to turn back clean sheets.
Her scent is sweet, so much like
apricot jam, I am dizzy. She looks at
the clock again and again, then scoops
me up and dumps me in a chair.

My fur coat is ratty. I'm patched, my right
arm tacked on. We've been best friends
since her tonsillectomy, but she has
a thing for this guy that makes her forget the
alphabet, the name of the street
she lives on, and me. I've seen the way
she looks at him, her eyes brimming
with sunlit honey. She sings as she
flutters to look out a front window.

Fly me to the moon and ... She's flat.

He's late. She waits until the night is
quiet as a butterfly's sigh. She comes
for me and crawls back in her cocoon,
holding me close. I am relieved he
didn't show. I don't like watching them.

February 15, 2007

I Draw the Line at Bloody Apes

Tarzan was undoubtedly dashing, though
quite inarticulate, at Greystoke's Gala.
He swept Jane off her high button shoes,
which she says she will no longer need.
But we didn't raise her to be *wild and free.*

And a tree house in the jungle is
a sticky wicket. Where will she put
the tea set, her cloaks and frocks,
underpinnings and petticoats?
Tarzan likely hangs loin cloths on twigs.
Oh, my darling daughter, Jane!
What will become of you?

We've always supported your choices,
however strange. Saxophone over piano.
Swahili over French.
A pity Miss Golightly's Academy
will be for naught.
Lawn Tennis. Flower Arrangement.
Elocution. Ballroom Dancing.

Tarzan may be a tiger in the bedroom,
but I dare say the luster of love will dim
when Jane tires of chasing chimps from
the tree house, baboons from the larder.

And what if she gets in a family way?
A proper nanny is an absolute must.
Not a bloody ape. Well, I'll cross that
rope footbridge when I come to it.

February 22, 2007

Beyond the Bridge

The last to leave
drift down to
rest on the bank
of a creek.
Bare branches
reveal a bridge
reaching
across a divide.
The tree in
full bloom hides
a time when
stark limbs
arc towards
a waiting sky.

March 1, 2007

A Way Out

Aggregate of crushed secrets
crammed into dark caves
of your mind, compressed by
time into sharp-edged stones
small enough to pierce
a ferret's heart, weasel into
the blood stream of sweet
dreams, stab sleep in the gut.
Turn up the volume. Dance
until you drop, hide a vial of
pills under the mattress,
a bottle of vodka in a drawer.

March 12, 2007

Betty Crocker Took a Sip of Cooking Sherry, Turned to the Pillsbury Doughboy and Resumed Her Lament

Nobody understands. General Mills thinks
I'm the Energizer Bunny. Nonstop Bake-Offs,
Editing cook books. Testing new recipes.
Plus I'm fed up with this red dress and
the pearls. You can't imagine what it's like.
Wearing the same clothes for decades!
No, Honey, you can't. Look at you!
Bare ass naked. Silly chef's hat and kerchief.
Don't you want to break out in Gap pants
and cool shades? I've aching to shake
my booty. Came to work Tuesday in
my new jeans with bling. So humiliating
to be sent home to change. The General
got all red faced and roared like
Tony the Tiger. *No trousers in the kitchen!*
How will I ever get the Marlboro Man
to notice me? My sex life is in the cellar.
Honey, hand me the bottle. Thanks, Sugar,
So anyway, Mr. Clean's always coming on
to me, but I don't trust a clean freak.
Know what I mean? He probably checks
for dust under the bed before he hops in.
Those muscles and that earring don't do
a thing for me. Then the dorky Maytag Man.
He wants to take me bowling.
Whoopdedoo! What's that, Honey?
Oh, yeah, Mr. Goodwrench. Can't forget him,
though I'd like to. Suffice it to say,
I was well-oiled at the time. Say, Sugar,
you know the Marlboro Man, don't you?
Give me something I can use.
Does he like brownies?

March 12, 2007

Since the Death of Her Husband

she redecorated the bedroom.
Rosebud pink quilted spread and
flowered sheets with eyelet ruffles.
Now it's *hers* though she misses
the light blue and cocoa brown
of *theirs* where they slept snuggled.

She signed up for a computer class,
never had time to learn the internet
when her husband was alive. And
took a cruise to the Bahamas. Met
a lot of widows with tight smiles,
could hardly wait to get home.

She braved Home Depot solo,
bought her very own tool box.
Metallic green. Fixed a loose
drawer front and hung pictures
all by herself. Monet prints to
replace cowboys in the den.

Now it's she who pays the bills,
and no one to complain about
so many long distance calls,
Visa charges. And she doesn't
have to watch endless ball games
on TV, which is a very big plus.

She doesn't have to fix lunch,
or dinner, for that matter. She grabs
every plus she can, hangs on
tight in a lonely sea of minus one.

March 18, 2007

The Demise of Sylvester the Cat
As related by Claudia Barnett to her mother

The big black and white furry cat,
came to Claudia's bedroom and
let out a death breath. A little while
later he died. So strange she still
can't believe it. Teresa is as stunned
as Claudia. Sylvester seemed fine
a couple of days ago. Not sick to
their knowledge. Every day the girls
feed the cats who live for their food,
and now one of them is dead.
Claudia thought it might be that bad
cat food in the news, the recalled food
that's been killing cats. Teresa said,
*Maybe it's been going on with him for
a while, but it just seems so strange
he would go like that.* She cried all day.
The girls hate to think they are bad
animal owners, although Claudia
always says they have too many,
especially cats. Three dogs and
four cats...well, now three. *And one
less to feed, to put flea medicine on
and take to the vet for shots,* Claudia
confides to her mother on the phone
from the office where she works.
*One down and three to go, is the way
I see it, but don't tell Teresa I said so.*
In answer to her mother's inquiry
as to the whereabouts of Sylvester's
remains, *I'm not saying,* she replied,
*but don't look here in the dumpster.
I hope the trash gets picked up today.*

March 19, 2007

The Trail Blazer(s)

Turning to give her a hand, pulling her along,
he led the way blazing a trail up the mountain.
He's gone after all these years, and she knows
she will have to find her own way. But she can't
think about that now. Together was how they
got through the brambles and together found
a place in the meadow to dance and to feast.

Now she's sunk in a deep well of tears, so
deep she could drown. Sooner or later she
will climb out and go looking for food. Yes,
she will eat again, drink again, laugh again.
She will even get angry at him. It's not fair!
*Why did you leave? You made everything
so easy for me. Now I have to fend for myself.*

She can't know how strong she will become,
the muscles she will discover in her flabby arms,
how calloused her hands, how tough her legs,
slogging through household accounts, repairing
neglected parts of the old place and of herself.
She will continue to seek his advice and will
perceive his answer in the trees he planted,

their branches swaying, *Good job, Baby.*
She will hear his harmonica coming from
the canyon, his whistling in the wind, and be
comforted. She will blaze her own trail with
confidence, maybe even invite someone
to join her in the meadow, in which case,
she will ignore any whistling in the wind.

March 19, 2007

Study of Broken Down

She moans, holding a hand to her head,
leans and examines a bruise on her leg,
black and blue laced with pea green,
shaped like Fiji in a sea of pale thigh.

Tequila, her tabby cat, yowls.
Shit. Out of cat food again.
Almost as bad as out of gin.

That biker guy at Laverne's Lounge.
Did he, ohmygod, bring me home?
She's on her own couch. That's clear.
Same sag, same broken springs.

March 22, 2007

Solitaire

Red 9 on black 10
He's late.
Ace of Clubs up.
Black 8 on red 9.
Candle wax drips.
Red 5 .....
Is that a knock?
..... on black 6.
Queen of Hearts.
No place to go.
Jack of Knaves
can go to blazes.

March 29, 2007

False Alarm

A warning bell
told her to retrieve
deep secrets
from dark places
under shelf paper.
She snipped them
into tiny pieces,
although her chest
pain proved to be
bronchitis.

March 31, 2007

Shoes

I

The little girl threw her arms around her mother's neck.
Please, Mommy, please! The shoe store owner tacked
metal taps on heels of shiny new black patent leather
Mary Janes. Soon as they arrived home, the girl,
cradling a shoe box, skipped to her room, put on
magical Mary Janes, became Shirley Temple.
She twirled and scampered to the basement.
Her mother looked up, smiling at the sound of
tap tap tapping from the concrete basement floor,
sound of last innocent dances before tarantellas.

II

She looked smashing, her long tan bare legs
in white open toe pumps with four inch heels,
and wearing a hot pink polka dot dress that
barely covered her ass when she leaned over,
which was a lot, always dropping her lighter
and cigarettes wherever she went. And she
went a lot...Happy Hour, party, open house
of somebody who was a friend of somebody
else's hair dresser or dealer. She lost a lot...
sunglasses, memory, keys, wallet, shoes.
Took to going barefoot in summer, keeping
it simple, heading straight for the bar and
leaving with any guy who'd buy her drinks.
She cried a lot, mourned everything lost,
especially shoes...white open toe pumps,
T straps, ankle straps, sling backs, slides.

III

Medicare.
Discount fare.
Dr. Scholl's.
Inner soles.
Sensible flats.
That's that.

April 7, 2007

What a Wonderful World

Slivers of fear pierce my mind where sight
resides, and I think to myself, what
a wonderful world fades in front of my face.

White winged birds fly under a bridge
that spans a vast divide between worlds,
one where *I see skies of blue, clouds of*

white, and the other of darkest darkness.
Sweet scent from my bedside waltzes in
my head and I see violets, red roses too.

Sound of footsteps announce the approach
of a gurney to wheel me into a cold tunnel
connecting a place where I see colors of

a rainbow dazzling in the sky, and another
where everything is black as a crow's wing.
An I.V. drip in my arm and I slip away to

lovely la la land, floating over two worlds,
and from somewhere among the Pleiades,
the husky voice of Louis Armstrong singing.

April 13, 2007

They Paved Paradise

Joni Mitchell

She drives her red VW bug into a slot
marked by white stripes. It sits
in the shade of gasoline thirsty SUV's
where there used to be trees.
Don't it always seem to go that you
don't know what you've got till it's gone?
sang her idol, Joni Mitchell, strumming
a guitar when not smoking cigarettes.

They paved paradise and put up
a parking lot. Joni was referring to
The Garden of Allah, Hollywood
Hotel on Sunset Blvd., torn down
in 1959, even though the landmark
building had been a mecca to literati.
F. Scott Fitzgerald lived and wrote
there, no doubt drank there.

But hey, America! Parking lots, banks, fast-
food drive-thrus with trans fats is where it's at.

Not too many VW bugs chugging
along anymore. Hers was a steal.
Primo paint job. Rebuilt engine.
She found it on eBay. A reminder of
hippie days, love beads, tie-died tees,
Joni, Jimi, Janis, grannie glasses,
Riders on the Storm, turn on and
tune in teen years long gone

She takes pretty good care of it,
changes her own oil. It's her baby.
And she doesn't have to empty
the ashtray any more since she quit.
Had a tough time kicking the habit,
is glad The Insider blew the lid off
tobacco companies, now peddling
"cute cigarettes". Camels No. 9.

Watch out, Joni! Don't let the smokes get you.
You don't know what you've got if you're gone.

April 15, 2007

Letters from Korea

My Marine Corps husband would have scored
D - in penmanship. Bless the typewriter he
occasionally found to pound out a letter to me
from Korea. The letters, my lifeline in a cold
sea of separation, his words a bridge across

a cruel chasm called War. I have them still,
in a packet tied with one of his shoelaces,
though I donated the shoes to Good Will
long years ago. Fingering his inky scrawls
draws me closer to him once again.

October 20, 1951 Korea K1
My Dearest Darling Sweetheart, Have you
checked on the procedure for sending
a dispatch to me when the baby is born?

Yes. Our first child. A year was torn from our lives
when her daddy was overseas in Korea. And we
were among the fortunate. He came home to us.

April 21, 2007

Tick Tock Tick Tock

I need no second hand
to remind me of time's

determined rush toward
night. I turn away from

numbered faces that
once held me captive,

counting down hours
crammed with endless

minutes. Evening, then
the shining time of your

arrival, now marks end
of day, setting of sun

April 28, 2007

Parsley, Sage, Rosemary and No More Thyme
For Miriam

Two minutes ago, leaves limp as boiled greens,
quiet as dying campfires down at Cardiff Beach,
then *wham,* yawling like cats fighting in the alley
behind The Shanty where boozers lap it up.

Branches tremble and shake. Leaves
rattle and wave. Somebody out there is
trying to get my attention. It's Miriam. She's
calling in her Mississippi accent. *Hi, yawl!*

She's up yonder with her plastic bags of
herbs.....basil, sage, pungent plants
from her garden. She's all set to sprinkle
them into a savory celestial stew that will

forever replace ambrosia at the heavenly
table. I envy spirits gathered round the pot.
Even Faulkner who lived next door and
never spoke to her when she was a girl,

will get a whiff of Miriam's herbs and
hear the sound of her peppery words.
He'll be first in line for her specialty.
Two things I do not know...how long

I will have to wait to taste the stew, and
how to season with herbs. Last spring
Miriam brought me a chart outlining
specific uses for each one. I lost it.

And she brought two big plastic bags
stuffed with bunches of various herbs
that I dumped when they became
slimy in my fridge. My little secret.

I could never tell her I trashed her gift.
But what the hell was I going to do
with herbs? God knows I don't cook.
Now, of course, so does Miriam.

June 17, 2007

Citizen Kane and I

spent an afternoon together
back when I was a kid and
didn't have a clue he would top

everybody's 100 Best Movies list.
Except mine. First of all, the film
was in black and white. Clunk.

I needed technicolor to put luster
on my tarnished day. More. He died
and I cried, not for him, for the child.

I missed the point, as I had
missed the bus to grandma's
house for Thanksgiving goose,

was stuck at St. Mary's with
the rest of the homeless kids
who had no place else to go.

An extra piece of pumpkin pie
with lots of whipped cream
served as my consolation prize,

but the piece de resistance
was free movie tickets to
The Lamar Theater on

Lake Street. Orson Welles
in Citizen Kane. Thank God it
wasn't Bogart in Casablanca,

or Rick's American Cafe might
lurk in my mind along side of bitter
sweet potatoes and tough turkey.

You can have your Citizen Kane.
I'll keep Casablanca, watch it
for the hundredth time and say,

Play it again, (Sam.).

June 26, 2007

Problem Child

Your cat pisses
on the rug.
Again and again.
You say, *Bad Taffy,*
spray water on her,
slap her butt.
She still pisses.
You say, *Shit,*
grab and wrap her
in a towel,
head sticking out,
take her yowling
to the pound.
Shebang!
Problem gone.
No tears.
It wouldn't work
with a bad kid.
You'd cry
all the way home.

August 13, 2007

Echoes of the Past

I learned early on the art of leaving
from my mother. Bright smile, quick
twist of the wrist and don't look back.

I never asked her to move to be close
to me and my baby, my man gone to war.
Hadn't I long been a pro at coping

without her?   without her   without her

I guess she planned to spend days off
with me and my baby. I had other plans.
Like lunch with a friend in the country.

But sure, she could ride along for part
of the way and take a bus back to town.
I dropped her off at a dusty bus stop.

Bright smile, quick twist of the wrist.
No looking back. I could have taken
her with me, but I drove off

without her   without her   without her

August 25, 2007

The Passage

They wore each other like vintage
undergarments, all-over close to
the skin. Soft as fog, as cobwebs.

Married for decades, he's naked
without her. Bare. Exposed.
Loneliness seeps from open pores.

Everything reminding him of her.
A Bergman movie with English
subtitles. Jane Austin novels he's

reading again. New Yorker magazines
she subscribed to. Her still life paintings,
on the walls of their tiny apartment in

a retirement complex. The two chests
of drawers. One his with shirts, socks
and sweaters. The other hers, empty.

He starts to write poetry about her,
about the blank space in his life without
her. And the more he writes, the more

the process fills his blank spaces,
crowding it with craft. Time consuming
craft. Like building a ship in a glass bottle.

Painstaking craft. Striving to find precise
perfect words like white sails billowing.
Building lines until he has created a ship

called *Poem*. He sails away on unfurled
words to a place called *Peace*, still missing
her when he isn't busy at the wheel.

September 3, 2007

History of Addiction

Her first kiss,
forbidden kiss.
Her uncle's tongue.
slippery lips,
taste of bitter gin.
So it begins.
Trysts and buzzy
highs, never quite
like that *sizzle*.
Still turns her face
red, makes her
breathe fast
looking back
at that kiss.
So bad. So good.

September 7, 2007

Stamps and Stuff

Where do you keep your stamps?
Perhaps in an empty stationery box,
presuming you write enough letters
to have an empty stationery box.

Or a pull-out dispenser, a gift from
your granddaughter, maybe brass,
matches the letter opener you never use,
preferring a knife.

I keep mine in a cigar box.
Don't smoke, just collect the boxes.
Great for junk and stuff. Stamps.
I suppose you do have stamps.

For monthly utility bills, of course,
but also for all the letters you write.
The letter never sent is
the letter never answered.

Empty See's candy boxes hold
my precious cargo of saved letters.
They are sweeter by far than any
soft centered chocolate bon bon.

Jenny may have kissed Leigh Hunt, but
I have a letter from my grandson in
a candy box in my desk drawer. Say I'm
growing old, but add, Davey wrote me.

September 11, 2007

Hot Dry Spell

no rain in weeks
each blade of grass and limp leaf
dusty

no cloud in sight
cruel sun beats down on cracked
ground

show me the man
with strength enough to sing Earth's
praises

he has air-conditioning

September 12, 2007

Pieces of Possibilities

Sherry met that curious marshmallow man.
at a coffee house. Short, pale and puffy.
The discussion turned to hobbies.
Hers is needlepoint. Marshmallow Man said,
My hobby is book binding. How odd.
Is it possible she had met him before?
Deja vu? How many people bind books
for fun? Now she had met two. Or had she?

When I woke this morning I couldn't shake
my dream of a craggy man with a wooden leg.
He said, *I own a castle, but this secret gazebo
is more precious because you are here.*
He unscrewed his leg and he screwed me.
I see myself leaning to kiss his stump.

But maybe too bizarre. I could write about running
around naked like Mary-Kate Olsen. She is quoted
in today's paper as saying, *I love running around
the house naked in heels, naked with jewelry.*
I see myself bopping around the house in the buff,
bangles and blubber bouncing. Nope. It will never
happen. There's not enough jewelry in the world.

Time out. I'm off to the store to buy another set of
china plates and a ream of paper, just in case.

September 17, 2007

Sunday Morning Chapel at St. Pat's Girls Camp

In a wooden chapel, thick
with incense and dozy girls,
the sound
of droned responses rose
to wormy rafters.
Sister Prisca
of the perpetual frown,
sat in back keeping track
of gigglers and whisperers.
I was among
both and added to my
basket of mischief, jabbing
Cecie in the side while
by rote, I prayed
for absolution.
Sister Anne Marie
of the benign open arms,
lined up girls scrambling
out after the final blessing.
Our transgressions.
Mystical body.
One day I'd come
to understand
those fuzzy phrases
with the help of
Father Frank
of the crooked smile.

September 21, 2007

It's Only a Diner but She Gets Big Tips

She sticks a bobby pin
in her brassy blond frizz,
pack of cigs in a pocket.
Her slip peeks beneath

a green waitress uniform.
Two buttons missing on
the bodice make it gap
when she leans down

to pour a cup of coffee.
Even a guy at the counter
with a frown on his face
looks up and smiles

as laughter spills from her
Max Factor Rowdy Red lips.

September 25, 2007

Obituaries

I've got to quit
reading obituaries.
Ages close
to mine pop out
like neon signs,
reminding me
the end of the line
is round the bend.
I'll pretend
the obituary page
is missing from
my paper, turn
to the crossword
instead. I've read
working puzzles
keeps the mind
alert, memory sharp.
One across:
an eight letter word
for notice of death.
What can I say!
There's no escape.

October 2, 2007

Miss Narcissus

I loved the sight of me
in my aqua skirt
twirled and caught
a flash of my smile

in a shop window
tripped on a crack
in the sidewalk
crashed and cut

my kneecap
dimes scattered
lunch money gone
blood on my

aqua skirt torn
beyond repair
now my knobby
knuckled finger

traces a faint scar
remaining from
a fall at the sight
of my own beauty

October 5, 2007

Narcissus and Me

We were both in love with him
and I lost out to the one more beautiful.
God! I wish you could have seen him.
All those golden waves, peacock blue
eyes and bright white even teeth.
No surprise he himself was my rival.

The lake was cold, of course, and he
sank fast, the weight of his ego
holding him down. I tossed rose petals
on the water, red for love, though he
probably would have found orchids
more fitting. A rare variety. Expensive.

October 7, 2007

Weeping Goddess Fountain

Her trickling tears ease
my fever, slow my pulse.
As I gaze at closed eyelids
on her weeping stone face,
calm like a bright white
wave flows over me,
quiets my crazed appetite.
I could lift my arms
and fly halfway to Africa,
but am content to lie
on a garden lounge,
surrounded by trailing
vines in a leafy haven,
floating in a green sea
of unfamiliar peace,
released from a need
for momentary remedies.

October 19, 2007

This Old House and I

Kevin stops by to change
a ceiling light bulb, and Dave
calls to say he'll spray for
white fly on shrubs tomorrow.

Dean advises, *Cancel the*
termite contract, Mom. It's a rip-off.
Claudia phones from Portland
to warn about climbing ladders.
I say goodbye to the Avon lady.

Now alone, we speak to each
other, this old house and I.
The house hums and I sing
what words I can remember to
Streets of Laredo. My husband's
favorite. A kitchen floor board
creaks and I nod agreement,
Yes. I miss him too.

A broken window rattles and
I reply, *Soon. Soon.*
When the new roof's paid off.
Walls crackling, tap tap tapping
of glass louvers tell me to put
down my book and look up.
Just like he used to. *Yes.*
You're right. We do need music.

The house likes country.
I like jazz. We compromise
on classical and listen while
shadows of the past gather
and settle down on our laps.

Melting sun low over the ocean.
Evening closes in and we lean
toward each other. It's enough.

October 20, 2007

City of Carlsbad Calls for Voluntary Evacuation

Into the light of a dark black night
Paul McCartney

We forgot the goldfish
swimming circles in a tank
in Grant's bedroom.
Left Max behind. That fat
black cat no way no how
going to get in a crate.
We remembered dog food
for Deacon, big black
Newfoundland and Jake,
yippy Yorkie. Couldn't find
a carrying cage for the birds.
Mimi, 12, unseemingly
handy with an ice pick,
punched holes in a box,
popped cockatiels inside.
She, Grant, 14, and I, their
Nana, raced like runners
in a relay, handing off
clothes and snacks. Grant
grabbed photo albums.
video games, his guitars,
acoustic and electric
Shoved them into any spare
crack in the back of the van.
Loaded up, we drove
through air dense and dark
with smoke and soot to my
house on the coast to wait.
For flames to recede.
For their parents to return.
For how long we didn't know.
But we had music as Grant
strummed, *Blackbird*
singing in the dead of night.

October 29, 2007

It Was the Wine

The third goblet
and her eyes, kohl lined.
A snake bracelet tattoo
on her left ankle.
Crazy quilt skirt twirling
as she danced barefoot,
bangles on her arms.
Her eyes dared me
to tear the yellow tape
around her danger zone.
She laughed. Her lips,
pillow soft lips parted.
When next we met at
a school PTA, she
in jeans and sneakers
looked away.

November 3, 2007

The Way It Wasn't

I always skip the part
about the cop
stopping me when I tell
how it all went down.
Fuck the cop. Nobody
needs to know I got
busted and ended up
owing Chuck big time
for bailing me out and
he's looking to collect
before my old man
gets back in town.
Digger's in Jersey
trying to score a gig.
But with his thumb
broke from a fight
with Fish and those
guys, he don't strum
so good. Anyways,
Rosa and Bippy left
me holding while
they went to pick up

wheels. There I was
on a corner looking
like you know what
when this cop shows.
But this part about
winning the lottery,
flying to Vegas for
the Elvis Look Alike
contest and meeting
Wayne Newton, then
dropping the rest of
my loot in the slots,
hitching a ride home
with an old guy
who used to work for
Howard Hughes.
And had a walk-on gig
in that movie with
Brad Pitt or was it Leo?
That's the part that
blows everybody away.

November 5, 2007

Time of the Crow

Sly mist settles on fence,
quiet as death's sigh.
Where are the crows?
Up the hill a dog howls,
sounds time to go inside.
Sudden thunder of black
wings flapping. Raucous
caw caw caws. Murder
of crows crowding sky.
Overhead they circle, dive,
attack a red Honda parked
at the curb. There are no
more paperboys on bikes.

November 20, 2007

Roses after Rain

grateful petals glow
in today's sun
yesterday's dust
washed away
sweet fragrance
rises as Mimi leans
and snips a stem
places it in a vase
Bob smiles at
a gift of love from
Mimi's garden

December 5, 2007

Mother at the Mortuary

I didn't pick out the coffin
and never knew the cost
which seemed irrelevant
at the time. I had flown
two thousand miles
at great cost to me,
and moreover, leaving

month end accounts
in complete chaos.
Her bossy sisters
arranged everything.
Church, prayers, hymns,
mortuary, best in town,
selected the clothes for

her to to wear in the coffin,
which was just as well.
God knows I could never
please her, would have
chosen the wrong dress,
although that might have
given me final satisfaction.

December 10, 2007

I Tripped on the Moon

I tripped on the calloused crust
of the moon which looks
slippery as stainless steel
from below.
Imagine falling into crevices
stuffed with helium dreams
and ballooned desires rising
to hold the moon aloft.
I hovered in space close to
star light, star bright, first star
of the night blinking and
hoodwinking silly saps who
can't get the job done.

2007

THE TRISH DUGGER COLLECTION OF POETRY

2008

Nightmares

Did you ever
drive drunk, your kid
in the back seat
screaming,
his knees bloody
from falling
onto gravel in a park,
the swing
pushed too hard
by a red-eyed fiend?
No? I envy you,
good mother,
your sweet dreams.

January 26, 2008

Woo Hoo Day

When you find my wine-stained journal
beside a leaning rock on a cliff
next to the boisterous sea, you will read...
*Today is the day I tore a page from
the Good Book and fed it to the shredder.
No thank you, Moses.* Today I covet my
neighbor's hubby, steal his heart along
with the key to his jeep, speed to
the frozen yogurt shop and command
the delicious shop boy to mound my cone
with creamy swirls of Frooty Tooty Delight.
And lots of sprinkles. I will bow down,
dance around and worship a fat-bellied
idol, stuff myself with insanely sweet
strawberries. Did you know? The colder
the nights, the sweeter the strawberries.
The lonelier the nights, the colder
the toes. Mine nearly froze. I will tell you lies.
No, I never did that. Show me.

January 31, 2008

It Started with Brown Brogans

A pair of worn brown brogans
stand to the side, guard my front door.
Mighty size 13 to fit the feet
of a man magnificent in proportion.
Deterrent to would-be burglars.
My son's idea. He worries about me
living alone. He'd worry more if
he knew I leave the door unlocked,
and even more if he knew how
this phantom man has my attention.
My new guy is six foot three, strong
as a Brahma bull, demands steak
and eggs for breakfast. I stock up
on T-bones, fill my cart with makings
for manly meals. He likes country
western. I download George Strait.
I catch myself thinking *We*, as in
We will watch an old John Wayne
movie on tv tonight and *We* will stroll
to the beach on such a lovely day.
Maybe *I* should be the one to worry.

February 4, 2008

Mattresses Revisited

tops the list of poems
I will never write
with Bar Stools of Stockton
close behind.
Seedy Motels of
Barstow and Beyond...
way up there too.
You don't need to know
and I frankly forget
seedy details.
But sour smells and
grungy rumpled beds
seep into my lines.
Watch out for
shattered glass
on the ground
under sassy pansies,
their roots
planted in ashes.

February 6, 2008

Valentine to the City of Encinitas

Roses are red. Violets are blue.
Sugar is sweet. Life here is too.
Hearts and flowers, love divine,
Encinitas, you'll always be mine.
From Olivenhain to the Pacific coast,
This is the city I love the most.
From Leucadia to Cardiff by the Sea,
This is the place I want to be.
Encinitas, both old and new,
I call you Home and I love you.
Five communities combined in one,
Our paradise under the sun.
Quail Gardens and Moonlight Beach,
Trails and parks, something for each.
Encinitas folks have spirit and heart,
An ear for poetry, an eye for art.
Our grand new library we celebrate.
What a wonderful start for 2008.

February 14, 2008

Violets Are Blue

Valentine's Day. Raining.
She grabs an umbrella,
runs out to check her mailbox
walks back empty-handed,
shoulders sagging.
Inside she picks up the phone,
punches numbers for a plumber.
Hangs up. Looks for a bucket.
Puts it under the kitchen sink.
She kneels and wipes
her eyes with a sleeve, the floor
with an X LG tee he left behind.

February 14, 2008

True Love

The deep crease between
her brows, gone.
Smooth as sea glass.
Crinkles at the sides
of her eyes vanished
like her bank account.
She smiles in a mirror.
Again. And again.
Says to herself,
Yes, ten years less.
Maybe fifteen.

February 18, 2008

Code Blue

The bed, rumpled sheets.
Coffee pot sputtering.
Scent of orange peel.
An unshaven man in
slippers and robe
on the ground.
Newspaper in
plastic sleeve at his feet.
His eyes closed,
skin cold as dread.
A woman kneeling
strokes his face, lifts her
head at the sound
of a blue jay.

February 19, 2008

It Started with Alice

Day narrows down to remote control,
tv guide, his big feet in boots
on the coffee table. She pours cups
of tea in the kitchen. He reaches for
the remote. Evening and Larry King.

She tells him to turn it down a bit
and picks up a book from a stack
next to her easy chair. Mysteries in
large print. On nearby shelves,
a colorful crowd of slightly tipsy

friends leaning into each other like
patrons at a neighborhood bar,
including Alice, inscribed, *To Patsy,
Christmas 1939*. Alice showed her
the way to a Wonderland of her own

where she found Nancy Drew and
the others, searched for clues with
Nancy in twisted candles and clocks,
solving cases with Miss Marple.
Bloody dagger in the potting shed.

Muddy footprints in the vicarage.
Elementary. But why does
the cable bill keep going up and
where is the lost remote control?
Not a clue. Where is Nancy Drew?

February 25, 2008

To Cardiff by the Sea

When my family settled down
in Cardiff by the Sea years ago,
it didn't take us long to know
we had found paradise.
Now 56 years later, driving
down Birmingham from the top
of the hill, it's still a thrill to
see the vast expanse of blue
in front of me. It still takes my
breath away to this very day.
Our town is rare with a charm
like no other spot. Look what
we've got! A beach and lagoon,
Cardiff Reef, Glen Park, Pipes,
VG Donuts, Seaside Market, Ki's
on Restaurant Row to name
a few, each with a killer view.
Our two miles of coast has
more than most to boast about.

Along our two miles of coast,
camping at a state beach park,
and kids of all ages having fun
in the sand and sea and sun.
We have our own library, our
own post office and zip, 92007,
which naturally rhymes with
heaven. And we have our own
bronze surfer dude. Some think
he's cool, some think he's rude.
Cardiff people care and work hard
to keep Cardiff special and unique.
When all's said and done,
what's the one town under the sun
where anybody in his right mind
..... or not ...... wants to be?
The answer is Cardiff by the Sea.
We must have done something right.
Let's celebrate our town tonight.

March 2008

Shades of Love

At dinner I told Bernardo about
my offshore bank accounts.
He smiled as he reached for
more Lobster Thermador
and poured another glass
of Chardonnay.
How soon do we sail for the Cape?
His eyes the azure blue
of his cravat.
I love him. He loves my money.
We both love the Cape.
How do we know what we love?
Our pocketbook tells us.
A shop girl in an upstairs flat
loves herbal tea and her cat.
And when my money and
I are spent,
Here, kitty, kitty.

March 1, 2008

Maybe It Happens Out of Boredom

a walk in the dunes, each grain of
sand shifting where the wind went.
She places her fingertips on
a tumbleweed and it becomes
a fruited branch. He'd never had
the slightest idea she yearned to
dance, never dreamed she longed
to see him kneeling beside her.
Finally one stolen night, an old story
unfolding, maybe in a hotel room,
they enter their blank page.
How would you write it?
All lust and tumble? The words he
wrote, touching her in slow motion,
showed her what it is to live
where light falls on her soul.
It's worth knowing that today,
in the privacy of their own home,
she unbraids her gray hair.
He, limping down the hall,
still quickens at
her voice calling his name.

March 7, 2008

Buses and Trains

Passage

Kids in scruffy coveralls pressed
against a chain link fence, eyes
wide, mouths in a round, *Ohhh!*
as a streamliner zooms by.
A steam engine down the line,
its faithful red caboose trailing,
pulls a freight load of coal as
it chugga chugga choo choo-s
into Once upon a time land.

Once Upon a Bus

On a Bluebird Bus grumbling along Route 66 to
grandma's house for holidays, her brown paper sack
of extra clothes on an overhead rack. Howling past
Chicago's rusty monster factories, past wide fields
of corn, fields of green grass outside the state prison.
Borders of pretty red and blue flowers along tall tall
brick walls. She knew to duck so the bad people
inside couldn't get her. Dark night when they finally
arrive at the station, her head pounding from bumps
against the window when she drooped and snoozed,
dreaming of Grandma in plaid jacket and flowered
print dress. Waiting for her. Waiting and smelling of
fresh baked bread and honey. Waiting and watching
for a little girl who'd run to her grandma's open arms
to catch up on hugs. A fairy tale ending she never
tired of, never stopped believing, even when Orville,
the hired hand, whistled and called out her name in
the station and reached for her brown paper sack.

Nocturne

Night train's mournful horn
owl replies *whoo whoo* full moon
gleams on dark wings empty arms

Learning to Fly

Leggy girls scramble
to catch the el train,
running to make it
on time so they won't
get docked. A job
working for pennies
at a candy factory.
They toss peanuts
from a penny machine
on the train platform,
laughing at
pigeons scrambling.

March 16, 2008

A Thing About Spring

Tulips wiggle their roots, stretch,
yawn and blink at Spring's sunny sky,
and an old apple tree in the side yard
pulls spring clothes out of
a bottom drawer, puts on flirty flowers
as if it were young.
Impossible blossoms.
And fruit it continues to bear, still tasty,
though a trifle tart,
like words from an old poet.

March 21, 2008

Crow Controversy

It's All about Who Laughs Last
Sometimes a cigar is just a cigar
Sigmund Freud

big black crows congregate
strutting on bare branches
of her cottonwood tree
a caucus of crows squawks
she shakes a broom at the sky
shouts *Hey you shoo fly away*
they stay pay no mind
what's next maybe a sign
No Crows Allowed
then she'd have to teach
them to read though signs
don't stop skate boarders
clacking on sidewalks
across the street kids and
crows enough to make
an old crone lose her cool
what's the world coming to
once she thought she knew
something to do with silence
is golden or was it everything
in its place no sleeping dogs
that's it let them lie but who's
going to clean up the crow crap

March 22, 2008

Mockingbird

There's not much I can say about To Kill a Mockingbird that has not already been said except maybe this:

Our world would be strange
to Atticus Finch, Scout and Jem.
Ipods, cell phones, laptops and such.
Much has changed but much has not.
If Atticus, Scout and Jem were here
today, I have no doubt they'd be
checking out their limit. Remember
how they ended most of their days?
Jem in bed with a book. Scout at her
father's knee or on his lap, Atticus
reading to her. The three would be
happy campers with all the books
in this wonderful new library. But
they'd shake their heads at DVDs
and say, *What the heck are these?*

I suspect they'd pass up DVDs in
favor of books. You see not only did
Atticus teach his kids to be kind
and to give others their due respect,
he taught them to love the printed page.
No matter what your age, when you
open a book to read, you open yourself
to adventure and suspense, to laughter
and surprise. A book you love is your
friend for life. *To Kill a Mockingbird* is
a friend to visit again and again, to meet
once more with Scout and Jem and for
me, to think about the dad I never knew,
wondering if he'd have been like Atticus,
dreaming he would have read to me too.

March 28, 2008

The Best Laid Pamela

If you're stepping out of your panties,
it's too late for Plan B. Trust me.

Actually, I never had a Plan B or
any plan at all. I maureened

down the farley path to where his
lips led. That was humphreys ago.

Losing the keys to my car, house,
indeed my life, ended in reginald.

Had I known the final phylllis, would
I have said, *vince* instead of *when*?

His lester and loretta philliped me
with a cynthia I'd never imagined.

Now I'm stranded at the janice craig,
glass shards of yesterday scattered

behind me. It's clare that I must brock
and bleed to return to the other side,

to get back to candace where brad
began, before the bruce of bridget.

It would be easy to remain in hillary,
to wendy my time in painless walter.

I'm no good with blood and gordon.
So look for me in the garden of denise.

The weather is pleasantly pauline and
I'm learning to clancy with new clydes.

March 31, 2008

Nobody Warns You

I climb seventeen stairs fast as I can,
gasping to a second floor apartment,
Steady, I say to my impatient heart.
Nobody warns me I'm losing it.

I knock on the door at the top and wait
for my dolly under the Christmas tree,
my pearl in an oyster, my pot of gold.
Nobody warns he'll grow up too fast.

My daughter at the open door holds him
wiggling on her hip. Eyes bright stars.
He smiles and squeals, reaching for me.
Nobody warns he'll move away.

We spoon sand into muffin tins, bake in
pretend ovens. We go pretend fishing
in pretend boats. He catches a big shark.
Nobody warns me to not go overboard.

But nothing could've stopped my runaway
heart. No words of warning could've kept
me from tumbling for a toothless charmer.
Call it temporary insanity. I'm a grandma.

April 4, 2008

The Seventh Child

The story was good for a laugh over drinks,
a seventh child we had put up for adoption
because he was allergic to dust, poor babe.
Our tumbledown house layered with dust,
rocked with kids gone amok in toy trucks
I dreamed up features for the seventh child.
One green eye, the other blue. Sandy hair.
Widow's peak. Dimple in his right cheek.
Our five sons could not have cared less
about one more boy in an already packed
teepee, the tribe fighting over everything.
Top bunk, baseball bat, last piece of pie.
But my daughter, our oldest, begged for more
about the baby she couldn't remember.
What was his name? I thought a bit. Trevor.
Always liked Trevor. Hadn't used it yet.
His birthday? May 8th. Nice spring date.
She insisted we celebrate. Party hats.
Streamers. Poppers. Balloons. I went
along, play pretend always big in our home.
The story has grown like Jack's beanstalk.
The afghan I'm knitting for his next birthday,
almost complete. It's green, his favorite color.

April 14, 2008

The Sleep Experience

I sleep solo in silky sheets.
600 thread count. Pale blue.
5 down pillows fit for a queen.
Sweet dreams guaranteed
like you and me tustling in
muslin sheets, those wild
nights when we didn't give
a fuck about thread count.

April 16, 2008

Dashed Off Tuesday Morn

Marte's great poems tend to be long,
full of angst and images dense.
Dolores' poems are like a song,
take us to China in the past tense.
Ivy's dreamy lyrical poetry flows.
and often back to Warsaw it goes.
RT's wonderful poems range far,
from California to an Indiana bar.
Dick keeps us all socially aware.
Tight concise lines written with care.
Look for Kate in the mountains high.
searching for an old Chinese guy.
who was last seen talking to trees.
And now Kate recites to the breeze.
Elaine's poems increasingly delight
with each new revision until it's right.
Connie insists she has nothing to say
while she continues to blow us away.
Lenny Lianne is our southern touch
a wonderful sound saying much.
Mai Lon serves us Chinatown in verse,
delicious images, vivid and terse.
Duke continues to grow as a poet.
She is amazing and we all know it.
Harry''s our mentor and the reason why
we stay together. He's our Poetry Guy.
Trish writes limericks raunchy and rough,
X-rated rhymes about fucking and stuff.
A limerick's 5th line ends with a punch.
Maybe that's why (It's just a hunch),
Trish tries to tie up her poems at the end,
which is, of course, a terrible trend.
Punch line or not, they could be worse.
They could be written in rhymed verse.

April 22, 2008

Survivors

Early dark before stars declare night,
hushed hearts in a holding pattern.
Wary minds tiptoe over foreign ground
inside a dragon's mouth.
They sit, little hands in their little laps,
instructed to wait on a back porch
of a strange house. Through a window
they see their new foster parents
eating potatoes and meat.
After the table is cleared, the man with
gray whiskers shows them where to
put their things, where to sleep.

April 27, 2008

End of the Line

Hot gusty wind sweeps dust
and gum wrappers round
a bus stop bench.
A woman with white hair sits,
one hand to a black straw hat,
purse on her lap. She leans
and fingers a run in her hose,
frowns. Dampness shines in
lines of her neck. She checks
her watch, pulls a transfer slip
from her purse, stands and
peers down the street, her
swollen feet in rundown heels.
Sunday afternoon. August.
Corner strip mall stores closed.
Donuts. Thrift Store. Pawn Shop.
Tarot Cards/Fortunes Told.

April 28, 2008

Disappearing Bees

No bees. No crops.
No money for the farmer.
No honey for bread.
No hum.
When all is said
and hung out to dry
in the sun,
most of all I will miss
the hum, its swarm
of calm, counterpoint
to life's uncertain song..

June 30, 2008

His Body Clad in Black

was found on a stained
and faded
green chenille spread
covering a queen
in Room 23 of a cheap motel,
west edge of town.
Missing *V* in blinking neon.
ACANCY ACANCY
and, according to whispers
among parishioners,
two empty bottles lying
at his surrendered side.
Aspirin. Jack Daniels.
Those who exposed him
in The Daily News
expressed regret.
And one old woman
on the prayer chain,
alone in her dusty home,
back bent over in pain,
answered the phone,
winced as she heard
the hushed words,
sordid and lost soul,
said, *Yes, of course,*
to a request for prayers,
then slowly hung up,
and added a couple of
items to her shopping list.

July 10, 2008

Let's Go Back

to sweet days of feet in pajamas,
gripper snaps holding tops to bottoms,
the bottoms bulky with damp diapers.

Let's go back to bedtime stories,
dwarfs in caves, handsome heroes
who saved the day, slaying dragons
and demons in time for sleep.

Let's go back to nighty-night tuck-ins
and teeth under pillows, belief in tooth
fairies, reindeer in the sky when a kiss
on the knee could make it all better.

Let's go back to you and me
in each other's arms at end of day,
before unpaid bills, too many
gin tonics and a note in your
inside coat pocket got in the way.

Let's go back to a time when we
didn't pretend to sleep, silently lying
on opposite sides of a king size bed,
back to when a kiss on the lips
could make it all better.

July 22, 2008

THE TRISH DUGGER COLLECTION OF POETRY

Bye Bye Firefly So Long Honey Bee

A temp at the front desk took a message:
V.P. Joe Bono is waiting for a tech
to recalibrate his breathing machine.
His bp dropped so low the doctor feared
he'd go into kidney failure so,
No, he won't be at the company's
annual Labor Day picnic.

The pullout book section of
the Sunday paper is a thing of the past
along with fireflies and honey bees.
Who doesn't love fairy tale endings?
Also disappearing. Who knows if

Betty's broken hip might have been
prevented by a bone density test
and treatment with Fosomax?
Since health benefits were cut back,
few have bucks for an office visit
much less a box of Band-Aids.
Five guys in the warehouse got laid off
last week and the shift cut to six hours.

The Labor Day picnic starts at
11:00 A.M. at Last Pine Park
on Rt. 65A by dry Lake Mondo.
Hot dogs and coleslaw.
Free pop and ice cream. B.Y.O.B.
Softball and horseshoe pitching
if it doesn't rain as predicted.

September 1, 2008

Girls Day at the Del Mar Races

All the Pretty Horses
Cormack McCarthy

It's not a sure thing on an inside tip, but the girls
are ready to run and the odds are on lots of fun.

Free parking at the track for the last two races
takes precise timing. One second after 4:30 P.M.

when the guy taking money folds up for the day,
they drive in, then cruise round the lot to spot

an empty space, park and pile out, four girls in
bright shorts. Tees and flipflops, Mimi's ponytail

flying as they make a mad dash to the paddock in
time to see jockeys in bright shiny silks mount up.

Blinders on the gray. A frisky bay kicks, swerves to the side.
What's your pick, Mimi? She's long-legged filly,

not quite thirteen, a beauty with excellent breeding.
Two across the board on the long shot, she replies,

passing her money to Aunt Claudia to place a bet.
Nana swears by her own surefire system:

No. 7 in the 7th to win. Then Nana and Claudia,
Mimi and Teresa hotfoot it to the betting windows,

pushing through crowds, laughing and shouting,
Wait up! Wait for me!, winners even before

all the pretty horses reach the starting gate.

September 4, 2008

When I Consider How

When I consider how my light is spent,
John Milton

sudden fog blurs a faint horizon
and thunderclouds expand,
early dark's black burlap wraps
around last glimmers of light,
casting a shroud over sight.
No more north star to guide me.
An icy needle jabs my insides
and I grope toward your scent,
hint of woodsy pine and musk.
Then your voice, husky, low,
the familiar warmth of you near,
hushes my fear as you unfold
your umbrella of calm and
take my arm. *Careful, Baby.*
Three steps up.

September 11, 2008

Lettuce Lettuce Lettuce

rise above petty peas and caramelized carrots.
Once and for all we must squash rumors
of rutabagas rabble-rousing among radishes.
It has been disclosed the rumors were
started by malicious scallions and onions
with bok choy motives. There is some truth,
however, to current reports that turnips
are turning tricks in soup tureens.
This must stop, of course, for the good of
decent folk everywhere. Furthermore, free
brussel sprout handouts must end before
they become a drain on our economy's
cabbage. The people have spoken.
They demand the government stop clear
and present parsnips with an artichoke
hold on democracy. Together we can
overcome kale. Never forget that this is
a country where freedom from broccoli
and spinach is guaranteed. Thank you
and God bless all our sweet potato pies.

September 12, 2008

Losing It

An inky black lake
floods green fields.
I sink into coal dust
with a thud on
the crust of a scream.
Where did it go,
this thing called *sight?*
It fled in the dead
of day, stealing away
what was left of light.

September 15, 2008

London Bridge

We drive out to Morristown to check on
Grandma's cousin May and her husband, John.
Last spring his rheumatiz was acting up
and May's eyesight failing, her knees creaky.

London Bridge is falling down

We take jars of Grandma's preserved beans
and beets, gleaming like jewels in the sun
and will explain why Grandma couldn't come.
Crick in her back. Can't sit too long.

falling down, falling down

We arrive in time for tea and fresh baked ginger snaps.
Spicy ginger can't cover acrid smell of cat pee.
We frown stepping around seven saucers of cat food on
the floor near the screen door coming off its hinges.

falling down, faling down

Cousin May turns on a dripping faucet at the sink,
fills a dented tea kettle. We chase cats, tabby,
black and calico, off chairs at the table and sit.
Watch out for that broken chair leg, warns John.

London Bridge is falling down

May's dress, faded blue, powdered with flour, hangs
loose on her bony frame. A slip shows below the hem.
Her silver hair spills from a bun on her head and
handles of her glasses are held in place with tape.

falling down, falling down

John shuffles a bit, taking baby steps as he brings
a plate of cookies from the flour dusted counter.
With his spare hand patting May's rump, he smiles,
his pale eyes sparkling under shaggy brows.

my fair lady

September 21, 2008

At the Supermarket with My Visiting Sister-in-Law

We had it out in canned tuna.
Right there in Aisle 15 of Piggly Wiggly.
A tiff over Star of the Sea and Bumblebee.
Me and Ruby Lee, self-proclaimed
Queen of Smart Shoppers.

The storm had been gathering
through produce and dairy.
Her mind processed numbers
at the speed of rising prices.
She compared brands and
announced cost per fucking ounce
of each item I dropped into the cart.

After one too many *tsk tsk* from her
skinny lips, I screamed, *Ruby Lee,*
you are in deep shit if you don't shut up.
A torrent of how I'd been managing
very well on my own for years.

And how she could go back to Kokomo
on the next boat. Her hand flew up
to cover her mouth and her eyes
grew wide as Lake Okeechobee.

Then she laughed and said, *You sound*
just like Emmy Lou. She gets so riled
when I'm trying to help. Her daughter,
Emmy Lou, left home at an early age.

After the terrible Tuna Tiff in Aisle 15,
after the storm had subsided,
I took Ruby Lee's advice, starting with
Bumble Bee over Star of the Sea and
saved enough money to add a bottle
of Gilbey's Gin London Dry to my cart,
another diamond in Ruby Lee's tiara.

September 26, 2008

To a Caraway Seed

Curved
like a tiny
dark scimitar,
you hide in
a slice of rye.
I bite into your
heart, slightly
sweet but
bitter,
releasing
oil of
Byzantine
nights,
sights
along the
Bosporus,
sunlight on
Topkapi as you
glide under my
bridge, return
to hiding and
my tongue,
a crusader
after an
infidel.

October 4, 2008

Too Many Towels for One Person

Neat stacks of thick terry cloth
sit on shelves in my linen closet
crowding sheets and pillow cases.
Towels, mostly white, a few bright
turquoise, royal blue, barely used.

I reach for a favorite in front,
pale pink, once rose, snip loose
threads at the frayed edge and
hang it on a towel bar in the bath
where I dried his brawny back.

He used to turn and grab me.
We would laugh as I dropped
the thick rose towel to the floor.
All that steam between us,
and sometimes when I wrap

myself in the pale pink I tingle
as I see him glistening, wet
like Neptune. I touch the worn
towel and think yet again,
it's good for one more wash.

October 19, 2008

The End of Innocence

Blood from the pig's slit throat
pooled on the shifting ground alive
with millions of screeching crickets
sounding alarm. She watched,

her hands pressed to her mouth.
Strung up by its hind hooves from
a corn crib rafter, the pig, massive
as a battleship to a ten year old.

A curly tailed pig stuck with a knife
by Grandpa, and on the same day
Grandma wrung a chicken's neck,
plunged the bird into boiling water,

plucked it clean, then hacked it
open and ripped out its innards.
Splattered blood. Awful squawking.
A ten year old hid in the house,

and closed her eyes, but couldn't
hide from bloody images shoving
out sweet dreams. She had seen
with her own eyes and she knew.

October 27, 2008

Night of the Grunion

We sip gin and tonics
at Bongo's Beachfront Bar.
Floodlights dance
on waves licking a sea wall.
We lean into each other,
touch knee to knee.
I finger your thigh. You point
to a heron as it lands and
stands facing open ocean.
Suddenly the surf flashes
and shimmers with fish,
elusive grunion coming
ashore to mate, an urgent
ritual seldom seen,
said by some to be a myth.
We abandon drinks and
run barefoot on the beach.
I giggle and reach for
slippery fish spawning at
high tide under a full moon.
Silvery little grunion wiggle
and twist in damp sand.
I hold up my skirt, briny wet.
My legs sting with sea salt.
We hurry home to undress,
wriggling under a full moon,
beneath a pine in our side yard.

November 1, 2008

A Poet's Perfect Day

She's in junior high. *Nana, will you come
and get me?* I would drive to Tallahassee
from the California coast to pick up Mimi,
pixie smile, teeth still in braces,
sky blue eyes, shiny fall of blonde hair.

She wants to hang with me. We drive
through KFC on the way back to my house.
Kevin, her dad, and David, my oldest son,
just happen to stop by in time for lunch.
Chicken and biscuits and cheesy mac.

Then Mimi and I, cozy in afghans,
snuggle on the couch to watch tv reruns,
Malcolm in the Middle. Her laptop on
her lap, during muted commercials she
reads me her homework assignment:

A horror story like one of
Edgar Allen Poe's, macabre mood,
gory details. I shudder and marvel.
Where did this perfect girl come from?
I didn't write a poem, not even a single line
on this perfect day, but I lived a sonnet.

November 11, 2008

2009

New Year's Day

The scarf,
maroon wool,
soft as snow,
lay folded in
a drawer ten
lonely years.
He had worn it
chilly mornings
on their walks.
Yesterday his
widow phoned
to wish *Happy
New Year* to
their grandson,
who's flat on his
back, says he
feels like crap.
She can't take
chicken soup,
but flashes on
a warm remedy.
She resurrects
the scarf from
its dark drawer,
wraps it to send,
then takes her
own cold bones
to the computer
and googles
eHarmony.

January 7, 2009

The More Things Change

I'd sneak away from the playground to
a haven of steam, wet sheets and Julia.
Her ageless arms, brown and strong,
lifted laundry all day long in the basement

of St. Mary's Home where we both lived,
me in a dorm, she in a room down the hall,
small as a cell in a convent or a dungeon.
I'd help fold clothes with jejune white hands,

and listen to tales of her youth in Georgia.
When Julia revealed that she'd been born
a slave, I dropped a pile of pj's and stared.
I'd just seen *Gone with the Wind* in color,

about the Civil War and slaves and stuff.
I adored Scarlett's gorgeous gowns,
and dreamed of living in a grand house
like Tara, with a black butler to bring me
biscuits and honey whenever I rang.

Today Melia and Sasha held their
daddy's brown hand after he became
44th President of the United States.
Neither Julia nor I would have thought
such an outlandish thing could ever be,

but dreams come true in this country.
I watched the event on a large flat screen tv
in my own grand home in a gated community.
No black butlers, of course, no slaves,
although, hispanic gardeners and maids.

January 20, 2009

Dear Tony,

Are you still writing about your father?
Tony Hoagland

Yes, I'm still writing about him,
struggling with sestina repeat
scheme, adding to a lifetime
of lyrical lines residing in 3 ring
binders and spiral notebooks.

I can almost hear your reply,
What the fuck is there to write?
(were you as profane as I).
He left before you could say Daddy.
You don't know squat about him.

Good point, but here's the thing,
my bottomless need to make
him real burns like miles of dry
pines on fire. I improvise with
poetic license and every word
I write is another way to say *Why?*

Sincerely,
Daughter of an Abstract Artist

January 31, 2009

The Gospel According to St. Valentine

And it came to pass
that he and she lay down
in a green field
and did it.
And verily I say unto you,
it was good.

February 8, 2009

Yesterday's Storm

unbridled limbs
writhing in wind
a wild tarantella
and now
how quiet
the boughs
serene
the leaves
their secrets
intact

February 10, 2009

The Way of All Things

Rain thrashes the roof patched
with pitch. No leaks. No drips.
Maybe I can sleep tonight.

Last week, my knees creaky,
I limped placing pans to catch
drips puddling on the buffet.

My house huddles in the storm.
I stay warm, snuggled under
an afghan crocheted by Aunt Cora.

Fingering variegated green yarn,
I think of hankies edged with lace
tatted by aunts Cora and Bess,

both gone along with their art.
Does anyone tat anymore,
or for that matter, use hankies?

February 16, 2009

The Parable of Forbidden Fruit

She saw a *Do Not Enter* sign
in red letters on the door,
her hand on the door knob.

She hesitated six seconds before
opening the door, undressing and
entering a place ancient as Eden.

There is no way back, but who
would want to leave a grove of
such exotic succulent mangos?

Behold! It has been foretold,
the time will come when even
exotic fruit rots, grows moldy,

paradise turns cold. She will
long for home, her own furry
blanket, an ordinary Jonathan.

February 23, 2009

Down but Not Out

A vintage charm fixer upper,
tan siding and patched roof,
built on fill in a canyon,
sits a bit off kilter, wears
a slick new coat of varnish
on its warped front door,
like an old bag lady,
shoulders sagging, who
pops a posy on a bonnet
snatched from a dumpster.

A neighbor lady in the gray
Cape Cod, gimpy hip and
a partial plate, snips pansies
that persist in neglected beds.
Back inside her house,
she leans into a cracked
hall mirror, frowns and
checks crevices in her
forehead, murmurs
Yes. Time for botox.

February 26, 2009

The Valentine

Scent of spicy carnation wreaths
clings to memories. Mom in
blue gingham, cast iron skillets
and pots, chipped Fiesta Ware.
Even some of Dad's things kept
through the widow years.
Campaign ribbons. Tie tacks.
Masonic ring. Bags for Goodwill.
Bags for trash. Time-outs to swap
stories about a life we thought we
knew so well. Or did we?
Black silk evening bag with
rhinestone clasp in
a bottom dresser drawer.
Red chiffon gown in the closet.
I frowned and looked inside
the bag. Two ticket stubs for
Mama Mia dated last May,
and in her jewelry box,
a valentine signed, *Your Lover.*
Oh, *Mama Mia*, we assumed
your big night out was Bingo
or Bunko. Well, whatever game
you played, you hit the jackpot,
and that explains the satin sheets.

March 3, 2009

Pocket Full of Rye

Ragtag kids ransack
the castle. Four and
twenty blackbirds
swoop and flap wings
at dragons napping in
the moat. The castle
keep abandoned,
an unkempt queen
in tattered gown,
hair snarled, sprawls
on an unmade bed
weeping while the king
is in his counting office
counting out the money.
Not enough for bread
and honey. The queen's
head throbs at a bell
tower's gong. Time for
dinner. The cooks have
fled. The queen must
rise from bed and feed
the hungry throng. She
rubs her cinder eyes.
*One more drink, maybe
two, and I can do it.*
The recipe is tattooed
on her brain: Pasta in
the pot. Sip of Chianti.
Meatballs and sauce
in the pan. Sip of
Chianti. *Fuck. Empty.
If there's no cooking
sherry, I will kill myself
and fuck your dainty dish.*

March 16, 2009

Death of a Line

His pen paused, poised over choice words on
a line. Plump pulsing words. Evocative vowels

and curvy consonants stirred into succulent
syllables. The line was last of a sonnet about

Spring, how it makes the heart sing, a line
that seemed right, not trite or contrived, which

is the bitch of rhyming. But upon reflection, his
confection fell flat, lacked the spice of surprise,

that icing on a collection of *best words in their
best order.* So the dreaded task. Can the poet

take an ax to the last line? He lowered his pen
to scratch it out, to trash it. The hitch in the line

was its predictability. No surprise demanded its
demise. A sad passing. No proper burial. No elegy.

No final words.

March 23, 2009

Scene of the Crime

The sun dies in a graveyard sea
and brine boils. One by one
blinking lights come on
and lead the way to coals
glowing with heat of passion
spilled from cauldrons
cooking entrails of
sentences spoken in anger.
Pallid paper boats sail
for black caves of silence
until your third goblet of wine
when her eyes, kohl-lined,
blazed, and the snake tattoo
circling her left ankle spit
and hissed as she danced
barefoot, crazy quilt skirt twirling.
Mesmerized, you tripped
on the on the crust of the moon
and fell into crevices stuffed
with helium dreams and
ballooned desires rising to hold
the moon aloft. You hovered
over the evening star ripping
apart yellow tape surrounding
your own danger zones.

March 31, 2009

Bottomless Night

finally gone
with no
nighttime stuff
getting done
dawn arrives
too soon too late
too slow too fast
no sleeping
dreaming fucking
vast waste
of night
lying alone
awake
in moonlight

June 10, 2009

I Had Tea with Mary Oliver

last evening. She droned
on and on about spring
violets in soft forest moss.
She lost me in a bog on
the edge of a pinewood.
I smiled and nodded in
response to her tedious
musings about peonies,
wildlife creatures, fawns
and bees, ants, while
I dreamed of dancing
in a peony pink gown,
sleek satin, a hand
sliding down my back,
like tea with honey
sliding down my throat.

July 9, 2009

The New Priest,

slick black hair and a widow's peak,
winked at lovely Alicia Lyman,
an Altar Guild lady who nearly dropped
a cut glass vase containing calla lilies
on the marble tile sanctuary floor.

Bible Study class and Ladies Guild filled up
fast after petering out under the leadership
of the previous priest, portly with bad knees
and occasional bouts of gout who faltered
at friendly phases with parish ladies.

Dear Lord, he succumbed to a flu bug
on Ash Wednesday, stumbled through
penitent days of Lent, took a turn for
the worse on Maundy Thursday, and was
deceased by Easter. With an eager new

priest, potluck suppers got going good again,
Mildred Morris' creamy cabbage slaw, a big
draw, plus Lucille Munson's Brunswick Stew
and lovely Alicia Lyman's lemon tarts, so tasty
a treat the new priest always took seconds.

Soon he too, grew a trifle portly. And so it goes.
A wink. Shared laughter. Platter of goodies.
A pat on the back, the ass. Next thing you know,
somebody's home late from Bible Study class
and saved again. Amen.

July 28, 2009

Letter to Melekian from Cardiff
(after Richard Hugo's Letter to Kizer from Seattle)

Dear Slut: Thanks for covering for me when I didn't
make it back to work. I'd be out of a job if not for you.
It was one of those long liquid lunches. Did the gang
go to Bully's for the publisher's party? John's new
book is dyno. If advance sales are any indication,
we'll be celebrating big time. By the way, I ran into
John's ex working as a checker at a market on
the back road to Palomar Airport. I was on my way
to catch a commuter flight to LAX and I ran out of
cigarettes. I'm still trying to quit. I might try the patch.
Anyway, John's ex is now a redhead. Still a bitch.
No wonder John screwed around. She looks trashy
as Sharon in Fulfillment who almost wore that
amazing dress at the La Valencia bash. Remember
the backless strapless hot pink number? The cute
drummer in the band came on to me during
the music break. But I'm through with musicians.
They are so way not available. I used to have five
rules of standard for men: availability, money,
chemistry, humor and intelligence. I've pretty much
narrowed it down to availability. Especially after
LAX where I met a guy. Hungarian accent, killer
smile and wicked eyes. In Pharmaceuticals, no less.
We hooked up and decided to layover at that same
hotel where you and I danced on the bar. Remember?
it was Cinco de Mayo and Fernando made margaritas
fabulosas. We closed the place and you lost well
sorry to bring that up. Anyway, Phil (in Pharmaceuticals)
had great drugs and a wife in Glendale. I can't make it
to Stephie's blowout. I'm in a support group for ex-twelve
steppers. Recovering recoverers. It's called RR. My new
friend, Skippy, and I started it. He needs lots of help
and well, he's available. You've been a true pal. Sending
good vibes your way. I hope Surfer Dude doesn't split.
Take care, oh nicest of sluts. Love, Trish. Thanks again.

September 1, 2009

Otherwise

Seems like a long time since
the waiter took my order,

disappeared behind a swinging door.
I rearrange silverware, move a fake

carnation in a dingy glass vase
to the neighboring vacant table,

take out my paperback. A few other
solitary diners, moored to separate

small islands, lift forks and eat in
a sea of silence. I dog-ear my page

as the waiter reappears with
soup du jour. Friday. Clam chowder.

Once it was otherwise. Fridays.
Me and Dino at Bully's cruising for

seats at the low bar, shouting out
our orders over laughter and chatter.

Doubles. On the rocks. Extra olives.
I knew someday it would be

otherwise. When his ship sailed
or, as it happened, sank.

And a deep longing for gin soaked
olives sank its teeth in me.

September 3, 2009

Happily Ever After?

That is the difference between you and me.
Cloth napkins. It will never last.
With each new move we lose some sweetness.
And slipcovers? You don't get it.

Still, I admire your bravado and
to a slightly lesser extent, your thinking.
Like most cowboys, you are conservative.
I can look at that two ways, or not at all

if I want your boots beneath my bed.
We thought we could come to this bridge,
sit a while and find a solution.
Never has steelwork seemed so serene.

Every day as the grapes come in they
reveal a verdict on decisions made earlier.
I know you will never find snow peas
more attractive than beans,

or asian squash more handsome than
jack-o'-lanterns. You don't seem to mind
our differences, but I go to sleep wondering
what kind of person doesn't like sushi?

September 6, 2009

Lima Beans

Oh! To rhyme a lima bean.
Finest bean ever seen.
Better than a butter bean.
More shapely than a lean
string bean. Know what I mean?
Named for the capital of Peru,
early Encinitas farmers grew
fields hoping for yields of
round little, sound little
lima beans, hoping for means
to a healthy economy.
Not hominy like in the South,
but limas best for dry western sod.
God brought Encinitas forefathers
with lima beans to this scene
of parks and flowers that
reaches to fabulous beaches.
So thank you, Lovely Lima
for your part in our beginning,
winning a place in our hearts,
if not the tummy,
I confess some find you
less than yummy.

September 9, 2009

Building Muscles with an Echo Gas Trimmer

Chris loves the Echo SRM 230 trimmer.
Lightweight and easy to use, with a nice
big head so she doesn't have to keep
loading the string so often. She had never
trimmed, left that job to her husband but,
since there is so much edging with this
complex, Chris knew she was going to have
to learn. By the end of the second day, she
scooted right along with the Echo SRM 230,
claiming it as her own. Using it has helped
strengthen her shoulders as well as build
muscles in her upper arms. She had tried
using her husband's trimmer but it just
didn't work for her since she's left handed.
The guard on the bottom of the shaft
was on the wrong side. No protection from
flying rocks and debris. Chris says she tried
holding his shaft with her right hand but,
it felt too uncomfortable. It's raining today,
so they're taking a grass cutting break,
a time, she says, to practice her hand hold.

September 18, 2009

Honeysuckle So Thick

in the canyon, a kid can walk on it,
lie back on a honeysuckle hammock,
head spinning in mist of sweet scent.

He picks a blossom, pulls its stamen,
puts it to his lips, sips its one drop
of honey and floats, eyes closed.

Sudden frenzy of bees. Muffled
thunder of resounding hum sends
him stumbling from woozy wonder.

But now he knows how heaven feels,
the smell of its aroma, its honey taste.
And now he owns a secret place

where nobody can ever find him,
sunk deep in honeysuckle vine,
yellow dust on his bare feet.

September 21, 2009

Man Shot, Youth Held by Fugitive (AP 11-27-71)

Escaped convict gives chase in stolen car,
smashes into pickup in Von's parking lot,
takes off on foot, shoots a guy in the gut
who tries to stop him in the alley behind

VG Donuts, disappears into the canyon.
A house stands at the far end. Picture it
surrounded by cops. TV camera crews,
finally floodlights and megaphones,

cops calling for the fugitive to surrender.
Which he does. Like fucking Hawaii Five-O.
Little brother was safe and the FBI
search of the house revealed nothing

incriminating. *Hail Mary, Full of Grace.*
But when I saw that fucker, I freaked.
The same cop who swiped my weed
when he stopped me for running a red.

He was talking to my brother when
I got home after hanging with Boomer
all day down at Pipes, pissed I missed
the hottest action in town, but saw it

later on ABC, CBS and fucking NBC,
Boomer said it was the coolest thing
he ever heard. Mom said it got quite
dicey when cops threatened tear gas.

Dad nearly had a stroke what with
her turkey soup simmering on the stove.
Broth, leftover turkey, celery, thyme,
carrots, onions, noodles and boiled bones.

September 27, 2009

Race of Time

days drain away
at dismaying pace
minutes matter more
than ever before
sovereign sun decides
when to rise and set
yet seconds truly rule
see you in few

September 30, 2009

Scrambled

over easy   sunny side up
upside down   hash browns
               catsup on top
links on the side   order up
    hot cakes   cold case
who stole the bacon?
      all the king's horses
paw the ground   upside down
boiled and poached
sunny side over   french toast

he unzips me in back
      I   slip out of
inhibition   and   u n l o o s e n
    him in front   shake his
cool disposition
    we abandon all decorum
  in a scramble of
         arms & legs
I tell him stay the night
I wonder how he likes his eggs

October 1, 2009

Fly Me to the Moon

I escape outside for a few in cool night air,
look up at the vast black sky and see it,
feel its magical pull. Its full luminous glow,
and know I don't need a rocket ship.

A crackley voice from a sparkley new TV,
Magnavox center of my family's universe,
That's one small step for ...
Kids' butts in Goodwill jeans squeezed

together on our Salvation Army couch,
My old man, can of Coors in hand,
Shut the fuck up ...
As our wiggly kids squabble and squeal,

Neil takes a giant leap for mankind,
and I'm gone, flying to the Sea of Tranquility,
then past Mars where spring is radiant,
playing among the stars, tripping with Frank.

October 10, 2009

Liquid Pepper

Fiery fluid spills on moonlit sheets,
burns a hole in the soul of night.

Dawn arrives with a bowl of sunlight,
splashes it over cold carne asada.

Cool breeze of sleep's healing salve
whispers kisses on blistered skin.

They awake in an iceberg garden and
he, honors grad of The Pleaser School,

reaches for his liquid pepper, smiles
at his mistress, hears her gradual gasp.

October 15, 2009

This Was the Dream

Lost, I walked down a lonely
street at night, looking for
someone to show me the way
to wherever I was going.

This was real ... as I walked,
I felt a warmth by my side,
and a strong hand gripped
my arm and pulled me along.

Alone is more solitary at
night than I ever dreamed,
and *bereaved* more full of
sorrow, but I have found

solace in sleep, in dreams,
and I find myself thinking
less and less of loss,
and more of tomorrow.

October 31, 2009

Lost and Found

They were crazy to rise at midnight,
pile in their rusty Ford wagon,
drive to a pricey neighborhood
of sprawling Rancho Santa Fe.

Crazy to find their lost Deacon,
collie golden mix, last seen
on Avenida de Acacias where
son David with Deacon

riding shotgun, parked his
dusty red VW bug in front of
Ye Olde Drugs. His VW bug
with an open window.

Hey, it happens. Like when they
left their youngest at the beach
and frantic hours later picked him
up at Oceanside Police Station.

Parked in lush white-railed
horse country in the middle
of the night, they called out,
Deacon Deacon, baying

Deacon Blues at the moon.
Sipping from a thermos of
coffee laced with Old Grandad,
moonlight a silvery glow over

rolling fields, they hugged
in chill still air, so close they
found a long lost spark from
a time they were crazy in love.

November 1, 2009

Reel Dreams

A ten year old girl, short bob
and bangs, sits in the third row
of darkened Lamar Theater
in Oak Park, Illinois, itches to
be *Putting on the Ritz* with
Fred in his top hat and tails,
Ginger in white satin and taps.
She grew up on Saturday

matinees, magic carpet
rides to ritzy avenues, miles
of reels all the way to Moon River,
Holly Golightly's world of
tiara and pearls, cocktails,
Breakfast at Tiffany's, and
yearned to step into the real
streets of her reel dreams.

She finally arrived, excited to
take a bite of the Big Apple,
window shopped at Tiffany's,
floated over to the Palm Court
of The Plaza Hotel for brunch,
but her dream made real is
south of 14th Street, scene of
Washington Square, charming

tree lined streets, the vibrant
air of cafes and bars, shops,
and brownstones, ghosts
of Bohemians and Beats as
she walks the Village streets
in twilight patina and dines
with friends, lucky to snag
a table at Elephant & Castle.

November 8, 2009

Closing up Shop for Harry

we close poetry books
folders pick up loose
papers pens put chairs
back against the wall
all traces of workshop
erased tucked into
briefcase and purse
our hugs goodbyes
like a period to
the last surprise line
of a Billy Collins poem

November 18, 2009

Barefoot into the Beyond

She finally picked the gray suit
over a navy blue. The shirt
was easy. White button down.
And the tie? Not too busy.
Something conservative
for wear in a casket.
Red diagonal stripe? No.
Solid maroon looked right.
Shoes were hardest. Brown
or black? Oxfords or loafers?
She settled on black wingtips.
She'd never seen him in
anything but jeans and boots,
Strange as it was, poking
around in a neighbor's closet,
stranger still to be selecting
his final resting clothes.
She had supposed a sister or
a grieving aunt might show up
to attend to his arrangements,
looking through teary eyes
at belongings of a beloved.
Her own eyes were dry until
the funeral parlor director
waved away the shoes with,
His feet won't show.

2009

THE TRISH DUGGER COLLECTION OF POETRY

2010

THE TRISH DUGGER COLLECTION OF POETRY

Some Call It Saugatuck

When to the sessions of sweet silent thought
William Shakespeare

When I get to heaven, it won't be lined with streets
of gaudy gold, but sleepy blacktop roads
shaded by murmuring oaks,
their branches arched in a hushed canopy
over kids cycling to a ferry on the banks
of the Kalamazoo River. No bike?

Rent one from a lanky guy, freckles and cowlick,
who smiles and winks and calls you Honey.
He'll knock Frank Sinatra out of your dreams.
Take the ferry across the river to sand dunes,
climb to the top and slide down, wild and free.
Shake sand from your jeans and head to

an old fashioned soda fountain, marble counter
and twirling stools, irresistible scent of vanilla.
Belly up for a root beer float, then flop on grass
in the park beside a white gazebo,
and steeped in sweet silent thought,
find cloud castles in the sky.

As a teenaged girl from rowdy Chicago,
I lived in a dorm with a clutter of kids
across the street from constant clamor,
of el train tracks. A summer camp job

in Michigan became an escape
to a quaint storybook place,
quiet as a sigh and soft as twilight,
like a lullaby sung
by a faintly remembered mother.

February 8, 2010

The Demise of Black on White

The Daily Times
downsized
earthquake fire flood
headline
skinny sheets
pages
dwindle

bookstores closing
books
sold on the internet
books minus ink
on touch screens
Kindle

college yearbooks
phasing out
replaced by
Facebook
kids minus pens
text and tweet on
Twitter

magazines shrink
covers scream
see tv stars
botox breakup detox
buy miracle diet pill
hyped in thin
editions

love letters
no longer by post
too slow too bad
no more sweet words
inked on vellum
trishdugger
@cox.net

February 18, 2010

Vagaries of Spring

She continues to put out
even with fifty years tucked in her floral bodice.
The camellia, a variety called Mrs. Hinkley,
leaning by my back door, staggers
under the weight of lush pink blossoms.
It's spring and I'm thinking, *You rule, Lady.*
Still flaunting your stuff like the town slut
strutting down Front Street and nobody sees
your outrageous display except me anymore.
You and me, we remember the clothesline
along the fence where I pinned tees, jeans
and sheets to dry in spring breezes.
Stepping in duck poop, holding clothespins
between my lips, I invoked whatever gods
of gas dryers to favor me with kindness
and reminded myself our pet mallards mate
for life, a good example to point to while
reaching for my man's elusive hand.
Look, Honey, they're so devoted.
Today March blusters across my page,
tumbling down its days, heading for April.
Spring again and me without a glitzy top
in my closet. One of spring's *must-haves.*
So says an *uber* fashion guru on tv..
She wears a J.Crew utility jacket in paprika,
one of Spring's *must-have* spicy colors.
I seem to hear the nearly inaudible pining
of my haphazard wardrobe, similar to
the whining of kids for popsicles.
True, my dresser drawers are crammed
with drab tees and jeans in various sizes.
I'm not up to crying this morning
over remembrance of sizes past.
Small black tee. Size 8 jeans.
55 years ago April first. That cute sailor
in the window seat of a Greyhound bus.

March 6, 2010

L'Oreal Preference #9

She is blonde
who once was gray.
Eye crinkles plumped,
frown lines gone,
erased.
Perpetually serene,
she is shrinking
a la Jenny Craig.
Her closet reveals
hip new DKNY clothes.
And where
do you think she goes
inside her head,
lying alone at night
in a quiet bed,
tired from a taxing day
battling black mold
of advancing old age?
And what
will she say to her
grandson when
he comes looking for
his Nana and
can't find her anywhere?

March 8, 2010

Way before Farouk

The new Egypt arose from
the wrath of Ramses
O. K. Tucker

Semite slaves knew their place
in the old Egypt. Ask Pharaoh

why his royal subjects came to
fear the adult children of Judah,

indeed all sons of Abraham.
It is a story he loves to tell,

froth foaming from his throat
like an angry volcano erupting,

how he caught Moses taking
a piss in the royal bath and

saw lowly semite slaves spit
at pyramids. Pharaoh decreed

these vile deeds be inscribed
in stone and placed beneath

the Great Sphinx at Giza,
a day's journey by camel

from the sacred altar to Ra,
Sun God who summons dawn.

It was recorded that he,
mighty Pharaoh, banished

the 12 tribes from the banks
of the Nile and drove them

into the Red Sea. All Egypt
joined in spiritual mourning

for the old days and this
was way before the Brits.

March 10, 2010

Heaven on Earth

The Second Coming
Hallelujah
The Second Coming
Glory be
The Second Coming
Oh my God
The Second Coming
Oh Baby Baby
Oh Baby Oh
Oh Baby Ohhhhh

March 11, 2010

Better than Sex

16 and taller than his dad,
my grandson tells me that
his favorite poet after me
is Walt Whitman.
He says, *Nana, will you edit*
my story for English class?
and taking his folder, I reply,
I thought you'd never ask.

March 13, 2010

The Mistake Not Made

The black lace garter belt
not bought,
lies beside a scarlet
baby doll nightie,
both left on a counter
at Victoria's Secret.
The purchase not made
saved a woman from
maxing out her Visa
and possibly from STD.
The date not kept
gave the woman time
to pick up her kids
from school and to fix
Swiss steak for dinner
instead of leftovers.
At the end of a risky day,
she snuggled close
to her husband in bed,
the neighbor not fucked,
safe inside her head

March 14, 2010

The Old Woman's Defense

There was an old woman
who lived in a shoe

The reports of whipping
are false, grossly overblown.
A few swats on their rumps
to keep the kids in line, but
no whipping. I will bet you
that the Piper down the lane
turned me in to Child Welfare,
and we all know about his son,
Tom, and the purloined pig.

The one time I put the kids
to bed without any broth?
The coffer was empty
and my cupboard bare.
I didn't know what to do.
Anyway, their tummies
were full of puddn'n pie.
Georgie Porgie's mother
across the way is always
passing out sweets.

And screw the *unsuitable*
dwelling charge. My house
is fine as any in the lane.
Soft leather with a padded
sole, found by my son,
Buster, in an alley behind
The Gingerbread House,
an eyesore half nibbled
away by three blind mice.

A Doc Marten's lace-up boot
is a tight fit when all ten kids
are finally tucked in at night,
Timmy, the tiniest, in the toe,
but my brood is snug and safe.
You can bet your Wellingtons
my house has a Mother Goose
Seal of Approval. I rest my case.

March 19, 2010

Dear Gene Kelly

Extra dry with a twist
at the La Valencia
Whaling Bar.
Dark in a booth for two,
you licked your lips
between each sip.
Your leaps and slides
exciting
on the silver screen,
I dreamed of being
your leading lady
from the first time
I saw you at the Rialto,
singing and dancing
in the rain.
There's no explaining
chance encounters.
Bumping into each other
on Prospect in La Jolla,
we went reeling and
my packages scattered.
You helped me gather
them up and asked me
to have a drink.
To think a few martinis
would provide me with
a lifetime of daydreams.
I confided I was a poet
and recited my aubade
to Auden, and after a refill,
I spilled my racy limericks.
You laughed in your
raspy voice to choice bits.
I have no regrets except
you didn't ask me to dance
and I want you to know
that I can really cha cha.

March 28, 2010

We Had a Shredder Experience at Work Today

Myron in accounting who came up short
in the month-end report, darted across the office
and tore open his shirt, unzipped his chest,
ripped out his heart and fed it into the shredder.
Jenny, a steno, looked on in horror as thick
dark blood dripped on the newly carpeted floor.

STOP! STOP! Yelled Roger, the controller.
I said it would be your HEAD
if you didn't balance, not your HEART.
But by then it was too late.
Claudia, Accounts Payable, called 911.
Paramedics came and carted Myron away.

The shredder was trashed in the dumpster.
No one wanted to pick out sticky pieces
of heart clinging to the blades. Claudia called
maintenance to clean the carpet, then put
on her jacket and reached for her purse.

I hope this means we get to go home early.
The whole shredder experience has given
me a headache, as had the stolen computer
experience and the lunchroom microwave
meltdown experience of previous weeks.

A requisition for a new shredder will be
submitted, but funds are not available
until next month, because Myron
came up short in the month-end report.

April 6, 2010

Junk for a Buck

Miracle Bubbles 6-pack
sparkling jellybean green
liquid in little bottles
lighting the 99 cent store
aisle like a beacon
draws a big bald man
reaching for the boy
he left behind waving
a plastic wand in wind
laughing at bubbles
rising to the sun
then poof gone like
his youth somewhere
in space dumped into
time's waste basket
like the man dumping
his Miracle Bubbles
when he got home
why the hell did he buy
this shit God knows
where it comes from
Hecho in Mexico

April 9, 2010

Foster Home Pitfall

Kenny cornered me with a gun,
massive in his small hands.
Pistol... Revolver. I didn't know.
Like in a gangster movie.

A ten year old menace with
a crew cut, pointed a gun at me.
His dad, sober for once,
and his mom, a dragon lady,

had gone out while I baby-sat
Kenny with orders to watch for
stray matches. He had a thing
for fire. Guns too, it seemed.

Shaking, I persuaded him to hand
over the gun, then hid it in a desk.
A call to Mrs. Crane, my crusty
trusty Cook County case worker,

and I was out of there fast and into
yet another foster home minefield,
another high school crowd to crack.
But poor Kenny, his dad a drunk,

mom, a bitch who didn't let me wear
lipstick, he had no place else to go.
I could be wrong. A couple years
later I read in the newspaper about

a house on South Oak burning down.
Some bad ass kids I knew told me
the food in Juvie is pretty good.
Kenny's mom couldn't boil beans.

April 11, 2010

Of Grain and Pine and Rain and Wine

I had to take the whole fucking thing apart,
including the motor, and on the arbor,
which is the axle, I installed new bearings,
four of them at about eight bucks apiece at
Grainger's in San Marcos after driving there
to buy them in pouring rain, forget cats and
dogs, think tigers and coyotes, nearly
rear-ending a Volvo SUV, taking time from
the job Rocko had subbed out to me,
five wine racks for a new restaurant which
I'm behind on, which was why Maurice,
the owner, was breathing down Rocko's
neck, giving him shit about the delayed
opening and the cost way over budget,
ragging about his La Jolla location not
doing so hot, though it seemed a winner
on the drawing board, but that was before
the economy went in the toilet and before
I nearly chopped off my left thumb on
the chop saw, which is now finally back in
working condition for thirty two bucks and
change plus damn near a full day's labor,
putting me more behind on wine racks,
but to tell the truth, I don't really feel like
working on wine racks, though I could
go for a goddamn goblet of Cabernet.

April 25, 2010

Fitness Workout
Dedicated to Robert Van Evera

My body talks back to me,
complains like a pouty kid
told to do chores before
going out to play. It says,
What about my nap?
What nonsense is this
physical fitness business?
Have you lost your senses?
I answer, Yes, I know.
Eighty is a little late to get into
shape. Push ups and sit ups.
Like learning a new language.
I may never be fluent,
but I look forward to sassy
conversation with a supple
spine, limber limbs and
elastic muscles in the exotic
foreign country of my new body.

July 2, 2010

Hephzibah Home for Children

You took me there
and left me.
I couldn't know
it would be forever.
I knew nothing
about time, only the feel
of your lips on my cheek
when you said goodbye

Tulips in bloom,
so it must have been Spring.
Lilies-of-the-valley
crowded a side yard,
thick sweet scent so close
it made me dizzy, breathless,
like your whisper in my ear.
Be good. Be brave.

Stunned snowball bushes
dropped their blossoms
when you left,
as if a sudden cold snap
had attacked,
a blizzard of white petals
falling on the ground.

A snow globe turned
upside down,
my world turned topsy-turvy,
and in the side yard,
the silence of tiny white bells.

August 14, 2010

My Father Going Going Gone

he went   away
and left a crater
        of smoldering loneliness
he was   gone
his place in the family portrait
      a blank   space
    his smile   erased
no trace of eyes dropped
        into
                black caves
his voice
                like silent chimes
    his easy chair   vacant
      his absence   hollow bones
        my   father
his shadows
            t o o   s l o w
              f a d e s

August 19, 2010

In the Midst of Wolves

Behold, I send you forth as
sheep in the midst of wolves.....
Matthew 10:16

She never would have done it in church
if she'd been afraid of going to hell.
God is Love, Father Foley always said.

He was the first priest to reach up high
inside her skirt and feel her cool thigh
trembling like a sheep at shearing,
setting her on fire like something holy.

Besides, she'd already done it in
the back seat of Pete Coogan's Chevy.
It felt so good it couldn't be a sin and
beat Spin the Bottle every which way.

Though not nearly wise as a serpent,
she knew enough to say, *No Thanks*
to the church sanctuary with its altar
and candles and Christ on the cross,

making her feel like an offering to
the Holy Ghost. And all the saints:
Here is my body given for thee.

Father Foley's study with locked door
was just the ticket to explore wonders
of God's creation, mystic meaning
of heavenly and divine sensation,
the pinnacle of parochial education.

When Father Foley was suddenly sent
back to the Emerald Isle, she sighed
and went for a ride with Pete Coogan.

September 9, 2010

Over the Edge

How easily we lose parts
of ourselves.
My youth slipped over
the edge of a sharp pain.
We move in and out of
each other like
shadows through statues,
leaving traces and
grabbing what we can
on this invisible odyssey.
While sliding through your
spine, I placed an ache
in your lower back
You took my sense of
balance when you
roamed inside my brain.
My heart gallops
across the moonscape
on your nightmare.
My mother, slightly tipsy,
walks inside me. I can't
find my mind anywhere.
An English woman
woke up one morning
with a French accent.
I speak in tongues.

September 16, 2010

So There Too

I wanted to be your north star at midnight,
guiding you toward my magnetic field.
I could never budge your reluctance,
enormous and solid as a rock in Morro Bay.
Because I did not hop like a rabbit to your
commands, I fell into a cauldron of sarcasm
I would never drive to Baker in a pickup
without A/C in July, so why would I want to
lie in a dry arroyo with cholla? You tell me.
I could never be like my ex-sister-in-law
who has found Jesus and peace in tithing.
I want to squander money, take a cruise
on a luxury liner to the island of Corfu,
be seduced by a handsome young Greek.
I would wave goodbye to you as I embark,
watching your image melt into the shore.
I want to splash my satisfaction in your face,
catch you off guard, watch you stumble.
I could be happy as Eric Clapton on guitar,
singing, *Wonderful Tonight.* I will no longer
let you whittle my pride to a slice of a sliver.
I will say, *Hello. Do I know you?* if we meet,
and it will be sweet to see your confusion.
I could forgive the thief who steals my heart,
but never the man who trashes my poetry.
I will waste no time of my diamond days
while twilight subsides into night cries.
I will finger faint messages on postcards
you sent long ago, then throw them away.
I feel no need to reach for your fading face.
My skin tingles from a foreign embrace.

September 24, 2010

The Tea Party

He loved his tea at three or so.
I'd heat the dented kettle, pour
a stream of steaming water on
a tea bag in his Spode cup,
but that day I poured
steaming water on loose tea
in a new teapot and let it steep
while my old man put down
his rake and cleaned up,
smiled and winked at me.
I'd spotted the white china teapot
in a thrift shop of St. Barnabas,
a church on Oxford Street.
Rich parishioners' castoffs put
my prized chipped Spode
to shame. The teapot without
a defect for two bucks gleamed
like an icicle in moonlight.
I stopped at an A & P
on my way home, picked up
a package of Fig Newtons,
and I had the makings of
a tea party for my old man and me
I still have the white china teapot
high on a shelf I can hardly reach

October 10, 2010

The Crap Trap

Eyes closed, I froze.
My son, Dave, had set traps
after finding
tiny turds in my house.

My once keen eyes
might have seen tiny turds,
but I was happily unaware
of sharing residence
with rodents.

My sons had come over
to move their accumulated
crap stacked to the rafters
of their old family home.

My daughter, moving back,
will need all that space
to store junk and stuff
she is bringing in a truck.

I weed out my things weekly,
scatter them into the trash
like ashes of a life past.
What do I really need any more?
Some paper and a pen and

time enough to write it all down,
how home is where
the Hold on I swear,
it was here just a minute ago.

October 12, 2010

Trick or Treat

My girls have moved back home
just in time to wake up sleepy old me.
Quite a trick, but they work their magic.

Claudia drags me out for a walk
while Teresa bakes a treat for our tea.
She makes a mean peach cobbler.

A witch with a wart on her pointy nose
hangs on my front door,
and a black furry spider lurks on top

my mail box. Skeletons dangle from
the porch and fake head stones
stand scattered across the lawn.

Yellow dust of Chinese lantern trees
powders the path to my faded gray
clapboard house. Soon green leaves

will turn brown and tumble down.
It's almost time to turn clocks back..
Fall back in the fall.

October 15, 2010

McKinley, Chanel and Louie (Villanelle)

My girls have moved back home to be with me,
set up a small apartment down below.
They've brought their three chihuahuas and tv.

One hopes the little doggies will not pee
on carpeting, at least where it will show.
My girls have moved back home to be with me.

Teresa is the cook we all agree.
With pots and pans she's practically a pro.
They've brought their three chihuahuas and tv.

Claudia does the dishes then we three,
get cozy on the couch like long ago.
My girls have moved back home to be with me.

They've helped to decorate the Christmas tree,
put up a wreath and hung some mistletoe.
They've brought their three chihuahuas and tv.

Like puppies in this house that's by the sea,
we laugh and hug, run and play. Heigh-ho.
My girls have moved back home to be with me.
They've brought their three chihuahuas and tv.

October 17, 2010

You Can Take the Girl out of Chicago

He wanted to take a leak
in the Grand Canyon at dawn,
as rays of sunlight spill down
silent canyon walls.
There's something primeval
about that, or so it seemed
the previous night after 3 beers.
Man baptizing Canyon
with pee, pissing a stream
in the stream down below.
Breakfast in the west
is a trip all its own.
Grits on the side with
everything. Over easy & grits.
Hot cakes & grits.
What's an Eggs Benedict
and Quiche Lorraine girl to do?
Dalhart, Texas has to be
the windiest town in the USA.
That coming from a girl born
and raised in the Windy City.
We could hardly get the door
to the diner open, tugging
against walloping wild wind.
Inside was a hodgepodge
of dusty boots, cowboy hats,

grizzled chins, sizzling griddle,
down-home aroma of coffee.
A jumble of long legs
in faded jeans, wranglers'
rumps on stools crowding
a horseshoe counter.
I could have stayed there forever
in that most northwest town
of the Texas panhandle.
Maybe me and my man could
get jobs there.
He could sign on for the roundup
and I could sling hash.
We could live in a shack out back,
forget about wars, change
our names. I would ditch *Trish*
and become *Ruby*.
Doug would hide inside *Stretch*.
This poem is a lot like
like that trip.....
rambling, ruts in the road,
vast expanses of flat land.
I wanted it to never end,
that trip to the USMC base
in California where he
would ship out to Korea.

October 23, 2010

Because I Always
Tell the Truth
Richard Shelton

I must admit
sometimes I feel

so alone
like maybe I'm

the only one
who doesn't get

the red wheel
barrow

and the white
chickens

the rain yeah
I get the rain

so much depends
upon the rain

plants grass and
at last

the rubber boot
industry

which is huge
in Oregon

October 31, 2010

Just a Regular Kid

Hand in hand, two by two, we would walk
to The Lamar Theater on Marion Street
where we got in free. But only the good
kids got to go and it was so hard to be
good all week long when I was a kid
at the Children's Home. The best day

of the week was Sunday. That's the day
my Mom came to see me. We walked
to Walgreens for a soda. Lots of the kids
wanted to walk with us down the street.
My hand in Mom's, I was happy as can be.
Pineapple sodas were always so good.

I studied my school work. I wanted good
grades, did all my chores every day;
mostly minded and tried hard to please.
In winter I shoveled snow off the walk,
and we slipped and slid on icy streets.
Since I was the oldest of thirty-six kids,

I was put in charge of some younger kids
who didn't know the meaning of good,
didn't mind and threw rocks in the street,
I couldn't wait until the second best day
when hand in hand, two by two we'd walk
to the movies. All week I'd longed to be

Betty Grable in a gown of sparkling beads.
Not just one of the Children's Home kids
walking on Marion Street, a short walk
with kids who'd all week long been good.
I got in plenty of trouble. There were days
when I didn't go walking on Marion Street.

The two floor red brick Home on Erie Street
was not exactly the place I wanted to be,
but Mom was a maid for a family every day,
and she didn't have a place to keep a kid.
At the Children's Home I was treated good,
and on Sundays Mom and I'd take a walk.

Any dark days at the Home on Erie Street
were lit by walks with Mom when I could be
just a regular kid sipping a soda so good.

November 8, 2010

2011

My Sister Comes to Visit

My sister and I, side by side
on the couch,

a moldy album of black and
white photos spread over

our laps, the cover a mottled
red leatherette.

We guess at ages, places.
You must have been six

because I was eight, I say.
Tiny faces, Wide smiles.

Eyes squinting in sunlight.
Black and white, shades of

gray, like a life well lived.
We use a magnifying glass,

my sister and I,
to look at the way we were.

Our little selves speak to us
from the pages and say,

You look so old.
Gray hair and wrinkles,

We slam the album shut,
put it up on the closet shelf.

Time to pour the wine and
drink to those sassy lasses

we left behind. Last evening
we drank to past lovers.

Tomorrow, well,
we'll think of something

February 13, 2011

Sixth Grade Field Trip to Chicago's Orchestra Hall

poor Polly Robinson got stuck
next to Billy Borden on the bus
he caused such a ruckus
on our last field trip to
the Hostess Cupcake Company
that Miss Hopkins made him
sit on the girls' side of the bus
Billy Borden thumped his rump
against the seat and punched
poor Polly Robinson's arm
she screeched and he looked
all innocent when Miss Hopkins
glared back at him *who? me?*
they gave us free Twinkies
at the Hostess Cake Company
that was so fun I wish we
could go back there again
I sat across from Charlie Ross
on the bus and he sneaked
a couple of Snickers bars
in his pants pocket and tried
to hand one over to me
but I just shrugged him off
he's so ugh wears corduroy
knickers Polly and me we
call him Whistle Britches
it's a long ride from Oak Park
to Orchestra Hall to hear
Peter and the Wolf
Miss Hopkins played it
for us on the school Victrola
that's when Billy borden
got sent to the principal's
office for throwing spit wads
at Ruthie Thomas

we passed The Chicago Theater
downtown in the Loop
on the way to Orchestra Hall
what a super movie theater
Mom took me for my birthday
to see The Wizard of Oz
WOW and then a stage show
Henry James and his band
and a lady singer wearing
a sequined strapless gown
the lobby was like a palace
marble pillars and a grand
staircase WOW I never saw
anything so wonderful
Orchestra Hall was ok really big
the music was like the record
only louder violins for Peter
oboe for the duck and
bassoon for the grandfather
like Miss Hopkins told us
Charlie Ross grabbed my
program and folded it into
and airplane and Billy Borden
whistled in poor Polly's ear
next day we all had to write
a report on our field trip to
Orchestra Hall and I only got
a C+ because I didn't write
anything about the music
our next trip is going to be
to the phone company but
Billy and Charlie can't go
they have to stay at school
and write a paper about
how it's not good to be bad

February 18, 2011

THE TRISH DUGGER COLLECTION OF POETRY

Letter from the Canyon House
after Oksana Zabuzhko

Dear _____

The roof still leaks even after
the repair. I regret going cheap.
but my plastic is maxed out and
there you have it. Unfortunately,
we are running out of buckets.
Come soonest, Love, before
the septic tank backs up again.
I feel the honey wagon will no
longer attempt the rutted path
to the lower meadow. The last
rain storm made a mess of it,
as well as the wisteria dying
on the bridge. Remember how
its trunk grew up the supports.
its laughing lavender blossoms
splashing down to the ground?
Bruno says it got its feet too wet.
There's no bringing it back and
anyway, the bridge has dry rot.
We keep hacking at the bamboo
near the house. It grows faster
than the poison mushrooms
in the side yard. I would leave
the porch light on for you, but
the switch is loose and needs
fixing. Sweet Love, remember
please, to bring your tool box,
and be sure to include your
current address when you write.
My last letter to you was returned,
marked *Address Unknown,*
so I send this c/o your mother.

Kisses, love T.

February 26, 2011

9.0 Magnitude

The thing is,
this earthquake in Japan,
and tsunami
have seriously fucked
my shopping fun.

I mean like,
I get a mega high from
designer stuff on sale,
a Jones New York top
in lime green on QVC,
Victoria's Secret bra,
lacy shocking pink,
even Fieldcrest sheets,
600 thread count

at Bed Bath & Beyond
that feel like silk when
I slide between them
at night and dream
of strolling down aisles
piled high with ripe
juicy merchandise
inviting me to take a bite.

Now this: earthquake,
tsunami and a huge wave
of sadness which puts
a crimp in a buying binge,
but it will pass with
visions of half price sales
at Bloomingdales.

March 13, 2011

Life on the Edge

I can almost touch
the beginning of yesterday
out at the edge of
vague waves hidden in mist

a time of tenderness
its skin pink and thin
before tumbles and bumps
mark it with scars

each day in this
wind battered house
that borders a beach
doors lean a little more
and cracks appear
in porcelain sinks

the sand is strewn
with dried bones
of childhood
broken shells and kelp
tangled ropes
of abandoned hopes

these stiff bones lean
to pick up a piece
of sea glass
it gleams in sunlight
on my weathered sill

March 21, 2011

Resurrection

I finished sewing the hem at 2 A.M.,
stuck my needle in a fat red
pin cushion. Picked up scraps and
scattered Simplicity pattern pieces.
Tired and limp as a wilted lily.
I gazed at the wonder of my creation.
Hosannah to the light blue
nylon dotted Swiss Easter dress
with puffed sleeves, size 3T.

She stamped her tiny feet in
shiny black Mary Janes and
refused to wear The Dress,
and I took the Lord's name
in vain on Easter .....
that's all I recall of our first
Mother Daughter Dress Debate
so many Resurrections ago.

She still hates puffed sleeves,
but allows me mine as she
helps to ease a blouse around
my bruised shoulder, takes
my arm so I won't fall again,
and helps me rise from the bed.

April 4, 2011

Jimmy Crack Corn

Will and Kate parade across our lawn.
Will flaunting his male mallard attire,

turning his iridescent turquoise head
toward cracked corn tossed by the girls.

Kate dressed in subdued muted tones
waddles close behind. We think she

has a nest in reeds down by the creek.
The Chihuahuas go a little crazy with

frenzied yaps at the ducks' appearance.
We named them after Prince William

and Kate Middleton, of course. There's
no avoiding news of the royal wedding.

Friday, April 29th in the year of our Lord,
2011 at Westminster Abbey, London U.K.

April 21, 2011

The Curious Lizard

sunning on a fence in the Hopper yard,
keeps tabs on the neighborhood.
Less pricey than the Stafford cul-de-sac.
this Barcelona block is more exciting.
The pit bull incident, for example.
Del Morrison, the mailman, yells, Fuck
at the dog, limps to his truck, call 911.
Pronto an ambulance screams down
the street, stirring Stephanie Stone
into action in red hot culottes and clogs.
She waves to Gertie Davis next door
attacking shrubs with wicked shears,
while Mrs. Jones in scuffs and black
negligee picks up a newspaper at
the end of her driveway. Don Grimes,
(rhymes with crimes) two doors down
seems to be checking the oil in his
Jeep, but he's really checking out
Mrs. Jones. They got a thing goin' on.
This block is buzzing with gossip
of whose honey is sweet on who.
Down the hill a bored gray hamster
tired of the spinning wheel routine

all the livelong day, escapes from
his cage, races to a fish pond and
dives in just to chase the blues away.
Uptown in Polk's New & Used Books,
a lazy fat tabby cat sits on a purple
velvet cushion and purrs when Viola,
Mr. Polk's pretty part-time clerk,
pets him just to pass the time away.
Business is slow since the bus line
cut out the corner stop. Viola has to
rise up so early in the morn to walk
five long blocks from Belmont Street.
Mr. Polk on his break from the shop,
sips coffee in Dinah's Diner, waits for
Dinah to serve his eggs over easy,
but someone's in the kitchen with her.
It's a long wait and his coffee's cold.
He can hear the town bum strummin'
on an old banjo in the alley behind
the diner where a shaggy black dog
paws for food in a turned over trash can.
The B & O down the line's right on time.
Can't you hear the whistle blowin'?

April 28, 2011

Losing It

What's the name of that poem
by Billy Something.....
the one about losing words?
I relate big time, says Joanne.

She's starting to forget things,
can't recall where she read it.
I reply, *Collins.* She shouts,
WHAT? and I yell back at her,

COLLINS. Billy COLLINS.
The poem, *Forgetfulness,* in
his *Questions about Angels*
is right here on my bookshelf.

Hmm. Well, maybe over there.
I pick up a magnifying glass
to read yet again the faint
print of Billy's fine wry lines.

if indeed, I can find the damn
book among this dusty stack,
and my thoughts wander off
into the persistent mystery of

disappearing ball point pens.
My sister phones and says
she took a fall on the sidewalk.
Tipped over. Lost her balance.

I know she'll find it and maybe
I'll find my ballpoint pen.
I need to write the last words
to a poem before I lose them.

May 8, 2011

Waiting for the Blind Guy

The blind guy has arrived.
Not blind like a guy who
can't see, but one who steals
you blind to fix your blinds,
to replace strings and stops.
Not stops like *quits,* but
gizmos to hold the strings
when the blinds are drawn.
Not drawn like chalk art
on sidewalks, but pulled up
to let sunlight in. Anyway,
the blind guy just pulled up.

July 21, 2011

Here Lies Love

A few too many beers
the night they met

landed the laughing lass
in the bad boy's lap,

a Captain with a silver Jag.
That's how it began.

advancing to champagne
and dancing on a glass

ballroom floor, brightly
colored lights beneath at

the Knickerbocker Hotel
on Michigan Avenue.

When did they take
a lurching tumbledown turn

into dimly lit Hangover Square?
Bloody Mary mornings,

Mai Tai twilights, Dry Martini
evenings ending in laughing,

shrieking, weeping.
Their backyard a burial ground.

Tiger, a yellow striped cat
beneath the deodar cedar tree,

Boots, a calico under a rock.
Some graves marked, some not.

September 2011

La Dolce Vita

started in a bar in Abilene place
called Jake's

guy with a goatee walks in he's
wearin' a black beret

Stetson-topped leather faced cowboy
says by gawd now I seen everything

shots of tequila all around
whiskey too heard tell somebody

up the hill in the cemetery gone
plum loco knockin' over headstones

crappin' behind a mausoleum
over in Lubbock dude pulls a gun

shoots hisself in the toe hundred
miles or so across dust and rocks

a maestro busts out of a bamboo
cocoon waves a baton bouncing

a cuckoo clock off the wall falls on
a clown he's singing Rigoletto in

falsetto this is where I came in
I'm sayin' *arrivederci*

September 11, 2011

My Daughter-In-Law's Recipe

A timer on the stove tick ticks
toward zero, then *bing,*
the steamed rice is done.

Time to flip another page
of the calendar. Holy smoke!
Getting close to jingle bells.

Another birthday waits two
blocks sway, just a crone's
throw across a medi-gap.

We've time enough, at least,
for spicy red beans and rice,
time to savor Cajun cuisine.

Though I've more yesterdays
than tomorrows, today pass
the tobacco. Bon appetit.

September 24, 2011

Anyone for Porridge?

lost in the forest
of your chest
my red riding hood
flung on a bedpost
you deep in my
basket of goodies
and oh dear
what a big yes
somebody's been
sleeping in my bed

October 13, 2011

A Simple Little Arithmetic

would have taught me enough
to balance a checkbook
and figure a 20% discount
Add Subtract Multiply
a little Division
I would have been happy
with that I hated fractions
almost as much as I hated
Peggy Robinson,
the girl with perfect curls
who always raised her hand
when Mr. Van Dyke asked
who knew how to find
a square root or prove
a stupid theorem
Algebra was a yawn
all those x's and y's
and geometry worse
cornered in triangles
we all knew Jerry a guy
with zits genius at math
I smiled at him a lot
let him walk me to class
and help me with homework
jazzed when I passed
free of Jerry and math
but who knew what
Clearsil and contact lenses
could do he and Peggy
named Cutest Couple in
the yearbook go figure

October 20, 2011

Perfidia

Nadie comprende lo que sufro yo
Alberto Dominguez

I'll take a 5 star hotel suite on the 24th floor
with a window wall overlooking the bay.
You say, *What bay?* and I say, *Who cares?*
Throw in some palm trees, a few yachts,
suspension bridge across glittering water.

I'll take room service. You can have your
streets of gold where you'll meet good
people who kiss with closed lips tasting
of dead smiles. You tell me it's over,
big top taken down, the circus moved
on to another town. I was shelling peas
while clowns drove around in tiny cars.

You say the party ended, open bar closed,
leftover stuffed mushrooms dumped
in the trash. I was baking biscuits while
a jazz sestet played *Perfidia* and the hot
drummer made moves on a skinny
blonde with big tits between sets
and I washed another load of clothes.

I hated the game. Handful of nothing. His
peg already on 4th street. Me left behind.
The blackout brought it all back, how we
used to have fun, reaching for each other
in the dark. He could charm even mean
Mrs. Potts with his harmonica, playing her
favorite, *I'll be loving you always.*
She'd forget we were behind in the rent.

I get by. I've got Daddy Long Legs who slips
me a C note now and then when I read his
astrological chart in the back behind a heavy
red velvet curtain. I'm a student of Crystal,
the fortune teller next door to the donut shop
over by Lou's Liquor at the strip mall where
I ran out of gas.

October 21, 2011

Peeling a Tangerine

like
un-
zip-
ping
your
fly
find-
ing
ripe
flesh
in-
side
that
hides
tiny
seeds
and
such
sweet
juice
of
eager
fruit

November 3, 2011

To Her Young Lover

You don't know
the place where
iris eyes fade
to pale lakes,
and smooth skin
turns to parchment,
and maybe you
never will,
considering your
love of sky diving
and fast driving,
in which case,
I'll meet you on
the other side
where your
forever iris eyes
will burn a hole in
my haunted heart.

December 1, 2011

The Gingerbread House Is
Made of Cardboard

I know this street.
I once drove it doing 60
in an SUV with a bird
on the passenger seat.
I always grab thrills in
the afternoon, zoned out.

A lanky Scandinavian
carpenter in tight pants,
sexed-up, humming.
with his tool he traces
my body. We clank
and bang all night.

Next day I say, Don't let
your cell phone rest on
my bed. Pick it up and
speed dial your dog..
Tell him how good you
are at setting a nail.

Downstairs the German
boy counts numbers.
He plays Hansel in
a school play. A 2nd grade
Korean girl is Gretel/
The witch is a Greek kid.

About the bird turquoise
cockatiel It flew away
when I stopped at a red
at Wilshire and Santa Monica.

2011

The Last Time I Touched Him

his skin icy cold
this is all I know

of death
freezing cold

and how
the earth stumbles

in its search
for a lost sun

and how bleak
the struggle to keep

from sliding into
a night without stars

2011

Mozart Ave. Menagerie

Yikes! Julie spies a rat
prancing in the garden
between rows of kale.
Oh No! moans Trish,
although her home
has always been
Open House to all
critters in the canyon.
From skunks and
opossums, squirrels
and raccoons, from
lizards and frogs
to the shy gray fox
captured on film
with surprised red
pinpoint eyes and
the exotic peacock
whose cries of Help
Help, echo across
canyon walls. And
Ohmygod, a snake,
says the Sears

repair guy as he
retrieves a reptile
wound around the
motor of the dryer.
First time in his
20 years with Sears.
And the wolves,
the ravenous wolves
in flip flops and
tank tops and shorts
sitting on the porch
devouring plates
of potato salad
and beef kabobs
served by babes
slithering out of
the kitchen in snake
tight jeans and slinky
tees in wild shades
strappy sandals
and painted toes
bright as rosy boas

2011

Our Manassas

War in the kitchen again,
Mom clangs pots and pans,
whacks celery stalks with
a French knife, chops beef
with a cleaver as if it were
a saber. At dinner a final
dash of anger tossed on
beef stroganoff over noodles.
Something Dad did, I guess.
Or didn't do. He holds a fork
at the north end of the table.
Mom at her post on the south,
we kids on the flanks,
mealtime marauders, ready
to attack platters of food.
A truce to dish up noodles
and pass around the plates.
Dad takes a bite, looks up
at Mom and smiles and
her fury falls flat as a soufflé
at the bang of a cannon.
An uneasy truce then,
peace treaty terms to be
settled in the bedroom.

2011

Who Begat Who

Between innings I tell David
about tunnels beneath
solid granite cliffs of Utah's
Little Cottonwood Canyon,
tunnels with ceilings of curved
corrugated metal where
miles of microfilm are stored
with endless info about
who begat who
in the cool distant past.

David says, *Uh huh.*
My grandson Andrew's catching,
his pal riley on the mound.
Score tied, Man, those Vista High
kids look like giants at bat.
I tell David I've been researching
cities beneath cities.

David says, *Uh huh.*
Like the catacombs of Paris.
It took twelve years to move
all the bones from cemeteries
in the city into the catacombs,
and I swear I can hear faint
moans from piles of ancient
French bones.

David says, *Uh huh.*
Want a hot dog from
the snack bar, Mom?
Oh dear,
did we lose? *Uh huh.*

2011

2012

mmmmm

do that again
a little lower
yes there mmmmm
something baking
in the kitchen
smells like cinnamon
mmmmm
tastes like homemade
apple pie
clinking ice
in fresh lemonade
mmmmm
your wide smile
moments spiced
with mmmmm
make it worthwhile
to swim through
all the p's and q's
of each day's dull
alphabet soup
make bedtime sweet
shhhhh

February 6, 2012

My Other Self

fits into size 6 jeans with bling
doesn't nibble in-between meals
eats and drinks non-fat everything
brushes her teeth even when sleepy
walks 3 miles a day weighs weekly
sips virgin Bloody Marys doesn't
cuss or say fuck and I hate her
but she's the one he married
and he won't let me forget so .....
one of us has to go but which
my other self is an uptight bitch
wouldn't leave a single dirty dish
in the kitchen sink but he can be
a prick not at all the mellow guy
I married and he constantly nags
about extra pounds hounds me
to be more glamorous amorous
and I'm starting to wonder if he
too has another self more like
the nice guy he used to be sweet
as blueberry pie smiling at me
hanging out at the tavern where
we met but don't go to anymore
and it's clear to me now I'm the
one who has to go I'll grab my
bag and keys head for the door
I don't need any more of his shit
I'm off to look for his other self
I know we'll groove we'll move
to a loft downtown eat take-out
pizza drink Miller's from a can
and I'll make love with a man
who wants me just the way I am

February 9, 2012

Rash of Tuba Thefts in
Southland High Schools
L.A. Times Dec. 12, 2011

I can't get those tubas
out of my head. I can see
burly thugs in dark hoods
creeping down corridors
trying to hide humongous
tubas behind their backs,
crashing into lockers,
knocking over trash cans,
cracking windows.
I've never stolen anything
unless you count
Lucy Crane's boyfriend,
Corky Taylor, and I never
knew a guy who played
the tuba, which I can't
say I'm sorry about but,
Corky played a wicked
harmonica when we
weren't making out
behind the bleachers.

February 16, 2012

Writing a Haiku

possibly a sonnet but not a villanelle
no way a villanelle and definitely not
a pantoum and for sure sestina's out
but how about a brief haiku since my
time is limited and my attention span
decreased and I find complex verse
forms and confusing rhyme schemes
formidable challenges especially now
that my carpal tunnel syndrome has
taken a turn for the worse making
writing and typing especially painful
I suppose I could try a prose poem
but I admit the difference between
prose and prose poetry has never
been clear to me and perhaps the
workshop can help me with that
and meantime what the hell I'll try
haiku let's see I think it goes 5 7 5

flight of wild words
finds asylum in confined lines
folds wings in haiku

March 25, 2012

One Half Inch to One Foot

She hums at her work bench
alone in the garage, crafting
perfect little rooms to scale

with teeny tables and chairs,
itty bitty crepe paper flowers
in a wee vase on a wee tray.

It's quiet out here away from
tv, from squabbling kids and
her husband's angry shouts.

She smiles at her doll house.
No mess. No muss. Ruffled
pink quilt on a miniature bed.

A single place setting for tea.
Miniature cupcakes on a tiny
china cake plate. Petite treats.

She measures a little mauve
rug for the powder room floor,
then wraps the tape around

her delicate shrinking wrist.
Half inch smaller than last
week and this morning five

pounds lighter on the scale,
one inch shorter on the wall.
She picks up the tiny mauve

rug and fits it into the powder
room, adjusts a teeny mirror,
can almost see herself in it.

March 31, 2012

In the Infirmary

nice to be sick
with a temp
but no itch
Miss Miln in
crisp white
bringing juice
to my dry lips
nice to skip
school and
spelling tests
nice away from

the rest of the
swarm in the
girls' crowded
dorm Miss Baxter's
sharp tongue
cutting across
tattle and cries
and clatter of
cups clinking
spoons endless
dining room din

nice to
lie still
by my-
self in
a quiet
cocoon
of flu

April 2012

Belmont Avenue 1934

Parked at the curb,
the ice man's truck
loaded with blocks
of ice sparkling in
July sunlight. Kids
scamper for ice chips
like flies on garbage
in the alley behind
Saul's Deli. Barefoot
kids, scabby knees
and sunburned noses
hop up and down on
hot pavement, chase
each other to the corner
drug store with penny
candy bins up front,
beg Mr. Levinson for free
sour balls. He shakes
a broom, yells, Get out.
We scamper like rats.
I squeeze my eyes shut,
see it all in a flash that
glistens for a minute
like ice chips, then gone
along with my father's
movie star smile wide
as Belmont Avenue,
gone like ice melting
in a rivulet at the curb
when I am five.

April 9, 2012

If I Could Go Back It Would Be For Joey

to you and me at 17, running barefoot
through sprinklers on your front lawn
in moonlight, high on beer bought for
us by an older guy around the corner
who adored you. Your folks gone for
two weeks and me, friend trusted to
stay with you, the house left in our
care. To Do lists taped on all mirrors.
No surprise we left *Sprinkle Lawn*
until the last night when we became
slippery sprites, laughing, splashing.

It was a holy time, a sort of baptism.
The beginning of our new lives after
high school where we were brought
together by alphabetical order:
You, *Schaniel*, me *Saunders*. Me
following you through the four years
of Homeroom that saved me from
the loneliness of a foster child in
search of a North Star. Best friends
through the rocky landscape of life.

They are dead, those who told me
I was baptized by a visiting bishop
in a country church with no priest.
Was my father there? Did he hold
me in his arms? They are dead
who could have told me, but didn't.
Typical that I'd turn this poem into
a lament for a father who left me.

Did I envy you yours who seemed
to me a big strong story book Dad?
Maybe. I didn't know the demons
hiding in your seemingly picture
perfect home. You would spend
decades running from your father
while I sought mine. But that one
night has always been a beacon,
glittering as then when we were
17 and never again so carefree.

April 28, 2012

Looking Back

I can see signs replacing
our Ford SUV with a new little
Toyota easier for me to drive.
file folders with fresh labels

for legal papers. Phoning old
friends to say hello. Goodbye?
Makes me wonder how much
he knew. I never had a hint.

I was too busy making a list
of things I wanted him to do,
starting with our dingy kitchen.
I look at glossy white cabinets

and a built-in dishwasher that
I'd wanted with a passion but,
all I see is a solitary plate
in a dish rack on pristine tile.

May 2012

Memo to Terry

A black crow sits on a tv cable
outside my window,
watching waiting.
I think it belongs to you.
I don't allow crows on my lines.

It's enough for me that
the night blooming jasmine
blooms by day. A sin?

No more than day lilies
opening at dusk,
pansies poking up
where I planted poppies.

My dog howls at the full moon.
I lie awake thinking about
the audacity of wild flowers.

I decide to be more
like them,
wanton carefree
I'll fling myself
on a green meadow
and wink at the sun.

I suppose the crow is
an omen of darkness
or impending doom.
You'll find a use for it.

Ask the crow what it knows
about the disappearance
of paper boys on bikes.
The crow saw everything.

May 6, 2012

Positron Emission Tomography

Teresa pours another glass of wine.
Claudia takes her quiche out of
the oven, the crust burned dark as
charcoal, just the way we like it.
The wine's cheap. It's the running of
the Preakness on tv and Dino
arrives from Little Italy with Frankie.
Our three chihuahuas yelp and go
crazy chasing the visiting dachshund.
Claudia gets out the clippers to cut
Din's hair before post time.

Trish turns up the tv, tries to tune out
a dark horse rearing up in her mind.
Claudia yells, *Turn it down.*
Bill yells, *What?* He forgot his
hearing aid. He's 89, a sweet man
enjoying a glass of wine and burnt
quiche in this old topsy turvy house.

Now the long walk to the starting gate.
Gayle calls from Glendale,
says she's got a bet on the horse
that Nakatani's riding,
says she starts chemo next week.
Trish says we're all betting on her,
and when she beats it we'll go
to Disneyland.
Dino holds out his wine glass, says,
I'll Have Another.

May 19, 2012

Cook County Foster Care

Nobody wants two kids.
Hard enough to place one,
Even the cute little girl.
That would be my sister.

You go where they take you,
Your clothes in a brown
paper bag. You feel
like you lost something,

someone,
and can't remember
saying goodbye.
You don't cry.

May 24, 2012

Oops

I saved the page of the L.A. Times,
placed it on the side of my desk,

an article with a number to call
to donate my body when I go.

I put the article on top of one with
the number to call to donate clothes.

I wish I could find a number to call
to donate heartaches and pains.

You changed your number, didn't
tell me the new one which says it all,

so it's comforting to know that some
place will want my old expired bones.

I'll try to keep them in decent shape,
though their density decreases daily,

and my heart's not worth much except
for studying effects of too much vodka,

which I spilled on my desk, soaking all
of the papers and had to throw them out.

May 24, 2012

Hot July Saturday Night

he's doing 80 on the I 5
southbound in the fast lane
getting out of L.A.
in a gray Ford pickup
downtown lights on
his right and nobody's
going nowhere
at 10 P.M. but him
headed south
into the mouth of night
caught in the grip of
white line fever
bound for the beach
driven by visions
of salty kisses from
the lips of a girl he met
at The Hurley Bell
name of Misty
something like that
Biffy ..... Bambi
butterfly tat on her thigh
he wants to dive into
her wet kisses
and drive back home
Misty at his side
in the diamond lane

August 31, 2012

Oh Well It's Just Stuff

my sister says, speaking of her Ikea
furniture purchased just one year ago
for her cute new bungalow apartment.

My sons will move out the Ikea stuff...
dinette table, chairs, couch, bed, chest
and the rest before the lease is up.

A Hospice bed in my spare room where
my sister sleeps has an electric control
to raise and lower the foot and the head.

September 7, 2012

Bhutan and Petra and Harmony Grove

Bhutan, says Bruce, *definitely Bhutan,*
between bites of macaroni salad and
baked beans. Maureen, jingling silver
bracelets on her right arm. Pipes in
with *Petra* during a discussion of
the most beautiful spots in the world.
I sip an Arnold Palmer while sitting
In the middle of this well traveled group,
and I don't have a clue where these
two places are located. My offering at
the table begins with Harmony Grove.
Does anyone know Harmony Egg Ranch
on Country Cub Drive? I say I've heard
It's been sold to make way for 742
homes in a development that will include
a private equestrian facility and spacious
estates featuring half-acre cul-de-sac lots.
I like horses, of course, and find half-
acre lots quite nice, but is this progress?
Like the Mulholland Bridge demolished
as part of a project to add a car pool lane
to a section of the 405. I don't confide
I secretly desired to see it blown up and
worry a bit about what kind of person that
makes me. And does anyone really care
that old timey movie theaters are closing
because they don't have the money to go
digital. I've gone to Netflix although DVDs
that are paused in the middle and won't
go back to START even when STOP is
pressed can drive a body over the bend.
Happily I learned the solution from a friend.
Try pressing STOP twice like STOP STOP.

September 9, 2012

My Sister's Cell Phone

I speed dial my sister's cell,
listen to her sassy voice tell me

to please leave a message.
And I do. I say, we miss you.

It's so quiet since you passed.
No Hospice nurses in and out.

No meds and supplies arriving
day and night. No cousins

coming by to hold your hand.
Some lovely flowers from

the folks back east. Cards too.
And I can't do the crossword

without you. Your stuff slowly
floats away the tv to Dave.

Pauline took the bed. Your
wedding band to C, of course,

and the lever back puffy gold
heart earrings that I secretly

coveted? Now they're mine.
Well, that's about all for now.

I'll catch you up later on how
Louie's doing after C brings

him home from the vet and,
oh yeah, I still get mad when

I think about that bitchy T-Mobile
supervisor who wouldn't let me

cancel your cell, but oh well,
turns out I have the last word.

September 23, 2012

Autumn Rain

Well, it isn't the subject.
Richard Hugo

insisting itself into my house with
drip drip drips on a table near an outside wall.
It's been such a long dry spell.
I'd almost forgotten the power of its thrust
against my siding, stunning surge
of tingle in my finger tips from the kiss
of autumn rain on my skin, and no matter
what Richard Hugo says, the subject is
autumn rain, autumn fucking rain
that floods this place with reckless waves,
then gone almost as soon as it comes,
leaving me ragged in its wake.

October 2012

Life/Death/Sins/Angels on the Head of a Pin

We always held our breath walking past
Osgood's Funeral Parlor on Superior Street,
stepped across cracks in the sidewalk and
tried to avoid all the black cats in our path.

Our voices lowered when we talked about
Charlie Ross, a kid from the neighborhood
who died of polio, and how we might get
polio too, swimming in the municipal pool.

I never worried about getting into heaven,
even tried being bad enough to go to hell
where I'd meet up with my dad who bailed.
Mom used to tell me to look for him there.

October 12, 2012

Rain on the Roof & Mud in the Yard

and an old army blanket draped over
the dining table encyclopedias
holding it in place books without which
you cannot raise your children who are
under the table with flashlights and
graham crackers encyclopedias for
which you made payments and put
hamburger meat on a tab at the local
mom & pop grocery store when the
money ran out and the encyclopedias
were used to help make a little house
under the dining table the big books
holding an old army blanket in place
ever notice how easy it is to remember
exactly what everybody was wearing
just before lightning struck
me in jeans too tight from eating
leftover Cheerios and peanut butter
sandwiches likewise too tight black
sweater the encyclopedia salesman

in dark suit light blue button down
shirt red tie he knocked on my front
door in time to save me from dying
of boredom offered me a deal on
encyclopedias the sample volume
heavy on my knees its pages thick
and glossy vivid photos of Burmese
elephants and natives of New Guinea
places I will travel to only on pages
exotic adventures offered to me by
an encyclopedia salesman who
knew he had me I bought a set
and the previous week
it had been the Fuller Brush man
in tan coat and brown slacks who
knew a thing or two about what
I needed besides brushes
like lemon scented furniture polish
selling two for the price of one
and how could I resist

November 13, 2012

A Year after Your Death
after Czeslaw Milosz

I still smile at strangers
laugh at Tina Fey on tv
hum to songs on the radio
the world hasn't ended
after all
sorry Darling but I flirt
with box boys at Von's
and I confess I stuck
your silver framed photo
in a dresser drawer
when I had a visitor last
Friday but you know that
don't you
why else would he trip
and break his leg
while hopping into bed

2012

2013

So You Think You Can't Draw

No question. A course made to order for me.
Ms. Angelo Rm 25 7-9 Tuesdays. I used to
grab that Adult Ed. Catalog from a stash
of bills in the mailbox, much like my kids
went for Sears Toy Catalog at Christmas time.
Adult Ed., path to enlightenment and oh yeah,
my night out. Creative Writing. Spanish. Pottery.
Spanish. Semantics. Spanish. Phys Ed. Spanish.
Yes, I'd a crush on Mr. Castellanos, but it takes
years to get the accent right, as I reminded
my husband when he asked, *Spanish again?*

I showed up in Room 25 with my drawing pad
and pencils, sat in the front row and practiced
till I could draw a profile to please Ms. Angelo
of my husband as he slept stretched out in his
recliner after an early supper of split pea soup..
In Ms. Angelo's class, I learned that drawing
is really seeing what you're looking at, even if
you don't *want* to see shallow breathing and
dark urine in a bag at the end of a tube because
you know you are looking at the end of a life and
Adult Ed. is dying, pricing itself out of existence.

My friend Julie teaches watercolor. She says
her class is down to 5, and I tell her at Costco
just the other day, a checkout guy held high
a glossy green sunset tinged mango, stared
at me, said, *I can't sell this to you,* and I'm like,
Huh? Do I need a permit to buy a mango,
heavenly fruit of the gods? Then he grilled me
on the spot. *Did you pick this out of a box of 6?*
I stood guilty as charged. You have to buy
the whole fucking box.

January 17, 2013

Stumbling Feet and Crumbling Teeth

I'm 2 inches shorter than I was at 20,
but my feet seem to keep on growing.
My brand spanking new black
Reeboks are a clunky size 10
and make me stumble over my own
feet when I climb steep stairs to see
Lena who cleans my crumbling teeth.

I drive down Birmingham to the
bottom of the hill in my 18 year old
Toyota replete with dings, and I'm
dizzy with an ageless thrill that
rushes through me like a gust of
wind, starts my heart cartwheeling
at the sight of the sparkling Pacific.

I'm young again, alive, excited
and everything inside me tingles,
if it's not stumbling or crumbling.
I'd take your hand and place it
on my heart so you could feel
its impetuous beat but, well,
you might misunderstand and
I wouldn't want you to tell my kids,
like that time with the handyman.

January 25, 2013

They Are Hungry

The boy with skinned knees …
he's four, bites a fingernail, fidgets
as he sits between his sisters on
a back porch seat. The pudgy

girl is five, short blonde hair with
bangs, buck teeth, sucks her thumb.
The littler girl, three, has brown
eyes and dimples, eyelids drooping.

She leans against the boy's arm.
He pokes her side. Quiet as a kept
secret, they look through a kitchen
window of their new foster home.

A woman, gray hair in a bun,
wears a faded blue bib apron and
a man, shoulders slumped, shiny
bald head, sits at a table in brown

sweater and a frown. The woman
ladles stew onto his plate.
In the cold dark of the back porch.
the kids wait, lick their lips.

February 10, 2013

San Diego Public Library
Local Authors Reception

driving downtown
in the dark of a Friday
traffic lights sequin
the black velvet night

in the back seat
my eyes blink my
heart leaps
I tingle at the sight

of high rises and for
a brief while I'm
nineteen excited by
lights in the Loop

My grandson Andrew
hired to drive me to
my big night downtown
Meredith his girlfriend

at his side shudders
says she feels
surrounded closed in
by concrete giants

Andrew at the wheel
smiles says *Nana*
You should write a poem
about downtown about

tonight

February 14, 2013

Sweet Secrets

Stirring sliced zucchini in an iron skillet,
I turn to look up at my six foot tall grandson,
blue eyes the size of boysenberry pies.
He picks up an eggplant from the counter,
tosses it back and forth, hand to hand
while talking about tattoos. He wants one,
maybe on the inside of his arm, maybe
a map of his favorite surfing beach. He
says so many girls have cliché tattoos
like a heart or infinity sign. He wants one
that's unique. Talking fast, he squeezes
the eggplant, then stops, smiles wide and
blurts, *Wow. I never felt an eggplant before,*
Now the eggplant has him, its oval shape,
firm but soft, that gives like the flesh of
a teen-aged girl, its dark skin gleaming,
sleek, hiding sweet secrets. He places
it back down on the counter, pats it with
a grin, snatches a couple of snickerdoodles
from a cookie tin sitting on the counter.

February 15, 2013

Bedtime Stories

A winding road lined with iceberg roses
and magnolia trees comes to an end.
A foot path leads to a house with pillars.
A butler's pantry behind the kitchen
and a sun room off the parlor, buttermilk
and cookies on a tray in a breakfast nook,
music room upstairs with a grand piano,
broad porch across the back that
faces a sloping lawn with a croquet set.
Nobody lives there anymore, but
ghosts roam the halls and a child's cry
can be heard coming from the nursery.
Some say the old man, a retired banker
with Wells Fargo went crazy, attacked
the butler with an ax, split open his head,
or something deliciously wicked like that.
Everybody should have a haunted house
down the road. We kids shrieked and
ran at the sound of a pail clanking behind
a trellis covered with baby pink roses.
The gardener deadheads roses and
a cook chops the head off a chicken.
Almost rivals bedtime nursery rhymes,
visions of Tom, Tom, the Piper's son
getting beat, the farmer's wife whacking
off tails of three blind mice, *Sleep tight.*

March 4, 2013

Bowie on the Brain

Ziggy Stardust glitters after more than
four decades. Androgynous fashion.
The London Olympics. A new album.
But I might as well be in Dubuque because
everybody here is into The Walking Dead,
and I don't think they play music.

I'm glad to read that the pronghorn might
roam again in San Diego county. They're
the fastest land animal in North America,
I found facts like that useful in my days
of glazed eyes and cocktail party patter.

Today my one good eye tripped over
a title in a book of poetry. *Leftover Wine.*
I'm thinking, *Holy Shit. Never happened
in my house. Never any leftover wine.*

I see that Vacheron Constantine is now
in Beverly Hills on Rodeo Drive and that
Seattle has the Hernandez elbow issue.
Speaking of baseball, my son informs me
catcher's gear is called Tools of Ignorance,

but don't ask me why. That bit might serve
you well at a Senior Center Weekly Lunch,
but it's not as delicious as the auction of
Elizabeth Taylor's fabulous bling, bought by
Burton at Bulgari's on Via Condotti in Rome.

Don't you love it when allegations resonate?
Like a dude who sued McDonald's because
they refused him extra pickles on his burger,
which I totally get. I'm a pickle person and
I'm a dinosaur reading two newspapers daily.
It's yesterday's news, but Honey, so am I.

March 4, 2013

Office Politics

After the break for lunch
and before the group launched
into committees, the pretty
sloe-eyed dark skinned sylph
with easy smile reached for
paper from Barnaby's desk,
then gave a wave to Aaron
across the room. He frowned
and turned his head, ignoring
Sylvia. She expected him to
beg at her command.
Getting into her knickers was
not worth the humiliation.

Bruce called for attention and
the meeting resumed.
He said the company was behind
in total sales and would go
bankrupt unless cuts were made
in staff and various new projects
dumped including R & D for
x-ray vision, Clark's brainstorm,
but a pet project of Vance, a VP
whose enthusiasm for Sylvia was
an open zipper, got the go ahead.
Aaron got the ax. Sylvia got laid.

March 4, 2013

Like a Plural of Dry Martini

fog enfolds forlorn pines
in a forest of blind souls
blurs sharp curves and
shrouds early sunshine
hushes hungry cries for
rays of warm morning sun
days of buzzy honey haze

March 19, 2013

My Big Brother

Jack and I sit in rattan chairs
on the wrap-around porch,
I sip iced tea.
He drinks beer. We talk soup,
clam chowder.
We agree New England beats
Manhattan
on any given Friday evening,
We talk weather,
the dry spell, climate change,
coastal fog.
We talk baseball, how scouts
only look for hitters
and pitchers.
We talk around the pit
of his having passed out
on the couch last night
This visit he seems quite
broken, the phone pole
he once was,
struck by lightning.
His hand shakes
as he takes another drag
on his cigarette.
How's Dad? he asks.
He forgets we went
through Dad's stuff,
discussed what to do
with his WW II medals,
forgets he cried
at the nursing home when
Dad didn't know him.
I reply, *He's failing, Jack,
we're losing him.*

March 24, 2013

What's for Dinner?

imagine growing up with no take-out
fish sticks yes Sloppy Joe's yes
but no take-out we survived on
steamed rice and frozen pot pies
Mom opened cans of baked beans
plopped hot dogs in boiling water
my life changed when Jack-in-the-Box
came to town around the corner
Mom plucked a couple of bucks from
the cigar box kissed the top of my
buzz cut gave me a pat on the butt
and shoved me out the front door
I was first in line at the Grand Opening
Jack's smiling red rubber-ball head
going round and round on top of
the square box building inside at
the counter I too smiled at Inez as
her name tag read when she handed
me heaven in a bag double cheese
burger large fries large coke like
Thanksgiving on a hot June afternoon

Imagine my youngest son's voice relating
the above Hallelujah to the Drive-Thru
my oldest son in balding middle age said
Mom you never did made a habit of
serving a regular dinner at a regular time
did you note the accusatory tone
I laughed and replied *Why son that's*
the nicest thing anybody ever said to me
but his memory's not as keen as mine
I can see me then in frenzied nightly
efforts inspired by Betty Crocker well
that's bouillon under the bridge I've long
since said goodbye to Betty and the boys
are now men grilling salmon with the best
of chefs and the girls and I order pizza for
dinner from East Coast Pizza plus there's
great Chow Mein from Chin's and don't
forget Jorge's sopa de tortilla muy delicioso
and it makes no sense that I sometimes
miss my kids' persistent *What's for dinner?*

April 4, 2013

My Six Degrees of Separation

Yusef Komunyakaa follows me
on americanlifeinpoetry.org.
I'm Column 153. He's 154.
Thanks, Ted Kooser.
You'll further find
Komunyakaa's
Yellowjackets in lots
of anthologies while
my Spare Parts about
broken hearts may be
folded and crumpled
in some jumbled
junk drawers where
spare parts are usually
found, along with spare
pencils and pens,
paper clips, cancelled
stamps, discarded and
tarnished gold rings.

April 20, 2013

The Poetry Reading

My mind can't get past the handsome man
in a tan plaid cap and khaki slacks in the back.
Is he here to read? I haven't seen him before.
A woman at the door who's such a bore, frowns.
She's in brown Uggs. She shrugs, takes a seat
on the side up front. Her wide behind overflows.
I suppose more trite lines tonight. There's Lou
in a blue shawl, all in a stew about who to sit next to.
She finally slides in by D. A lady in gray waves
to the man in a tan plaid cap. A pretty young thing
in pink winks. He winks back. Who is this man and
why am I so entranced? From the front I hear
the tall slight guy with a trick eye, shout, *Hi Stan,*
to the man in a tan plaid cap...so...his name is Stan
and I am but. Enough! Where's my stuff? I'm up.

April 22, 2013

The Significance of Pi

A carpet of mustard creeps across
the desert while sea creatures do
what they do in the depths which is
mostly a mystery to scientists, and
all the great knowledge of the world
is hodgepodge to me. Take pi for
instance, its significance...how does
3.1415, (I googled it), affect my life?
I live on planet earth breathing air,
polluted yes, but tell me why the ratio
of the circumference of a circle to its
diameter which gave me such grief in
high school geometry, is so important.
I admit however, a fascination with
parabolas and asymptotes, lines that
are asymptotic to the parabola. My god,
if you love language how can you resist
that wonderful sound! And chemical
compounds, Wow! My chem major lover
recited them to me like sweet nothings.
Say what you will about innocence,
before pi in my life, when air I inhaled
was more pure than now, Alice fell down
a hole in the ground and I took a dictionary
from the shelf and looked up the word *fuck.*
I'd seen it scrawled on el train platforms
in Chicago. Times past more innocent?
Eve might tell you otherwise. My dictionary
came up empty so I had to learn on my own
which proved to be a lot more fun than
trying to learn pi, and though scientists don't
have a clue about what sea creatures do
in the deep, between you and me, I don't
think they're just swimming around in circles.

April 25, 2013

Deadline

I open the page to Death
Well, what can I say?
The poet's sister overdosed,
so the grieving poet writes
blah blah blah die dying died
Not exactly what I need.
Haven't I spent nearly a year trying
to catch a last glimpse of you in
that black tunnel or is it white?

On the other hand, I'm happy to
report my magenta Mandeville
thrives. It hangs in a planter by
my front door, a place a friend
calls The Kiss of Death,
due to my spotty watering of
various departed petunias.

Yesterday I smashed a big black
spider crawling in my bathtub,
and this morning I reached for Raid
to poison spray an invasion of ants,
all the while wondering what we
will do about Syria. And by the way,
it was rude of you to leave before me.

September 4, 2013

Blonde in White Convertible

Do you know me?
I am the blonde
in the white convertible.
Have you seen me
cruising up the coast
on a mango day?
Top down, honeydew
bandana holding back
my hair, juicy fruit lips
smiling, enticing you
into a day dream?
Have you looked for me?
I am said to be elusive and
you may not recognize me.
I frequently slip into
something more comfortable
inside the round
gray-haired lady who
lives in the canyon
and writes poetry.

September 4, 2013

The Dental Diary

Eve cracked a tooth in the Garden of Eden,
biting into a siren red apple that called to her
like a circus calliope, though the Bible
doesn't say so. Original Sin gets lots of mention,
but there's nothing among the verses about
root canals and implants, cavities and crowns,
scourge of man involving serious money and
heavy duty pain. Anyone with spare Vicodin?

And search as you will, no biblical reference
to the Tooth Fairy whose collection of baby
teeth is vast as all the gravel of the land and
rattles the heavens. Reportedly, the going rate
of exchange for a baby tooth under the pillow
is five dollars. Back when my old man played
Tooth Fairy to our kids, quarters did the job,
making me long in the tooth and minus a few.

September 14, 2013

Reading Poetry Naked

on Sunday Afternoon
while watching tv
anthology on the coffee table
open to Robert Pinsky
doors and windows
open to breezy
butterscotch haze
of a perfect day
butterflies flap happy
dusting their bottoms
on saucy blossoms
two minute warning
Chargers 30 Cowboys 21
scent of charred chicken
on the grill fills the air
time to put Pinsky's Shirt
back in the box
without even trying it on

September 29, 2013

Snapshots Taken with My Brownie Camera Given to Me by My Uncle Bob

that's Uncle Bob in uniform
a Chicago cop Mom says
he's on the take once I held
his gun and he let me sip beer
and ride on the back of his motorcycle
around the block holding tight

that's Aunt Dorothy in the fur coat
Uncle Bob got it for her at a giant
wholesale house I went with and
never seen so many coats in one place
and I got a free new Sunday coat too
with a dark blue velvet collar

One day when Uncle Bob didn't come
home again Aunt Dorothy said he was
full of shit and moved out so we don't
get no free Pepsi Cola any more and
there's fat Cousin Sheila who I babysat
stuffed into a dress with puffed sleeves

she can't even wipe her own bottom
yells at Aunt Dorothy to come help
Mom says she's a brat because
Uncle Bob gave her everything
my dad split so I don't get nothing
except from Uncle Bob and

that's Mom with her hands on her hips
wearing Aunt Dorothy's old
polka dot dress and that's me in shorts
waving and smiling at Uncle Bob

October 8, 2013

Chinatown Rising

A dark dragon inside me
never lets me forget
even after all this time.
It spits fire on dying
embers of a deed
I've tried to leave behind.

And you may need to know
although I take you
softly in my arms tonight,
once upon a time I didn't
look back at the one
I abandoned at a bus stop
near the end of the line.

October 12, 2013

The Affair

slivers of moonlight
slice deep
into a secret tunnel
of desire
no one can ever know
he whispers
she sighs *no one*

yesterday
soft moss beneath them
Crayola blue sky
above thick with
white castles
and impossibility

and an angry tiger
prowls
in an empty house
a rumble of thunder
followed by salty showers
raining upon denial
and leaving a stain
that never quite fades

and the tiger
never quite sleeps
and she
beside him smiles
in her dreams

October 20, 2013

The Good Bad Girl

She wanted so bad to be bad
and when he said,
Don't scratch my back,
she knew for sure she was bad.

She wanted so bad to go
where she'd never been before,
and when he added.
Next time don't wear scent,

she was thrilled to be there
in forbidden territory.
She wanted so much the rush
of a flutter in her breast,

and all the rest tingle of
fingers in damp places,
flushed faces and
all the while a secret smile.

She got so good at being
bad she almost forgot
to be good anymore which
anyway was such a bore.

And finally tired of running
around, she went home to
her man who'd been patient
and good, but found him

gone to the arms of a woman
wronged by a guy who had
said, *Don't scratch my back.*

October 21, 2013

A Modern Gothic Tale

Come to tea
in my secret hiding place
and taste
yummy poppy seed muffins
baked in my oven.
I plop an empty tin
on a pepper hot oven rack,
close my eyes and chant,
Make me a dozen
yummy poppy seed muffins,
and do a little dance.
Do you remember
my secret hiding place
in a hollow under the stairs
where you told me lies
when you said
you'd never leave me?
I'll spread my crazy quilt
on the floor, tell you
I still adore you, then
pour you a cup of my
special peppermint tea,
and keep you there
forever in the hollow
under the stairs.

October 28, 2013

I Woke Up in a Strange Bed

Miss Lilliana shaking my shoulder,
Patsy, what are you doing in my bed?

Clearly she was not a bear
and I not Goldilocks. I was nine or ten.

Short brown bob. Buck teeth from
sucking my thumb.

I must have sleepwalked from
my dorm down the hall and into

Miss Lilliana's room, her empty bed.
I loved her soft voice and

her smile was like a warm hug
when she helped take care of us.

Mean Miss Caswell, girls' matron,
had sharp teeth and a wide belly.

She tried to make me say
I did it on purpose, said I was bad,

and hit me on the wrist
with the sharp edge of a ruler.

No Saturday movies for a month.
Denied my escape

through weekly free movies at
the Lake Theater around the corner

from the Oak Park Childrens' Home.
I've never sleepwalked again but,

I admit there've been strange beds,
and times I've been bad on purpose.

November 4, 2013

2014

News from the Home Front

the talk is all about rats
how many traps
we've bought we've set
best store to get them at
Ace Hardware's nearby
but the wise guy clerk
with a doomsday *Uh Oh*
every time Claudia
shows up to buy more
traps ticks her off
so it's on to Home Depot
farther but cheaper
where nobody gives a peep
or even gives a shit
this old house a compound
exploding with energy
pulsing with purpose
since we declared war
my slow steps escalate
to a military march and

I've even chipped in to
the mounting cost of
a major frontline assault
my family the troops rally
David with tight lips and
quick deliberate moves
resets old traps after
a snappy salute to my
command battle-ready
Claudia her eyes like
searchlights and Teresa
on recon bent in grim
pursuit they bait new
traps with peanut butter
no more uneasy peace
with creepy little fuckers
not since Kevin spied tiny
turds on a kitchen counter
every morning we check
the traps count the dead

January 27, 2014

Just a Whisper of Vermouth

Two martinis away from my finest lines,
never to be penned, lost forever
in the sand of a land called Abstinence.

Thirst never goes away. it longs to be
on the rim of a pitcher of gin. The brink
of a warm Tanqueray haze and begin

a descent into a pool of words, flashing
like koi and string them into a necklace
of effervescent verse but quickly,

before a two martini glow goes poof.
The glow gone, blurred inky scrawls
on cocktail napkins fall to the floor.

A third and I weep because Billy Borden
picked Patty Anderson instead of me
for his baseball team in 3rd grade recess.

A fourth and I'm past remembering,
and worse than any lost verse:
lost panties, lost purse, lost way home,

and if it's a stretch to say sober steps
are a kind of ode, waking up in my own
bed with a clear head is pure poetry.

February 15, 2014

The End and the Beginning

I know what Heaven looks like.....
a vast green field where folks
hold hands and laugh,
dance around in a growing circle
singing a song that never ends,
and there's more, of course,

..... sweet scent of freesias,
whisper of breeze, tangy taste
of fresh lemonade on tongues,
young and old, and the tune
they sing in unison is a song
I'll never forget, coming from

your car radio the night we met.
And maybe we'll meet again
in that enchanted circle of souls.
but it feels good to know when
I finally go to sleep, a hand
will reach for mine and we'll sing.

February 17, 2014

Meeting Anita

Oh those burritos
from Carlos's roach coach
swarmed by workers
like ants on a discarded
cupcake in the parking lot
of Dyna Industries
at lunch break.

Carlos likes to remember
meeting Anita there,
she of the extra hot sauce,
a temp in Data Entry
with skin like cream and
a smile wide as
La Cienega Boulevard.

These days he drives a
a produce vending truck
in Pasadena where
ladies in tight yoga pants
and even tighter faces
saunter out and lean
to smell yellow lemons.

After work Carlos returns
to his home in Pomona,
to Anita and pinches her *culo*
like Pasadena ladies
pinch ripe tomatoes,
and unlike the ladies.
he leans to take a bite.

February 22, 2014

Tommy with Buckets of Laughter

shows up at my front door
walks right in and pours them
out on the floor.
We wade knee deep in roars,
splash, damn near drown
in a flood of laughs, flowing
into empty pockets of my day,
now receding, its sediment
strewn with shimmering smiles.

March 16, 2014

The Crow Connection

I swore I'd not write one more word about crows,
so I won't.
Nothing more about ominous big black birds
lurking in my catalpa tree, gathering on wires to wait.

Nada regarding raucous *caw caws* as they swoop
down upon my roof and thump thump around
as if inspecting the spoils.

I scare neighbors when I go outside and shriek at the sky,
Go away. Go away,
But I don't scare the crows. They pay no attention.

So I'm done with going crazy over crows but today
my friend Joey sent me a photo
of a painting by her artist son, James.

Nine black crows sit on bare branches of a tree.
Ohmygod. Spooky.
And today's featured poem on Writers' Almanac starts,
the crow's voice filters through..... Yes. It does.

Early evening creeps in like a latecomer to a concert.
I sit on the porch and look to the west, watch the sun
sink into the sea as it has done and will do forever.

Quiet as a butterfly's sigh, night wraps us in its black cape,
and I sit here waiting.

April 5, 2014

My Mother Cooked Kosher

for the Cohens, made matzo ball soup
and cheese blintzes, while I ate fish
on Fridays, usually tuna with noodles,
and gave up candy and ice cream
for Lent at St. Mary's Home for Girls
As a teen I got to sleep over at Cohen's,
shared mom's bed where she was a live-in,
ate bagels for breakfast and challah,
ate gefilte fish and sour cream on borscht,
chomped on chunky kosher dill pickles.
All by myself, all on my own, getting to
go on weekends, riding the rickety el
past tenements and factories, changing
trains in the Loop, catching the north
bound, catching a sight of Wrigley Field.
I explored Jewish delis on Howard Street,
the far north side of Chicago, home to
sliced corned beef piled high on rye;
pungent smells and men with dark beards,
an exotic foreign land to a school girl who
lived a few blocks from the last stop of
the Lake Street el in suburban Oak Park,
village of churches and neighborhood of
American cheese on Wonder Bread.
Mom lost her job when Mr. Cohen sold
a wholesale business and left for Miami.
She moved in with Aunt Mattie way out
in Kankakee and went back to cooking
corn fritters and grits. No more kosher
and I don't think she missed it, but I did.

April 12, 2014

Mercury in Retrograde

how else to explain the duck
at my front door
quacking twice and waddling off
to sit in the shade of an acacia

I woke up naked
my nightie on the floor
at the foot of my bed   I might
have had company last night

otherwise an ordinary Tuesday
champagne for breakfast and
poetry for lunch mostly sonnets
sweet and juicy and a few tasty

villanelles with Salsa Fresca
a dreamy siesta in a macramé
hammock hung in the catalpa
listening to music of Segovia

I'm reminded my flamenco's
a bit rusty   I must call Jose
for lessons and whatnot

April 21, 2014

To You Who Would Be a Winner in a Poetry Contest

Write a great first line unlike mine.
For example:
A one legged lady lies naked on the black sand beach.

Seize attention and be concise.
Don't write *nice*.
Nice is limp as a dead shrimp.

Be clear and/or mysterious.
Be dense and/or precise,
and always always be concise.

Display your sparkle and pizzazz,
and as poetry judges tend to lose
concentration, shake up fuzzy minds

by writing seductive lines, syrup
sweet juice sucked from ripe fruit.
Use words with verve and jazzy snap.

Remember that poetry judges adore
a metaphor and furthermore go gaga
over assonance and alliteration.

They seem to like internal rhyme.
It's time to try your hand at that,
and varied line length can add interest.

If you win, the prize will be your
poem in print on a page of some obscure
poetry publication or anthology,

and if you don't win, no apology
is necessary. Remember that
the real reward is in the process,

or so they say and finally, a great
last line is a must if you want to win.
Pick up your pen and begin.

September 1, 2014

Stuff I Don't Know

I don't know much about Estonia,
except it's a country so tiny
I need a magnifying glass
to find it on the world map
hanging on a paneled wall in
my dining area where I gaze
at continents floating in oceans
while I eat my BLT on toast.

And I don't know much about
the Federal Reserve Bank,
which my son informs me
is not a bank at all, nor even
federal. I suppose I *should*
know because I took Econ in
college, but it was springtime
and I was in love and, oh well.

Don't know much about electricity,
though I know enough to unplug
a toaster before sticking in a knife
to fish out a burnt English Muffin.
Don't know much about meteorology
but today's so hot I'm burning up,
and I don't know where the hell
I put the extension cord for my fan.

September 13, 2014

All's Well that Ends With a Nice Pension

They're hiring at the phone company,
Auntie had written. *Come to the city,*
apply for a job. Stay with me for free
till you're settled. A Fairy Godmother
to girls dreaming of leaving the farm.

Sick of slopping pigs and shucking corn,
three teen sisters, Elma, Gay and Dot,
set out for the city in pretty dresses
bought in town at Ward's, and bright
red lipstick from Kresge's 5 & Dime.

Matthew, their dad's hired hand, lanky in
bib overalls, gave them a lift to the depot
driving their dad's Model A. He dropped
them off, winking at Dot after secretly
pinching her arm and waved to all three.

Dusty busses pulled in and pulled out.
Honking horns and sputtering engines.
Fumes of acrid exhaust. The laughing
girls hurried to board the Express,
pushing their way through the crowd.

This story has no end, goes on for generations.
Icicles. Violets. Ripe cherries. Brown leaves.
Humdrum days. Minutes of bliss. Sweet seasons.
In short, Elma and Gay retired from AT&T,
and lived long lives with nice pensions.

Dot returned to the farm, married Matthew
sweet on her as you likely guessed, and yes,
she drew the line. No slopping pigs or
shucking corn, but she canned tomatoes
and beans, made biscuits and blueberry jam.

Turns out she loved life as a farmer's wife,
fell into Matt's arms at night, fell into sleep,
never had to count sheep, always counted
her blessings, including being left-handed.
No southpaw operators were hired at AT&T.

September 19, 2014

Pedicure Tidbits

Tina leans to clip toenails
six days a week.
She's Vietnamese and
speaks English.

Her black hair shines.
She wears a fine gold
chain with a tiny ivory
pagoda pendant.

Her patron, Maureen,
tight smile, trim hips,
bright titian hair, wears
diamond earrings.

She picks up a People
magazine and studies
its pages for the latest
hot buzz in show biz.

Tina's kid attends
UC Irvine. Her tips
go for textbooks
on biochemistry.

When Maureen departs
in glitzy thong sandals
her hot pink toenails
scream, *Look at me!*

September 26, 2014

Hiding within Silence

he cracks the silence
with a groan and all

heaven breaks loose
agate beads of desire

scatter across the floor
crystal cries sparkle

and tumble in sunlight
bubbly laughter floods

rumpled sheets
smoky moans float

up toward the ceiling
whispers slide off

the bed and hide
under a nightstand

and sudden sweet
scent like violets

popping up from
soft forest moss

after snow and ice
have said goodbye

October 14, 2014

Thimbleful of Thistles

Miss Mitchell, English Lit, bent her head
as she listened to me recite my winning poem
in the high school Senior Class Day completion,
and when I trumpeted my final line .....
da Da da Da da Da da Da da Da

something about going forth into the world,
she lifted her eyes to mine and said,
You have a lisp. You should practice saying,
Theophalus Thistleby with a thimbleful of
thistles to correct it before your presentation.

Stunned to learn about my lisp, I repeated
the name and the phrase endlessly and
in secret. I was already dealing with more
than enough teen impediments: Zits. Glasses.
Plus I was pudgy. A lisp could bury me.

I guess I did well burying the lisp. No one ever
mentioned it again and no one ever will. I've buried
my husband and many close friends and my lisp
is still a secret, though my slurred words concern
my family. By the way, this red wine has a nice bite.

October 17, 2014

Hello from the Bordello

The elevator door slides open on the 11th floor
and a stout man in a white turban steps out.
He carries a cage holding a bright green parrot.
Exotic people come and go through New York.

It's no Village of Secrets and it's not
Possum Grape, Arkansas where guys
guzzle beer before breakfast waiting
for the 67 Liquor store to open at dawn.

In New York's fine restaurants, waiters,
passionate about wine, know the pour
should be at most three fingers high,
leaving plenty of room for swirling.

Donald Hall says Frank O'Hara threw
the best parties, raging parties that
lasted far into the night swirling with
jazz and Pollack and de Kooning.

Friends too broke for cab fare walked
down Greenwich Avenue with its sneaky
little bars. I was tipsy there in a dream,
laughing and leaning into your shoulder.

In Arkansas I was denied a booth to sell
my artsy Bordello Posters at the Elks Fest.
Sometimes I think I speak a dying language.
My future is as cloudy as a craft beer.

Maybe I'll move to Venice Beach, California,
get an apartment at El Bordello Alexandra
with its rooftop Centaur, Poseidon, archangels.
Not just a building, it's a vibe. Saturated at

night in crimson and gold lights, people walk by,
say the place is crazy and neighbors complain
about loud music. I'll fit right in, wear a ruby
silk sari and invite you over for a Sloe Gin Fizz

October 26, 2014

Owl in Dead Cottonwood Tree

day drags its bundle of pain
stumbles toward the edge of light
the sun goes down in flames
dark wings arc a somber sky
evening arrives to apply its salve
soon cool moonlight gleams
on tombs and black pansies bleed
into the inky chasm of night that
magnifies fears about the lack of
a broom sturdy enough to sweep
dust from a room beneath the stairs

October 31, 2014

The Persistence of Tabby Cats

They all look alike to me, orange and white stripes,
and anywhere you toss your hat, you'll see
a tabby cat and they all sound alike when hungry,
same loud meow and when a neighbor down
the block phones and says, A dead cat in the road
looks like your Tiger, orange and white stripes,
my alarm bell rings Ding Ding Ding. My kids will be

devastated. Our Tiger, ten years a pet, feline
warrior, never neutered. I get in the car, speed to
the scene and park on the side. Sure enough,
orange and white stripes, dead and cold in the road.
I pick him up. He doesn't bend, put him in the back
of our Ford Station Wagon. I'm surprised by tears,
wipe my eyes and say to myself, Now what? I don't

have a Plan A or a Plan B, but I have a best friend
who has a very big yard out back. Will she bury Tiger
for me? I don't want the kids to see him stiff and cold
and dead. Somewhat reluctant, my best friend, or
more precisely, former best friend, pressed into burial
service, agreed. Home again to face my kids and
I wondered how to break the bad news when I heard

a loud meow coming from around corner of the house.
Ohmygod! Orange and white stripes. Very much alive,
Tiger, hungry, on the prowl for food. I scoop him up,
feed him Friskies and cream. So who's missing a tabby?
Tiger's long buried, my husband too with his famous
Stetson hat and I'd like to be known for a famous elegy,
but I'll always be the lady with the wrong dead cat.

November 9, 2014

Wind Farm

On the way to the wind farm, at the junction where
one road leads to Barstow, the other to Bakersfield
and beyond to Tehachapi, the cup of my soul
like a crescent moon holds the gleam of your eye
like the evening star in that rare occurrence called
the Venus planetary occultation, but which I call love.
Once seen, never forgotten. Reaching the wind farm,
long arms of wind mills slicing through dry desert sky
like your smile slicing through my heart, it doesn't
matter that I lost my sanity from the back of your
Harley slicing through the desert like a comet on fire.

2014

2015

What about Winter?

Too soon leaves turn brown,
tumble, crumple and scatter.

Breezes scurry them across
parched lawns, cracked sidewalks.

I'm lost in a barren neighborhood,
far from the fruited plain.

Apples shrivel on branches and
roses lower their dusty heads.

Amber waves of grain are scorched.
A patient snail waits for rain and

every blade of grass strains to taste
tears from a cloudless sky.

The sun no longer sleeps, reaches
deep into polluted water. Shrinking

icebergs melt in simmering swelling
seas. Summer sun swallows

spring's haze, autumn's crispy
golden blaze. And what about winter?

Winter persists, blitzes with blizzards,
grips cities in a vise of gleaming white,

multiplies havoc on traffic that chokes
America's roads from sea to shining sea.

January 19, 2015

I'll Be Down to Get You

in a taxi, Honey, sung to the strumming of
Uncle Bob's guitar, his whiskey voice and
black coffee eyes following me up the stairs
of the farmhouse, Grandma in a faded blue
denim bib apron, rolling out biscuit dough in
the kitchen, Grandpa in the high back rocker
tapping the foot of his good left leg, a cane
on the floor to the side, and me, sixteen, my
tingling body an unexplored Newfoundland,
my insides heavy cream churning into butter,
a strange creature with no face and no name
clutching me high up under my skirt and by
the time the moon rose up bright over the silo,
the creature had black coffee eyes and I had
a secret that burned and a thirst for whiskey.

February 5, 2015

You Will Find Me

close as I can get to this side of Hippieville
farmer's market street fair
open air stalls whole lotta tie dye's still going on
yesterday's Flower Child in granny glasses
has blossomed into Granny on Medicare

tee dump tee dump tee dump
falling upstairs in Topanga Canyon
tee dump tee dump tee dump
banging my head on a walnut bannister

an unfortunate Fortune Cookie incident
Beware the *Stairway to Heaven* uh oh
and meanwhile Jimmy Page
at Barnes & Noble peddles a picture book
that weighs 50 pounds and

costs enough to bail out Granny
but ohhhh that silver pony tail
pony tails ginger snaps snickerdoodles
Egg Foo Yung and Chow Mein Noodles
forget fortune cookies rely on relics

remind me to take my baby Jesus
to a shop in Boyle Heights to get his
cracked arm mended and maybe buy
him a new dress and the crèche is

a mess of moldy hay and the shepherds
ohhh Jesus their robes torn and
tattered dirty oh well
I'm already going to hell for
flipping off the Wise Men

February 7, 2015

The Cast Iron Clawfoot Tub

Yes, Will and Kate have returned, our mallards.
Too bad the creek bed is dry. I remember when
the kids caught crawdads down there and then
we were afraid it would overflow its banks after
heavy rains, can almost remember heavy rains.
Years ago we had an old cast iron clawfoot tub
in the yard so Duke and Duchess, our first pair
of mallards, could splash. Crazy Vito, a plumber,
hauled it down in the yard for us. Sight of a cast
iron claw foot tub made me dizzy, spun me back
to our first home, an attic apartment. We had to
duck to get out of the claw foot tub tucked under
an eave. Romantic, we said, laughing at our bed
shoved up against the slant of an eave, so that
we had to climb in at the foot before climbing into
each other at night, our tenderness nurtured by
limber legs, good teeth, extra bucks for a movie.
Too many cavities later, buried under a mountain
of dirty socks, lost in the jungle of hungry mouths,
stashed in a stack of unpaid bills, our tenderness
went missing. I retrieved it at least for that night
by asking my husband to wash my back in our
white ceramic tub after tossing out rubber ducks.

February 14, 2015

Remedial Chocolate 101

Shes wants to drop down the drain
in open showers at the girls' gym
fakes being sick to get out of P.E.
Sitting at the back of study hall,
she opens her book bag, slips
out a Hershey bar, sneaks a bite
and daydreams about dancing
at the Spring Prom with cute
Tommy Swanson who smiled
at her once in Geometry. She
eyes petite Debbie Duncan in
a tight pink sweater and sighs,
tugs at her own baggy black,
takes another bite of chocolate

February 18, 2015

It's Here Somewhere

I knock over my cup
of morning coffee
on the obituary page.

Can't read it anyway.
Print's too fine and
I don't know where

my magnifying glass is.
I wonder if horny old
what's his name died.

Too bad we lost touch.
If I find my car keys,
I'll go and buy another

whatchamacallit.

February 26, 2015

Understanding Feet

There are twenty-six bones in the foot,
as Teresa has learned on her new job
at Foot Solutions selling orthotics.
Plus, there are three arches in the foot.
A good shoe is all about support.

Try telling that to feet screaming,
Gimmie Gimmie Gimmie
when they see metallic green slingbacks
with five inch heels.

This morning as I ease into sure foot
sandals, I remember my tan bare legs
anchored in white pumps that I flung
off when I climbed onto the bar top
and danced to the Doobie Brothers.

From baby white high tops to shiny
black Mary Janes, penny loafers to
tennies, pumps and slides to thongs,
my shoes, on and off, have seen it all,
and I'm here to tell you it's not about
support, it's about stepping out.

February 30, 2015

The Serpent Told
Me To Do It

I go through on yellow,
and don't beat about
the lily pond.
A snail squished
is a daisy saved.
He loves me.
He loves me not.
He loves my
Dutch apple pie.
Eve, sitting in
the passenger seat,
dressed in
designer fig leaves,
turns to me and says,
It was a Winesa,
quite tart, hardly
worth all the fuss.
Then she goes off
on Adam, his wine,
how he ignores her,
and how the garden
has gone to seed,
says she needs
a good yard man.
Well, don't we all,
I reply, glancing in
my rear view mirror.
Uh oh
flashing red.
How to explain
an open bottle
of champagne?

March 15, 2015

Haiku

pelican wings low
over slow soft spoken surf
seek evening meal

moon floats in night sky
lovers reach touch each other
sail to ecstasy

March 20, 2015

Third Party Shipper Shit

I find this alternate universe quite comfortable,
cloud soft beds and great angel food cake.
There's no cable tv and I miss music on iTunes,
but I sing a lot and lyrics are coming back to
me since my mind is free of passwords and

pin numbers. I got locked out of my life when
my password came up invalid. Again.
So I reset it. Again. And this time...bingo until
I was asked for my pin number. Oh yeah, those
pesky pin numbers, elusive as tech support.

Apparently my life was low on megabytes.
I should have changed my media sync options.
My baffled mind stumbled on a reboot enigma.
Another option, which I chose, was to go bed
and take a nap. When I awoke everything was

clear. I don't need Google or Amazon which
anyway can't correct the incorrect shipment.
The customer must contact the third party
shipper with order info and a tracking number
from a fucking torn label. Good luck with that.

April 4, 2015

Night Survivor

I wake exhausted my arms heavy
limp from endless swimming
in a blurry ocean of night crawling
through swirling currents trying
to reach an elusive island of sleep
finally washed up on the rocky shore
of a nightmare my baby gone
swept away in a tidal wave my car
totalled in a ditch at the bottom of
a sea cavern my library card caught
in a riptide lost a continent of loss
when you left I lost my laughter
would that I could lose my memory
but then my new poem
how does it go? how does it go?

August 6, 2015

My Knitting Needles Sleep in Summer

A big bag of yarn yawns while waiting
for me to get going on the promised
afghan for my granddaughter, Mimi.
Variegated gray and silver and white,
exactly what she likes and she plans
to take it back to college at UC Davis
for her junior year. Ever the optimist.

Who knits in August with wooly yarn?
Apparently me. I shake awake #13
stainless steel round needles, grab
startled wooly yarn. What she wants,
she gets, my favorite granddaughter,
my one and only, and though wooly
yarn itches, I cast on 110 stitches.

August 7, 2015

Open Wide

I said goodbye to a molar
last night, back upper right.

I didn't even cry
though it's also goodbye

to thick grilled ribeyes.
My time on this planet

is marked by my teeth,
their fillings and crowns,

extractions and bridges,
receding gums with #5

pockets plus a very deep
cavity in my pocketbook.

But I still have sass in
my tongue, bite in my lines.

August 11, 2015

Floating on a Note

in a stream of melody
my soul sails free

slipping into a song
that carries me

away from cries
and screams

I drop a green glass
bottle over the side

the wind and sea
in frothy refrain

lull me to sleep
the message in

the green glass
bottle reads .....

Don't rescue me

August 13, 2015

Tanka

white paper blue lines
ballpoint pen runs out of ink
nothing more to say
though few words have been written
the ending is preordained

lowering sun drops
crimson streaks evening sky
beach sands invite footprints
we run into the soft surf
our chapel of evening prayer

cold wind on my neck
I put on my blue sweater
the one you lent me
and I never gave it back
it's all I have left of you

August 13, 2015

p's & q's

Some mind them. I eat them.
Tasty in a scramble with g's.
and j's. Lower case, that is.
But lower case doesn't cut it
except in a scramble. I use
cursive letters to write poetry
in a notebook. If you look up
"cursive", on google you will
find "cursive...joined-up letters"
and I'm wondering if that's like
"hooked-up" and should we be
concerned with cursive morals?
You might be surprised by some
of the individual traits of Capitals,
For instance, Z has anger issues.
Always last. Always fucking last.
Z thinks A stands for Asshole,
a smarty pants kid in class who
always gets an A, always first in
line, always first to raise a hand.
I have my favorites. Capital O is
so over the moon and romantic.
H and I are a friendly pair, but
I like to slip into a slinky sexy S.
When I'm sleepy, I crawl inside
the cozy curve of a capital C and
catch 40 winks with a capital W.
I'm partial, of course, to T and D.
I hope to someday sign them to
the last line of a new poem. T.D.

August 28, 2015

Without You The Stillness

your empty chair is full
of a melancholy quiet
and your empty place
at the table surprised by
large servings of silence

the pepper mill sits and
waits for you to lift it over
the pasta and twist its top
the tomato plant is thirsty
for your watering can's

attention not to mention
Louie's frantic yapping as
a car pulls into the driveway
his sudden stillness when he
sees it's not you coming in

August 31, 2015

Funerals from Now On

Bet you can't remember the last fun
wedding you went to, says Linda.
Big bash with lots of champagne,
sit down dinner at the country club,
5 piece combo playing a rhumba
you dance with somebody's
Uncle Gus who grabs your butt.

She's back from her brother's
memorial service in Porterville.
Gave a eulogy. Made up stuff.
They hadn't been close for years.
Happy to see her favorite nieces,
and hugged a bunch of cousins
with gray hair and hearing aids,

So many old people at the service,
and when she got home, flocks of
old folks on her block, one after
another who's had a bad fall or
heart attack, terminal something.
It's funerals from now on, laments
Linda but, in-between treatments

for rheumatoid arthritis, she's
already planning a fun wedding
for her junior high granddaughter.
Maybe at the beach, margaritas,
mariachis, an enchilada buffet.
We're praying Uncle Gus won't
bite the dust before the rhumba.

September 4, 2015

When the Moon Was Full We Sang All the Moon Songs

We took off, tin cans dangling from the rear license plate
of my new husband's dark green Plymouth business coupe,

a long ago September afternoon, destination Honeymoon at
a lake cottage lent by a friend. The road, never before taken,

bumpy in a couple of stretches, detoured through sleepy towns,
no marquees on Main Street. We tried to find a country inn

or nice place to stop for dinner. Finally a roadhouse, neon sign,
Big Foot Inn. How's that for romance? Knotty pine inside,

tables, long bar plus a jukebox. We had our choice of tables.
A weepy guy at the bar fed nonstop coins into the jukebox,

endlessly playing, *Jealous heart, oh jealous heart, stop beating.*
We did not dance to the music, drove on until finding a cottage

as far from *Honeymoon* as a fishing camp cabin. Spider webs,
bunk beds in the west bedroom, two cots in the other, a card

from our octogenarian friend, greeting the newlyweds and
writing that we'd likely prefer the east bedroom. Oh yeah.

What do you do but laugh and throw mattresses on the floor?
The third night my man found that the couch made into a bed,

We spent a lifetime laughing and reaching for each other in
moonlight in spite of lumpy beds, singing, *Fly me to the moon.*

September 18, 2015

Waiting for a Train in Union Station in L.A.

not really but I love the thought of it
the feel of it excitement at
the departure of the Coast Starlight
in 20 minutes to Seattle passengers
lined up to go through the tunnel
to the tracks my guy arriving from
San Francisco on time at 11:25
a woman across the aisle from me
checks her face in a compact mirror
paints her puffy lips poppy bright
smiles at herself her stained teeth
I tuck a stray curl behind my ear
my hair auburn long and wavy
not really but I love the idea of it
the station buzzing with men in
suits testosterone in gabardine
scent of Old Spice and bravado
a woman loses a shoe running
to the ticket window she limps
reaching for the strappy sandal
I'm meeting say an old flame
widow's peak wicked grin
he left me for a job as copy editor
at The Sentinel in a inland valley
town the paper just bought by
a big city Times his job phased
out he needs a place to flop and
blah blah blah in his gifted tongue
I got nothing else going on and so
ohmygod it's almost 5 o'clock
and I forgot sprinkles on the icing
again it'll be my ass the boss
says he can't run a bakery
with me daydreaming all the time

October 3, 2015

She Sees

a window in
the corner of
the hospital
room where
she waits for
surgery on
her left eye,
her right eye
blind.
The irony
of her bed
in a spot
where she
can't see out
the window
almost
makes her
laugh.
Her surgery
delayed,
she spends
the rest of
the day
getting in
and out
of bed for
one more
look to
memorize
sunlight.

October 9, 2015

A Little Excitement on a Sleepy Sunday in October

Past big black spiders and severed body parts
made of plastic, an abandoned car
sits in the middle of the intersection of
Mozart Avenue and Rossini Drive,
a looming hazard of symphonic proportion.
Claudia calls the sheriff to report…
it's just past our curbside graveyard
and witch's broom. Black car. Mercedes.
No tire. No wheel. No driver. Spooky.
Asks the sheriff, *License plate number?*
Oh, good question, replies Claudia and
walks outside with our landline phone,
toward the abandoned car. The sheriff
shouts, *I can't hear.* Claudia yells back,
I can't see the license plate number.
The phone goes dead. End of talk.
A tow truck shows up later in the day,
hauls the Mercedes away. End of story.

October 18, 2015

Reflections of an Old Poet

Of course, I wonder how and when.
what with my 86th coming up.

Not so much where anymore, since
I'm mostly here. I tend to reflect

now and then about whether I have
any little wisdoms to pass on.

Then, of course, I smile to myself
and pass on that ridiculous idea.

Nobody would listen. Everybody's
glued to texting and checking or

finding his or her lost cell phone.
The Chinese Checkers board is

on a shelf in the hall cupboard.
Where, oh where are the Dominos?

It takes two to tango, so I play Solitaire.
But last night the moon was full

and today October's clear blue sky
gives me a reason to smile and also

to hope I stick around for a while, at least
long enough to see how the story ends.

October 27, 2015

I Always Loved the Fireworks

A deodar cedar near the end of our
driveway blesses our yard. Its name,
from Sanskrit, means divine tree, and
sometimes I hear my husband's spirit
whistling in its branches, still hear him
jingling coins in the pocket of my mind.
Before our cottonwood trees shot up
into the sky, my husband and I could
see fireworks over the Fairgrounds on
the 4th of July from our upstairs porch.
He'd hold me close as the sky exploded
with razzle dazzle wow pop sparkles,
fireworks rivaling the Siss Boom Bah
of a new house with an upstairs porch,
a home exploding with sounds of life,
shouts and roars of four kids. Today
echoes of laughter and cries resound
through empty rooms, compel me to
pick up a pen and write, *I always loved.....*

October 30, 2015

Looking for Bernardo

I put you in a song I sing
at 2:00 A.M.
when everybody else
is sleeping.
My lyrics are incomplete.
and the refrain is
a sort of blues tune.
If I could play
the harmonica, I'd make
a howling sound of
lonesome notes that say
how down I am without you.
Our voices used to blend
like honey and wine.
What happened to our
harmony? Please tell me
the reason your love
for me went flat.

November 3, 2015

Keep Me From Going to Sleep

limit poets please
at monthly open readings
to a few haiku

November 9, 2015

At Ponto Beach

this beach pebble your eye on me
the sign you sent
breezes whistle in my ear
your touch and
trace of musk mix with salty air
we meet on sand
walk together in knee high waves
your face in clouds
dampness silky on my skin you
everywhere and
everyone we ever knew here
sprinkled like shells
from the sea as water evaporates
and ice melts
rejoining waves of those who left
returning to glisten
along the shore I knew you
as a mallard and
again you appeared as a wooly blanket
to keep me warm and
that pesky fly against the window always
finds a way into my world

I looked for a sign
from you and a crow scolding
in the middle of the road
told me to look in the tree by the bridge
in that low hanging
branch a nest at limp lilies after
a sudden rain and
listen because you are the patter of raindrops
hum of the fridge
squeal of kids on swings and the cat's purr
and so we go and return
Grandma is a peppercorn this time around
and stern Miss Baxter
a nasturtium and Jesus is an avocado
we love avocados and

perhaps my father is a 9 dollar Nicaraguan
Casa Magna cigar hand made in the Cuban
tradition and maybe that's why I collect cigar
boxes so this time he will find his way home

2015

2016

Smoke Screen

Burning trash down by the creek,
me, one of the older campers,
sifting through shit from councilors'
waste baskets, grabbing butts and
lighting up. My first secret smokes.
I went on to raiding cigarette boxes
at homes where I was babysitting.
So grown up. So glamorous.
The black and white movie Blonde,
luscious lips, waving a cigarette,
always gets the Cute Guy blowing
smoke rings from the silver screen.
As the movie ends, they drive off
in a racy roadster. At the premier
they drove off going through a red
on Wilshire landing Cute Guy in
traffic court. The judge, who had
a thing about actors, threw the book
at him. Cute Guy got fat and that
was that for Cute Guy parts, and
the Blonde? She sued her plastic
surgeon. That's Hollywood for you.

January 27, 2016

Special Needs

every kid needs a haunted house
down a dirt road deserted
broken windows clanking pails
screeching owl that triggers
running tripping skinned knees

every lady needs a gazebo
down a secret path secluded
clinking ice in gin and tonic
that triggers laughter tripping
over someone else's knee

what does every guy need
neighborhood bar or tool shed
in back of a garage I know
a few guys I could ask but who
knows what that might trigger

February 1, 2016

Rain Like a Rowdy Stranger

pounds on my roof
shouts at me to
come out see it pour

startles the canyon
washing down
its scrubby slopes

budges the creek
at the bottom
to get a move on

a red-tailed hawk
on a cable high
over the canyon

spreads its wings
open to the rain
three times while

my daughter and
I witness through
a window whisper

February 5, 2016

The Player Piano

It stood against a dining room wall of the farmhouse
where my Grandpa and Grandma lived. A bench in
front of the piano had a lid that lifted to reveal a pile
of cylinders, each one to produce a piece of music,
sort of like magic, but I never did hear anyone play
that piano except me. Not Grandpa. Not Grandma.
Not Uncle Ted who played a banjo or Harvey Ford,
a boarder who played pinochle with Grandpa. Not
Aunt Julie who was secretly sweet on Harvey but,
played hard to get. Nope, just me, and I played like
a barn on fire. I'd insert the Blue Danube and push
my feet against those pedals as if I were in a race
against the wind. My fingers raised above the keys,
swaying, I played to an invisible adoring audience,
a prodigy at age ten. Too bad I couldn't live there
forever but, summer over, I had to go back home,
and it was my last time there. Sad to say, they lost
the farm, had to move to a tiny house in town taking
some of their nice things with them, a china cabinet
with a cut glass bowl Grandpa won playing ring toss
at Will County Fair and Grandma's salt and pepper
shaker collection, little hollow men on the top shelf.
I never did know what happened to the player piano,
sadly waited too long to ask. Only lately has a more
intriguing question played in my mind. Where did
the piano come from? If my Grandma was anything
like me, I see a cute salesman in a Chevy drive up
on a quiet Sunday morn, wearing a snappy suit and
smiling like a movie star. He tells her she deserves
music in her life and has just the thing to put it there,
a fine player piano on easy payments. Free delivery.

February 11, 2016

Voilà

among anonymous pebbles
a piece of sea glass
iridescent shining perfect
to complete my mosaic

and I feel a crazy kind of joy
like when I find the precise
word for a poem *the* word
that sets the poem free

releases it from my brain
gives it wings to fly to rise
from a piece of lined paper
onto a page of your mind

February 14, 2016

Quik Disconnect
Page 28 in a Tool Catalogue

You Quik Diconnect
your hand from
my waist and leave.
We never see
each other again,
but at times I hear
your voice
in the night call
my name and
I feel the same
Quik Clutch
between my thighs,
Quik Tug
at my breast and
there's no
Quik Disconnect
strong enough
to pull you
out of my dreams.

February 20, 2016

Field Tripping

I packed my dancing-in-the-desert duds,
put everything else on ice
and here I boogie as cliffs exhale and inhale.
My fascination with finding
hidden canyons can seem strange,
and sometimes feels
as hit-or-miss as panning for gold,
but imagine drawing
something you've never seen before.
In my hand, a pad of
acid free paper and lined up on
a rock at my side,
my drawing pencils, sharpened, waiting.

April 3, 2016

A Trip Back in Time

I trip over the streetcar tracks of nostalgia,
fall into a pool of new school supplies,
thick blue Laddie pencils. Yellow wide rule
paper, rulers. So easy to stay down here
in a recess of dodge ball and hopscotch,
and not deal with the price of parts for
the power mower, cost of flood insurance,
protection plan for the washer, cable bill,
termites and dry rot or how the hell I got
down here sprawled on the kitchen floor.

My high school allowance of 10 bucks
a month took me on a streetcar to see
movies, over to Walgreens for sodas
served up by a cute guy with a cowlick
who asks me to the prom in my dreams.
I'm tempted to stay down on the ground
and reminisce, but the floor is hard as
marble and I wonder who put that box
in the doorway and how I'm going to
get up and where the fuck my cane is?

April 5, 2016

La Vida

Diego drove Rosa to Tijuana
to catch a bus bound for Sinaloa.

He last saw her in a window seat
near the rear, her shiny black

braids coiled on top of her head.
She smiled at Diego waving like

a windmill gone wild as the bus
pulled out of the crowded station.

He sees her in dreams, his face
buried in her hair loose to her

smooth shoulders. He counts
the days until she returns to him

in San Gabriel, prays *su madre*
recovers. He can't know the bus

veered off the road and tumbled
down a hillside as was reported

in The Los Angeles Times.
He plans to learn English when

Rosa returns. They'll attend ESL
class at the high school together.

August 10, 2016

The Mystery of the Missing Dragonfly

This morning I felt a soft flap by my ear
as I rinsed my face at the bathroom sink.

Startled, I looked around and *WOW*...
a dragonfly at least three inches long

with wide double wings in my bathtub.
I reached for a hand towel to swat it.

The dragonfly flickered, moved and yes,
I swatted it again, looked away and then,

it was gone. Small bathroom. Screened
window. Stopper in the tub. So *where*?

And who would swat a dragonfly *twice*?
A lady with white hair, blind in one eye.

who's sitting at a table all innocent like,
double winged shadow inside her mind.

August 15, 2016

Floods Fires Wars & Other Disasters

Fire in the high desert, floods
in the plains, Syrians fleeing.
and Chicago street shootings.
I can handle all these from afar,
but, when my printer runs out
of ink, I have tantrums, scream,
stamp my feet. Then I have to
take a timeout, breathe deep
and reach for a replacement
cartridge. Maybe somewhere
whirling in black space there's
a replacement cartridge for
earth, if so. I pray it doesn't
have an expiration date.

August 20, 2016

This Night

throbs with sound
crowded into a black box
sirens scream
cicadas screech
nightmares gallop
across fields of dreams
hiss of danger
seeps into my mind
as a car engine sputters
down the street
I'll never find my way
back to sleep

August 23, 2016

The Scarcity of Sharks

Nana's big black umbrella that popped open
at a press of a thumb, is forgotten in a closet.

Today the dry creek, lined with a regiment of
sand bags, waits and waits for El Nino rain.

There was a time screeching kids splashed,
trying to catch pollywogs wiggling in the creek.

Nana turns on a/c deep in winter, remembers
when she wore wooly sweaters, red mittens.

Everything changes, but nothing so much as
her desires. Iced tea instead of dry martini.

Cozy nap in bed instead of fucking on a futon.
The daily news instead of page turners, and

she smiles at a column about leopard sharks,
reads they are returning to La Jolla Shores.

The ocean, too warm for too long, is once again
cold, once again dotted with spotted sharks.

August 24, 2016

The Breakup

maybe I don't get the drift and
maybe I'm too straight for this shit
maybe if I didn't care that
maybe you just don't understand me
maybe enough to put up with
maybe days and nights of writing and
maybe assignments requiring
maybe hours of my attention then
maybe you'll take a hike or
maybe like last week when you threw
maybe half of my stuff on the lawn
maybe after grabbing all my cash that
maybe some day you'll pay back or
maybe not

August 30, 2016

Evening Prayer

We girls sang in the St. Cecilia Choir during Lent.
I prayed for Lent to be over.
We giggled and whispered behind our hymnals.
Mr. Jones, the organist, glared.
I stared at the back of Peggy Robinson's head,
her long blonde hair and sighed,
I stared at the altar, yawned, thought about Mary,
how If she really *was* a virgin,
she missed out on a lot of fun. I decided I'd never
be a saint. I liked boys too much.
Matter of fact, Father Matthew, the curate, would
never be a saint either.
He liked feeling up my skirt too much. I confess
I never went to confession.

September 5, 2016

Snow White and the Seven Dwarfs Motor Court

Happy. Yeah, Happy. That's the cabin I wanted.
Aunt Gay and Uncle Carl bought a motor court.
Cabins, chipped brown paint, dingy white trim,
stood round a patchy lawn, picnic table, broken
bench, a gravel drive past the sign-in office on
a main highway near Three Rivers, Michigan.
They had a plan to spff it up. I could have told
them it was doomed. Like who wants to sleep
in Grumpy? When I stopped there on my way
back home from Grand Rapids, I got Grumpy.
I'd been awake all weekend partying with pals,
so I didn't complain and slept for twelve hours.
But sure enough For Sale signs soon went up.
New owners renamed it Alice in Wonderland.
Mad Hatter cabin proved to be as popular, but
Dormouse is *always* vacant. There's no need
to make reservations. Just say Trish sent you.

September 24, 2016

The Woman in the Moon

has a lazy left eye and a mole
to the side of her upper lip.
She thinks perfection is boring
and, of course, she's right.

When she smiles, the whole world
sighs and shivers, glimmers.
She sees us behind closed doors,
sees all our indiscretions with

a *tsk tsk* of her puffy lips.
She sees fingers sliding down
the back of a red satin gown,
a hand cupping rounded flesh.

She hums a lunar lullaby and
the whole world yawns, a fussy
baby stops crying and a rumpled
drunk snores under a park bench.

She laughs at you in the top of
a sycamore tree in your front yard,
trying to get a better view, and
her laughter dazzles the night sky.

October 6, 2016

Downtown Jungle

I know nothing about wildlife
unless you count Aunt Jeanette
on Saturday nights getting ready
to prowl at a downtown tavern,
me perched on the bed
watching her paint Danger Red
on her unruly lips, ribbon of
smoke rising from an ashtray,
me leaning in to catch a whiff.
When Grandpa said she was
wild as a coyote in moonlight.
her laughter rattled the rafters.
I could see a lynx in her eyes
framed by lashes thick with
black mascara. Sometimes
she'd put it on me too and
I'd smile at myself in a mirror
and pretend I was beautiful.
She'd pat my head and say.
*You just wait, Kiddo. Your turn
will come* and she was right.

October 25, 2016

Bag of Oranges

One doesn't expect to find four apples
at the bottom of a bag of oranges from
Von's. Granny Smith. Green. The kind
of apple you peel and slice and sprinkle
with cinnamon and bake in a pie. Right?
Is this a sign? Is the God of Good Wives
sending me a message? Telling me to
get out my rolling pen or is it rolling *pin*?
I may actually have one in the back
of a cabinet along with a meat grinder
and a screwdriver which reminds me to
juice an orange and get out the vodka.

2016

Nesting

By day I scan the sky for wide pointed wings
and wear a leather gauntlet. You wanted to
come back as a peregrine falcon, remember?
And I'm caught in the claws of missing you,
Your lucky buckeye waits on the oak bureau,
your pocket knife too. Sorry, I can't find your
harmonica. I'll buy one at that music store
next door to La Paloma theater, remember?
By night my spirit sits on a stool in the diner
of *Nighthawks, the painting* we saw at Chicago's
Art Institute after walking down Michigan Avenue
laughing and hugging and diving into love.
You said Hopper should have painted us in it
because we were such night owls. Remember?

2016

Portrait of Eighty Something

9 A.M. her laughter splashes on a window sill
as she sees three mallards strut across the lawn
in iridescent blue green they seem to be on
serious duck business but she knows it's more
a matter of cracked corn at so much a bucket
from the feed store which works like chocolate
chip cookies did to keep her grandkids coming
back for more so many goodbyes ago since
then she limps a bit and little sounds disappear
to wherever sounds go chuckles under a rug
sighs behind a bookcase she winces at a pain
in her hip but her wrinkled skin still tingles at
another's touch and she smiles at a spicy scent
faint reminder of an aftershave that once drove
her crazy made her crave hidden kisses but
this is a time of a quiet kind of fun with ducks
books in large print kisses in silver wrappers

2016

2017

Darkness

Darkness dwells in all her rooms.
She remembers light when the sun
warms her arms on an afternoon
as she sits in a wicker rocker on
the front porch. Darkness has its
own muffled hum, its musty scent
She feels her way across the pit
of her living room, smiles when
she hears footsteps down the hall.
Ask her if she remembers what
Beautiful looks like. She will feel
your face and say, This is *Beautiful.*

January 20, 2017

My Brother's Scar

on his wrist and mine almost match.
He was running away from a gang
and smashed through a glass door.
I was on my way home from school,
took a shortcut through a vacant lot,
and crashed on a broken milk bottle.
Plus matching scars on our hearts.
from when our father cut himself
out of our lives. Faint jagged lines
on our wrists have faded, the pain
forgotten, but pain of his leaving
still throbs. Our smiles hide scars.

January 23, 2017

My Legacy

*He'd be there another week
he wrote on the postcard.
Why don't you write to
Daddy....A. A. Saunders,
13 Via Parigi, Palm Beach,*
when I was only four, not
reading, much less writing.

He lives at 13 Via Parigi,
Palm Beach, forever in my
mind, though I know better
than to try to find him there
writing another postcard,
palm trees and oranges
on the pretty picture side.

Ink faded, barely legible
after more than 80 years,
that and a black and white
snapshot.....all I have of
a smiling man, dark hair,
widow's peak, leaning
against a boxy black car.

Though Mom refused to
speak of him, she saved
the postcard for me, and
I recall as through mist,
when I'd had too many
gin and tonics, she'd hiss
at me.....*Just like him.*

February 19, 2017

On a Sunny March Morning

I sit and stare at my dining room table
still wearing bold red plaid with a shiny
gold thread running through it, and
I say to myself, *What are you waiting for?*
Time to switch it out for turquoise linen,
and ditch the red candles for pale pink
fake tulips and Voilà Spring again.
Reminds me that I could use a Spring
do-over too starting with Super Cuts
and Nailtopia.....maybe a new dress
from Ross for Less and oh yes Shoes.
Shiny black patent strappy sandals
to put some spring in my reluctant feet.
I wince as I reach for my cane and limp
to the kitchen with my empty coffee cup,
but in spite of white hair and wrinkles,
in spite of pain, I still feel a tingle in my
heart at the mention of *his* name, and
it's still Spring inside me at end of day.

March 2017

The Dinner Party

A catered affair in the backyard
of a plush Beverly Hills mansion.
Hunky servers, wannabe actors,
dish up potatoes-au-gratin, grilled
salmon, green beans almondine.
The emerald green grass is thick
and velvety rich under my feet.
La Vie en Rose from an accordion
floating over the buzzing throng.
Sparkling wine and fine cuisine,
diamond glitter, shiny white teeth
mingle on the patio, And me,
second-cousin of the Assistant to
the Business Manager of the Host.
And me from Redondo Beach
in a thrift shop polka dot mini.
This is where I click my heels and
turn into a princess in peach satin.
Not. But hey. I snagged one
of the servers who was peeking
at my cleavage, got a ride home
on the back of his Honda and
we had our dessert on the beach,
and I'm not talking ice cream.

June 15, 2017

The Return of Mules

Mules are coming back says my shoe guru,
granddaughter Mimi, who's on a mission
to find the perfect flat. She informs me that
denim mules are very cool. I tuck that bit of
info under my granny cap. The perfect fit is
also an on-going conundrum. She's one of
the two people in the whole world who own
a pair of wooden shoe stretchers, her dad
the other with his own peculiar shoe issues.
My needs are quite simple ..... stylish flats
long enough to fit my 9 ½ size feet, cheap
enough to fit a lean budget. One would think
it a reasonable objective. I'm mulish enough
to keep trying while wearing flip flops and
waiting the arrival of denim mules. Mimi
rules.

June 21, 2017

She Still Dreams

battered sprinkling can
in her gnarled hand pours life
into sweet pea seeds

August 12, 2017

The Highest Point

Highest point in town they say,
grassy low hill in a park at
Oak Park Avenue and Lake,
Mom used to take us there
on Sunday afternoons
when she came to visit us,
Billy and Gayle and me.
We'd take a short walk
from the Children's Home
past the Post Office, past
Gilmore's Department Store,
Billy and Gayle and me.
In winter rosy cheeked
kids just like us on sleds
squealed all the way down
to the bottom of the hill.
I used to love to feel
the soft furry collar
of her black wool coat.
In summer she wore
a silky light blue dress
that matched her eyes.
We'd stop at a corner
Walgreens on the way,
She'd buy us popsicles...
grape for Billy, cherry for
Gayle, orange for me.
The park, only 4 blocks
away from The Home,
but a whole world away
for Billy, Gayle and me.
I used to pretend we
could stay there forever.

August 13, 2017

Not a Love Poem

He moved his hand over her body
like a blind man reading Braille
in slow motion, over long words
with slippery syllables, and she
sighed in reply which translated
means, I like how you read me.
Fluent in an exotic tongue, his
liquid whispers seeped into deep
crevices of her being. He said
he adored a thing she did with
her finger, that he loved the soft
skin on the inside of her thighs,
and they lingered past the limit
of stolen moments. Memories,
confetti snow in the mind of
an old woman. Some bits glitter.

August 31, 2017

Wonders of Woolworth's

Evening in Paris perfume in royal blue bottles,
and Princess Pat lipsticks, a young girl's paradise
in the cosmetic aisle of a nearby Five & Dime.

A quarter in my pocket, plump full of possibility.
But I found my Nirvana in double features
at the Rialto Theater on Saturday afternoons.

Popcorn in the lobby. Cute guys in maroon
uniforms slicing dark aisles with flashlights.
Heaven, seat down in front, box of Milk Duds.

September 8, 2017

The Mysterious Disappearance of Red Cars

black black white black white silver gray
screech beep beep
red? only a rare red car fire engine red racy red
blood red danger red gone gone lipstick red
screaming red exciting red fun red gone gone
Grant calls me from his gray Toyota on his way to
work in L.A. says
What are you doing, Nana I say writing a poem about
the mysterious disappearance of all the fun red cars
these days all the cars are black and white and gray
he says yeah but there are lots of shades of gray
I say *Hmmm like 50.* He replies his family had
a red car but it was no fun at all why not ? because
a minivan is a *Mom Car* black black gray white
black gray silver *white* Claudia in the kitchen
pitches in says she was in the middle of a swarm of
red cars the other day on the freeway like it
was totally alarming being surrounded by red cars
like on their way to
a red car demonstration I ask *in Rose Canyon?*
she replies *No...Fire island*
screech beep beep black/black/white flashing red

September 14, 2017

The Canyon

my branches arch a bridge crossing a ravine
to a kingdom ruled by a matriarch with a dark
secret she has summoned Amazon to deliver
a myriad of mysterious packages I have seen
the arrival of snakes and possums in the garden
an invasion of honey bees my gold dust pollen
drops on the bridge with dry rot and termites why
do folks love it so I remember kids gathered
around my trunk and getting drunk on beer I have
heard shouts from the house and noise from boys
having a crack at each others' backs a girl's shrill
voice protests at her brothers invading her space
I drop my leaves all over the yard and it's hard
anymore for the old lady to rake them up but hey
my day is more important than hers she sees my
dark red seed pods as a nasty mess I see them
as my beautiful babies maybe we have more in
common than she thinks we both embrace this
place of life in a canyon holding us both in its care

September 27, 2017

Diana's Birthday Dinner

A gathering of the family to celebrate
at Jake's seaside restaurant in Del Mar
The slim and tan and chic like to graze
on Jake's tasty gourmet catch of the day.

Set sail at Jake's seaside restaurant in Del Mar
where a touch of ginger seasons the butter.
Order Jake's tasty gourmet catch of the day.
Watch waves frolic up on the sandy beach.

A touch of ginger seasons butter for rolls
hot out of the oven and straight to your table.
Watch waves frolic up on the sandy beach.
You might catch sight of a gray whale spout

Hot out of the oven and straight to your table,
served to a gathering of a family celebration.
Did they catch sight of a gray whale spout?
When's the next birthday? Make a reservation.

September 30, 2017

A Summer Rental

by the shore and a mailbox at the end of a gravel path
where she kept an eye out for the mailman. He'd greet
her with a grin, extend his hand that held fliers and bills,
She would feel a spark where she touched his fingers.
She, lonely in her empty summer, the cottage once full
of laughter. With the mail came a muscled man, she
eager to meet someone to ignite dying embers inside.
But the end of summer and the rental and a change of
address put that desire to rest, and dashed dreams to
marry the mailman. A pity, but back in the city she has
her eye on a burly guy at the corner dry cleaners, and
everybody knows she has the cleanest clothes in town.

October 1, 2017

We Dine by Candlelight

A Greek guy seated on my right.
Sleepy eyes. Widow's peak.
Wine in crystal. Flaky salmon.
Lemon slices on the side.
The Greek guy leans and
whispers in my ear but
I can't hear over The Beatles
in the background. A bearded
guy across the table knocks
over his wine glass. Cabernet
seeps into creamy damask
The Greek guy's hand is on
my knee. We rise. He nods
toward the door. I later heard
dessert was a great success.
Meringue with brandy sauce.

October 19, 2017

Monday October 23rd

Last night I decided to write
a novel in rhymed couplets
about a dashing Lithuanian spy
with a speech impediment.
The plot revolves around
a mix-up due to the fact that
Lithuanian spoken with a lisp
is quite difficult to understand.
This twist might not sound
compelling but wait, there's
a love interest with a busty
blonde Bavarian barmaid
who also works undercover.
This morning I'm trying to
decide on a title. Has to be
catchy like *Danger in Bavaria*
or *Caper in the Caucasus*.
My God. I'll do anything
to avoid paying monthly bills.

October 23, 2017

A Case of Temporary Blindness

You left my bed but never left my mind.
I still can see your boots lie on the floor.
I saw you as my prince but I was blind.

I trusted you would not leave me behind
like careless lovers I had known before.
You left my bed but never left my mind.

Tough but tender hands are hard to find.
They handled me in ways that I adore.
I saw you as my prince but I was blind.

We celebrated daily, wined and dined.
You filled me so I never wanted more.
You left my bed but never left my mind.

These nights I sleep alone. I am inclined
to dream about a sheik. I'm told I snore.
I saw you as my prince but I was blind.

Looking back I see my friends were kind,
comforting when you walked out the door.
You left my bed but never left my mind.
I saw you as my prince but I was blind.

October 29, 2017

Consideration of Punctuation

Forlorn semicolons
lie abandoned, limp
and forgotten
at the bottom of
a punctuation pool.

Commas, in great
demand, insert
themselves at every
chance, into every
turn of phrase.

The period, as we all
know, has the final
say which gives it
a certain standing
and special status.

I'm fond of the dash - - -
and use it a lot.
It has pizzazz, has
attitude. Who cares
if it's incorrect?

I'm the poet and make
my own rules I don't
use punctuation at all
sometimes not even
a fucking period

Have I left anything
out? Did I neglect
any major punctuation
mark? Did I say it
well? Was I clever?

Oh my God! I forgot
the exclamation
point!! I'll never live
it down!!! How can
I be such an idiot!!!

November 13, 2017

After Midnight by Moonlight

He walks her home from the diner,
takes off his jacket, puts it over her
shoulders, slips his arm around
her waist, bends toward her face.
They linger under an oak near
the corner, the tree trunk rough
against her back. A street light
makes shadows of leaf upon leaf
all the way up to the umbrella of
night sky. This moment shines
when her sight has grown dim
and she no longer remembers
his name or where he came from.
Somewhere out west. Yuma or
Albuquerque or maybe Santa Fe.
But she never forgets the hungry
look in his eyes and his huge
appetite for chicken fried steak,
deep-dish apple pie and deep
delicious kisses and cowboys
were always great tippers too.

2017

After Sundown

Twilight, whisper soft,
a cashmere shawl
in muted shades
of blue and gold
over the shoulders
of diva Evening for
a brief appearance.
Night arrives in its
quiet way like a late
comer to a concert,
slips into an aisle
as a black velvet
curtain descends.
Stars twinkle and
nod at applause,
and one little star
falls off the stage,
a front page item
in tomorrow's Times.

2017

The Asian Lady

Driving home from the Promenade,
he sees her walking backwards
down the street, She stays with him
all the way into his new apartment
in a strange neighborhood, roams
inside his mind and seeps into his
frontal lobe, hides behind his eyes.
He needs to ask her, *Why?*
And were you coming or going?

Need grows like a weed after rain.
At night he dreams of long black
hair, dark almond shaped eyes.
By day he drives the side streets
looking for the Asian lady, longs
to catch her walking backwards.
He prays that she speaks English,
that she'll let him walk beside her
backwards. He's getting good at it.

2017

Breaking Out of Writer's Block

Try sitting in a different spot, in the gray easy chair on
the opposite side of the room. Stare out another window
with a view to a sycamore. Use a new ballpoint pen with
a startling shade of ink. Green. Write in a purple binder.

Try listening to the Coldplay album that your grandson
downloaded to your iTunes. Words will come, will shove
their way through cobwebs onto the page. Let them spill
where they will like jigsaw puzzle pieces dumped out on

a dining room table along with dust of cardboard, soft
and gray as brain cells sitting too long in the box. Fiddle
with the pieces. Fit them together like words on a line.
This one over here. That one there in the corner and so on,

until the last piece of sky is pressed in place, and it's not
at all like the picture on top of the box...the Eiffel Tower.
No, it's the Brooklyn Bridge. Your fingers walk across
it to the other side where you see a piece of paper on

the ground. Fine script. Green ink. Bingo! Your poem!
But no, the last line reads *Anonymous*. Fuck. But you
knew it was never going to be that easy. So it's back
to the waiting gray chair, back to the sycamore tree.

2017

Department of Loose Screws

Someone please tell me where to find the
Department of Lost and Found Memories.
I lost mine somewhere between the dump
at the end of Second Street and Broadway.

An elusive thought sneaked out an open
car window. Something about a new easy
guaranteed method to keep from going
crazy. I saw it on the internet or maybe

QVC. I need something serious to keep
from going back. I've been there and it
is really fucking freaky, hard to describe.

Think psychedelic tangles of tarantulas,
kaleidoscopes exploding into rainbows.
I'm talking about the good weed. And you
in Birkenstocks and silky milky yoga pants,

insisting you didn't swipe my memory of
gymnastics on a waterbed with a bearded
guy from Temecula, I wouldn't put it past
you. Get lost in the ashram. Shit. I missed

the turn to the Department of Lost Souls.
I have been meaning to scope it out for
*The One That Got Away Noooo Not
the bearded guy.* Do you think I'm crazy?

2017

Fruit Salad

apricots speak primarily to
other apricots
whereas bananas well
you know *bananas*
they peel so readily and
then there is the issue
of splits and such
apples of course are
multilingual and therefore
quite cosmopolitan
one might call them smooth
which is not to say slick
cherries are complicated
some sweet and some sour
like people in that respect
and don't forget about
the pits now on to grapes
as is commonly known
they are grown in vineyards
and eventually become
hmm oh my this vintage
is robust and fruity on
the tongue well let's just
fast track the kiwi
and the kumquat and
pour another goblet of this
very fine wine

2017

Full Circle

My hand circles a white pottery plate
with a red checked dish towel, as my
mind circles back to pastel Melmac

on a yellow Formica table top and tv trays
in front of a black and white Zenith.
Hot dogs, baked beans and Bonanza.

Today my kids, senior citizens, eat
organic, watch The Walking Dead on
giant flat screen tv, while I reach for

a big button remote, turn up the sound
to watch Wheel of Fortune, only to nod
off dreaming of my man waking from

the dead, walking over to the couch,
leaning to kiss me, and reaching for
the remote, switching to a ballgame.

2017

The Journey

We will travel by train,
an old fashioned train
with a steam engine,
and we will reserve
a sleeping compartment.
A porter will bring us
tall cool drinks and I'll
fan you with a paper fan
shaped like a palm leaf.
The train slows as we
chugga chugga along
a river. The water is so
clean we see boaters
reflected in it, Folks
along the banks are
eating picnic lunches
spread out on cloths.
The sun lowers. We
join other passengers
in the dining car and
I think we will have
champagne. Yes.....
an expensive French
champagne and I will
not get drunk. Other
passengers stop and
greet each other as
they pass by to their
tables set with crystal
and silver on linen
tablecloths white as
a baby's new tooth.

But there are no babies,
no children to divert
us from each other.
I think we must be
traveling through
heaven. At least,
the food is heavenly,
has been prepared
by an invisible chef
in another car. We
have been served
and have dined on
lobster and shrimp
and finished it off
with crème broule
followed by a snifter
of brandy. Dishes
have been cleared
away. Passengers
in another car play
card games and ask
us to join them but,
we smile and decline.
We want to be alone
on a train to nowhere,
all our needs and our
desires attended to.
So why do I wonder
when we will arrive
at the next station?

2017

Play It Again Sam

In a previous life my name was Suzanne.
French class. Sixth period. Oak Park High.
All the students assumed French names.
Which is why, when the other Pat in class
appropriated Patrice, Miss Bissonette
appointed me to be Suzanne and voilà!
I laughed louder, wore tight sweaters,
bright scarves. A Parisian at heart, I said
Mais oui and *C'est la vie* a lot. My bored
lunch buddies said, *Get over it* and I did
in Beginning Spanish. *Olé.* Too bad for
Suzanne. She had the spirit of a poet,
wrote passionate sonnets to a cute boy
slumped in front of her in American Lit.,
aspired to write free verse like Whitman.
My spirit is a love struck girl like Suzanne,
but I write like Pat, and sometimes I wish
myself back to where I began a love affair
with words, with French, with the sound
of *L'amour. Mon coeur.* Je vous adore
words I never heard in a low urgent tone.
No, what I heard murmured against my
cheek was, *Baby, Let me buy you a drink,*
and I tumbled for a guy that I met at a bar
in the Loop. We had a grand passion that
couldn't last. He left me to go back to a wife
in Kansas but, we'll always have Chicago.

2017

A Poet's Love Letter to a Poet

You scribble lusty words
on my blank page
and make me blush.
I want to fold myself
into a plane and do
loops around the moon.
Your bold ink gives me
a rush and my blood
bubbles. Oh, we
could make beautiful
free verse together.
I want to whisper sweet
similes in you ear and
kiss your epigraph.
My ex, a haiku kind of
guy, left me hungry,
wanting more. I adore
your syntax and
your alliteration makes
me tingle. Let's mingle
in the margins and get
lost in assonance.
Are you up for a slam?

2017

What Calls to Me

dust under the bed calls to come blow it away
and while you're at it make the bed
the washing machine calls come come fill me
with dirty clothes overflowing the laundry basket
the broom calls me to come grab its stick and sweep
dirt from behind the fridge
windows call come wipe grime from our panes and
dust our filthy sills
the gin bottle in the upper cabinet calls *oh baby baby*
you know you want me
the pile of unpaid bill on the desk calls saying *overdue*
overdue pay me pay me
the dishes in the sink call me to come and wash them
and put them away
the car calls me to come vacuum its interior where kids'
muddy sneakers mucked it up
the gin bottle calls to me from the kitchen counter and
the dryer calls me to come remove clothes
the stove calls for a pot to boil and a burner calls me
to get a move on with dinner
the gin bottle calls me to unscrew its cap and the phone
calls me to answer
a tumbler calls for gin to its rim and a doorbell calls me
to open the front door where
a stranger calls me to come to God and I call to powers
that be to pour me a drink
the cat at my heels call me to feed it I kick the cat

2017

THE TRISH DUGGER COLLECTION OF POETRY

2018

Yard Work at the Condos Next Door

Quiet coming apart
by a leaf blower's
vicious screech.

Quiet fleeing from
a power mower's
deluge of growls.

Quiet returning with
a silence so sweet
that I can even hear

a sigh and swaying
of a cradle of peace
when the work is done

January 20, 2018

Another Day in the Life of a Senior Citizen Homeowner Poet

It came in the mail yesterday, four page flyer
from San Diego Gas & Electric, their logo on
the front, shades of light blue on the top half,
lots and lots of bold print headlines and many
columns of fine print blah blah blah and where
the heck is my magnifying glass? Something
to do with a new payment plan. I tossed it on
a pewter tray in the middle of my ancient oval
oak dining table along with two lottery tickets,
a Sprouts flyer touting veggie specials and
a Pay Up or Else notice from People which
I subscribe to only for book reviews because
who the fuck can recognize interchangeable
faces and names of Jennifer and Jessica,
Jonah and Justin. Well, there's Usher. But,
he's talented. Meanwhile, a family member
with beacon eyes may come by to decipher
the ominous flyer from S.D.G. & E. but for
now, I flip a switch. The light still comes

January 25, 2018

Forever Thine

His Prayer Book bound in black leather,
worn at the edges, faint gold cross on
its cover, kept in her dresser drawer all
these years along with his Marine Corps
maple leaf pins and a Valentine cut from
red construction paper, inscribed in his
scrawled handwriting, *Please Be Mine.*

February 8, 2018

Prompt: Write About a Kiss

Strange to be writing about April
in February, but you know how

April shows up in any month at
the mention of a kiss, a breeze,

a sweet new love. It was April.
I lounged on a brown leather sofa

bordering a hallway at El Toro's
Officers Club and leaning back,

I looked up at a tall tan marine in
khakis drifting by, wings pinned

above a pocket. Our eyes locked.
He turned toward me and stopped,

smiled and bent to meet my lips
with the soft tenderness of an April

dawn and then with sudden hunger.
Like honey bees we sucked sweet

nectar from each other and just as
suddenly, he was gone. I would title

my sonnet, A Kiss to Remember but,
that's a bit overdone. I never knew

his name and never saw him again.
The squadron left for Korea the next

weekend. Maybe he didn't come back.
I'll never know. It was so long ago but,

I was quite likely drinking martinis and
wearing that strapless black satin.

February 8, 2018

A Brief Encounter

Jennifer Somebody will play me
in the movie.....me at 29,
an age of many brief encounters.
I'm thinking *Film Noir*...split screens,
slow zooms, a barrage of fades
and dissolves. Hint of kink.

Opening scene.....deserted street
in a seedy part of town. A cat yowls
near an overturned trash can.
Cement block building. Graffiti scars.
Corner bar. Blinking neon. JAKE'S.
Pavement slick with drizzle.

Mysterious woman in black (me)
steps out of a yellow cab and after
glancing over her shoulder, she
grabs the heavy door and goes in.
You get the drift. I'm thinking
French director...Jacques Somebody,

an Indie Film Company to produce it,
and a premier at Sundance Festival
where I meet Robert Redford. We
have a brief encounter in which he
smiles at someone beyond me and
shakes my hand and.....it's a wrap.

February 17, 2018

Sidetracked

There are no new stories.
Boy meets girl. Boy loses girl.
Boy gets girl or.....maybe
girl meets another girl and
boy's left holding his dick.
That's a twist, but hardly new.
Hello.....there are no surprise
endings except maybe mine.

The tracks of my life led me
to a nearby library that gave
me a way out of feeling alone.
I found my friends in books by
John Steinbeck, Anne Tyler
and others who fed me the
old stories in new ways with
words juicy as ripe mangos.

Train tracks at the end of my
block lead to a nearby station.
I knew I could walk there and
buy a ticket to get out of town
on a really crappy day, go to
L.A. and disappear and never
look back. It was July, a Friday.
I bought a round trip ticket.

March 5, 2018

The Dream

A swarthy man with a black mustache
put his arm around my waist and
took my hand to tango. I was wearing
scarlet with ruffles around the bottom,
and the sound of castanets peppered
the night air. It was so real that I spoke
with a Spanish accent when I awoke.
Perhaps a Spanish omelet I ate late
was responsible, so tonight it's French
toast. I've always thought a French
accent was sexy. Worth a try, n'est-ce pas?

March 12, 2018

Ode to a Self-Threading Needle

On a pedestal of puffy red
pin cushion you stand tall
and proud, tower over lowly
straight pins.....regal stem
gleaming in sunlight, your
one tiny eye seeking mine.
Retrieved from the depths
of a sewing basket, buried
under a clutter of buttons
and spools of thread, your
split head an answer to my
quandary.....how to mend
a seam when I can't thread
a needle. I slide a strand
of silky pastel pink thread
across your split head and
it pops down into your eye
through which it now glides.

Oh, Savior of Split Seams
and Drooping Hemlines,
your sharp point pierces
tattered fabric, also stabs
tender skin of my pinkie.
I suck blood and carry on.

Oh Goddess of Torn Garments.
bless a self-threading needle.
And bless a myopic seamstress
with a Band-Aid on her pinkie.

June 10, 2018

Blame It on the Weather

looming ferryboat plows through
the Sound soundless hour long
ride in thick dark night and finally
pulling up to a silent island with no
lighthouse a bit daunting having
lost my cell along with my mind
and how to find my way home when
I wake in a clammy bed of rumpled
sheets so many hot summer nights
can lead to crankiness according to
my newspaper but for me having
already arrived at crankiness many
root canals ago waking up reminds
me I'm still alive and can write about
surviving another hot summer night
if I ever find my fucking notebook

August 24, 2018

I Burned a CD and Labeled It "Moon Songs"

and every night I float out on a sea of sleep
listening to a lullaby of *Moonlight in Vermont*,
a little light blue CD player on my bedside table,

Willie Nelson's guitar strumming, his cozy
cowboy voice caressing a dream into being.
Sometimes *Blue Moon* seeps into my sleep,

and a ripple of *Moonglow* too. *Moon Shadow*
and *Moon River*, alas, remain to be heard but,
I'm sure a little bird outside my window flaps

its wings when Sinatra sings, *Fly Me to the Moon.*

August 28, 2018

Heritage

I come from
a sparkle in
my mother's eyes,
she a farm girl
who smiled at
the dark lanky
hired hand.
He responded
with a wink.
I think I have her
big eyes
and maybe his
full lips
that whispered,
Goodbye,
before I was five.

August 31, 2018

NPR at 1:00 A.M.

sleepless I fumble for a radio
by my bed press a button and
hear a voice sounding deep as
a canyon like that of an actor
in Hamlet droning on about
celebrity chefs and stock pots
exotic recipes bouillabaisse
I nod off at something to do with
truffles a ceiling fan's whirring
stirs my dream I'm swimming
in a sea of green papaya soup
I wake hungry for
Arugula and Pistachio Pesto Quiche
settle for corn flakes

September 1, 2018

Are You Tired of Rose'?

reads a headline
of the L.A. Times
Food and Dining
section,
and I'm thinking,
Unbelievable!
Are you fucking
kidding me?
(I read the Times
and Bukowski).
Those same
assholes tired of
drinking Rose´
likely eat fondue
and meditate.
Give me a break.
And what's with
this Aperol spritz
suggested as
a change from
humdrum Rose´?
I *dream* of Rose´,
long to wade in
a stream of Rose´.
I could go on but,
I'm running late
for an AA meeting.

September 3, 2018

On the Scent

Never a Chanel N° 5 girl,
she dabbed
Schiaparelli's Shocking
behind her ears and in
the V between her breasts,
sweet valley of secrets,

hint of musky scent
wherever she strayed.
Her bureau displayed
a collection of cologne
sprays which seems to
have gone the way of

high heels along with
her sense of balance.
Don't misunderstand.
She's not into lavender
sachet and lace shawls.
The thing is, she's lost

her sense of smell. But,
oh well, her memory is
excellent, reaching back
to Shocking times that
make her smile as she
nods off in a rocker.

Don't wake her from
her dream. She's seeing
without clouds in her
eyes, walking in a garden
without a cane and oh!
the roses.

September 4, 2018

Whatever Works

Follow your inner moonlight
Don't hide the madness
Allen Gwinsburg

I write countless words on lined paper
in pursuit of my *inner moonlight*, and
cross out words, crumple endless sheets
of paper into lumpy crumpled balls
And meanwhile, I reach for my old
How To books to get words to flow.
I'm tired and don't need this shit. So I'm
thinking I'll quit and take up Raku and
Wine Tasting where I'm more likely
to find my *inner moonlight* anyway.
And I'm thinking a glass of Bordeaux is
a fine way to start Wine Tasting.....right?
I'm *rethinking* Raku.

September 12, 2018

What Would Billy Collins Do?

What's a five letter word
for *procrastinate?*
This Times' crossword calls
for another cup of coffee.

Like that ...Billy would begin
in a conversational tone.
He'd mention the neglected
red notebook on a nearby
table, open to a blank page.
The table would be teak,
it's rectangular surface
gleaming, the room perfumed
by tangy scent of lemon oil.

Sometimes I wish I were
Billy Collins. He makes
it seem as easy as shelling
peas, popping out a fresh
crop of words, pulling
you in like a slick con man
with his smooth lines.

I gaze at the notebook,
imagine it has scooted
over closer, chiding me,
reminding me to write.
I finally pick it up and
a folded piece of paper
drops from its pages.
In faded ink on note paper:

Darling, What took you so long?

You've been avoiding me.
And by the way,
your five letter word is
DELAY,
as in..... Please don't.

September 25, 2018

Weather Report

It rained last night and
this morning everyone smiles
and everything shines.
Did you hear it on the roof?
My buddy Linda's voice
overflows with wonder.
My daughter, Claudia, shouts,
Water's running in the canyon!
We run to look out a window.

Daughter-in-law Teresa says,
*Our tomatoes got a good
drink of water.* She's thinking
of future BLT's. I try to think
of when we had our last rain.
Even my memory is dusty...
maybe many months ago
when rain prompted me to
renew my flood insurance.

When my husband was alive
he had a French drain dug
so the house wouldn't flood.
He replaced leaky faucets and
dried my tears and made me
chuckle at life's muddy puddles.
He'd be happy with today's
forecast: intermittent laughter
over split pea soup and cornbread.

October 7, 2018

Directions for Writing a Poem in a Hurry

write it short...10, 12 lines
and for the love of God...
Don't Rhyme...throw in
an image and be sure to
use a simile like sweet as
a slice of Key Lime pie...
sprinkle in a metaphor...
the door shudders and
groans as Marvin pounds
its rich mahogany mantle
Do Not Add *and the wind
moans.* Sign your name (or not)

October 15, 2018

Cloaks

You wrap yourself with light as with a cloak
Psalm 104:2

As I sit on the sofa in my Calvin Klein
jeans and beige cashmere sweater,

(bought on credit from Amazon and
from QVC on an easy payment plan)

reading Psalm 104 from yesterday's
bulletin for the 22nd Sunday after

Pentecost, it occurs to me that I've
never worn a cloak nor owned one.

And I don't think I ever saw a cloak
in the Sears Roebuck catalog which

had its place next to the Bible in my
grandparent's farmhouse. My sister,

Gayle, and I played store with Sears
catalogs using pebbles for money.

In my next life I'll own a black velvet
cloak and *clothed with majesty*, I'll

go to the opera in a limousine to see
Aida, feeling like a queen, providing

I have a next life, which at this point
is a bit uncertain seeing how easily

my mind strays from scripture, goes
to cloaks, clothes and easy payment

plans where, as grandpa used to tell
my grandma, the devil may be hiding.

October 21, 2018

Cribbage

The board, somewhere in the back of
the built-in buffet where patient vases
wait to be summoned for thorny stems
of flowers he snipped from the garden,
the board, scarred by wear from games
gone by and sadly replaced by solitaire,
the board still winces at pokes of pegs
scoring points, triumphant stabs, and it
remembers sounds of laughter, shouts
of *fifteen two, fifteen four, and a pair is
six*, ruffle of cards and the board mourns.

October 29, 2018

High Price of Smiles

Until she knew the meaning of Safe,
she sucked her thumb. Buck teeth,
high price to pay for comfort, made
her smile with her lips closed tight.

You could pick her out right away
in old black and white snapshots,
young girls in Sunday dresses in
front of St. Mary's Home for Girls.

Her teeth straightened, paid for by
St. Mary's, she found her own wide
smile, and it was better than finding
a prize in a Cracker Jack box and

she smiled a lot, but not when she
thought about Billy, her little brother,
his silly grin, and she wondered
where they send little boys to live.

November 4, 2018

Saturday Eve Service at St. Peter's

The church bell tolls
twelve times for those
who died in the shooting.
In prayer and chants
we search for answers.
Dark in the church yard
after service, black as
broken hopes, somber
as hearts of those who
survived. Twelve times
the church bell tolls.

November 11, 2018

The Chinese Lantern Tree

like a lovely lady
with tangled hair
to her shoulders,
dusty green gown
trailing behind her
strap dangling on
her graceful arm,
crumbs scattered
at her feet from the
muffin she ate with
a cup of oolong tea.
She's beautiful and
messy, so what are
you going to do but
clean up after her...
rake brown leaves,
sweep up gold dust,
tawny seed pods,
slave to a cycle of
seasons, pleased
to be in the shade
of her embrace.

2018

When I Consider

Light rays slide into my room
at the side of a drawn blind
and my eyes are open wide
at the sight of another dawn.
And I consider how the light
chases away dark of night
without a sound, how light
surrounds my days. I rise
and dive into light, splash,
and laugh at the way light
makes me feel giddy, free,
as if I had wings to lift me
up above clouds. I feast on
luscious colors that I see
with feeble eyes, dress in
scarlet red and dusty rose.
And though I know night
returns with its blanket of
dark, my candle still glows.

2018

2019

THE TRISH DUGGER COLLECTION OF POETRY

For Gayle

Holding her hand
as she slips into
the deep mystery,
as her heart beat
slows to peaceful
passage beyond
pain, all I know for
sure is that when
I go, her light will
show me the way.

January 18, 2019

Victor the Boa Constrictor

I forget how long
my boys had their
pet snake coiled
on a log hanging
from the ceiling
of their bedroom.
Where the hell did
Victor come from?
Probably a trade
involving alligator
lizards, a rosy boa
thrown in. Maybe
I should've asked
more questions,
but some things
you don't want to
know. And I was
too busy, almost
frantic, trying to
find tiny white rats
that broke loose
from a cage in my
daughter's room.
Is it any wonder
that cocktail hour
came earlier every
day? I found one
can become quite
fond of snakes
and tiny white rats
after a couple of
tall gin and tonics.

January 29, 2019

Chance of Scattered Showers

Rain is a fraction of cloud
multiplied by thunder.
Life can be explained
using basic arithmetic.
For example, one *Me*
plus one *You* equals
disaster as has been
proven a million times
Sunshine is a common
denominator. Times it
by moonlight and you
have Aquarius. Cool
numbers include four
and five. For example,
The Fab Four plus
The Jackson Five
equals Rock 'n Roll.
Subtract me from your
call list. That should
solve the problem.

January 31, 2019

Check the Dryer

A smooth wooden darning egg moans
at the bottom of a dusty
sewing basket, buried under buttons,
feels smothered, longs for the warm
hand of the seamstress
pulling it from a nest of tangled thread,
misses the thrill of sliding down
into the toe of a sock
to reveal holes in the heels and toes.
It feels neglected and mourns a loss,
the disappearance of
the art of darning socks, it's unaware
socks too have disappeared, gone to
wherever lost socks go,
the seamstress, her kids, carefree with
bare feet in flip flops, sockless in Keds.

February 8, 2019

An Otherwise Quiet Afternoon

a plane pursues clouds

and here on the ground
the bamboo bends low

whispering to crickets
occasional caw caws

of pesky crows punch
holes in the afternoon

my rocker speaks out
with a wheezy squeak

a cane leans against
a table near my side

my magnifying glass
and a book in my lap

a few more chapters to go

February 17, 2019

Red Satin Nightie

under black tights
in her dresser drawer,

saved to wear for
a special friend,

lace trim on a deep V,
and tucked in its

folds, an obituary
from a newspaper.

It's been a while...
a size or two ago.

Time to clean out
the drawer, shop

for a gown more
comfy and warm.

It's off to Goodwill,
a nightie like new.

And the obituary?
A long last look at

the past and she
tosses it in the trash.

February 20, 2019

Babushka, Fashion Accessory, 1940s

A snowy winter afternoon
when Mom came to visit,
she brought me a babushka,
bright blue triangle of rayon,
with a fringe of white yarn.
I'd written to her, begging
for a babushka, convinced
it was my ticket to fit in with
the smooth girls at school.
Her tired eyes squinting and

calloused hands gripping,
my mother had hemmed it in
her room across town where
she cooked and cared for
someone else's kids, her own
daughter in a foster home.
I popped it on my head, tied it
under my chin, turned to Mom
watching me with a wide smile
that I had missed like forever.

I gave her a hug, didn't want to
let her go. I had a new babushka
and more, for a sweet wink in
time she was all mine...until we
said goodbye and then we kept
it light with a quick kiss kiss and
I didn't smear her lipstick or cry
any more. Today with my own
kids grown and gone, I know her
tears were hiding behind a smile.

March 14, 2019

Fake Yellow Rose

in a glass vase
on my kitchen window sill,
petals leaning low,

I know how it feels…
a bit tacky, its pizzazz passei,
too tired to stand tall,

but happy to still
have its spot on the sill with
life's vital items…

Aspirin, Jergens and Tums.

March 21, 2019

The Constant Gardener
apology to John le Carrei

The seed of a poem was planted
in the loam of a young girl's mind

when she spied a violet beside
a path edged with an icy crust of

snow, its brave burst into spring.
The seed sprouted and she wrote

with a thick blue Laddie pencil on
wide ruled paper, her first poem,

first time digging for words, aching
to say the best way how the violet

had lifted her spirit, sent it soaring
like a bright red helium balloon.

She would spend a lifetime digging
for words in her mind garden, for

words with wings to lift a poem
from the page and send it soaring,

a fantasy that keeps her sleepy-eyed,
up at night to revise, revise, revise.

March 29, 2019

To The Birdwatcher

cockatiel folds into sleep tucked
under the wide spread wings of a seagull
in the aviary of my awareness
red tailed hawk scans the scene
from its perch on a cable between
two lobes of my brain frontal and temporal
humming bird of sweet memories
hovers behind my eyes and
my heart flies to you watching in the beyond
no need for your Nikon binoculars

April 3, 2019

Moon

barely there moon
piece of a pie crust moon
round rim of a raisin muffin moon
barely seen by a coyote
on the prowl in a backyard in
Escondido on the scent of
a frisky feline silent slice
of a moon smiles at slinky tabby
hides its shadow from paws
of a night marauder waning moon
disappearing under a black afghan
a shroud of cloudy sky rind
of a yellow grapefruit moon and
tart not a sweetheart moon
where did the rest of you go
who knows where the man in
the moon goes baby moon better
eat your Wheaties moon are you
coming or going moon and are you
Gorgonzola or Mozzarella

June 27, 2019

Rattled by *Ink Blots* in Rattle

I'm stunned by the sting
of a memory.....a spill of
indelible black ink on my
new foster home rug,

light sage green at the side
of my bed so long ago that
I can't recall what I said.....
but *Fuck* seems appropriate.

My fountain pen, bottle of ink,
notebook of poems along
with hand-me-down clothes
in a battered tan suitcase,

a history of goodbyes, and
now.....*this* hideous stain
that will ruin my pathetic life.
Well, it was the far side of

the bed and nothing was
ever said.....and I survived
to write a few more poems,
and to subscribe to Rattle.

July 25, 2019

Kerosene Lanterns

Grandma lined them up before sundown,
I'd see her striking a match to light them.
Little round lady in bib apron, brown hair
pulled back in a bun, serving up platters
of fried chicken to harvesters from nearby
farms, chickens she'd wrung by the neck
out in the yard, chopping off their heads,
with seeming glee, laughing and cackling
and dumping them in a vat of boiling water
before plucking and cutting them up to fry.
Little round lady who bore eight babies as
easy as shelling peas she said when I told
her I was going to have a baby. She raised
six, my mother the oldest, and helped raise
me, my daddy gone off. Up before dawn,
fresh baked biscuits every morn made with
a pinch of this, handful of that, and topped
with a slab of butter made in the butter churn
that I helped hand crank, a dab of cherry jam
that I got to lick, cherries from an orchard out
in front of the farmhouse. Grandma and me,
we had a game. I'd beg *Pleeze Pleeze* to get
her to pop out her false teeth. When she did,
I'd shriek, *OH NO*. She'd laugh in her mother
hen cackle. I'd hide behind the player piano
(where one day I'd play The Blue Danube
in two minutes flat.) Before sunset. Kerosene
lanterns lit, grandma and me, we'd yawn and
fall in bed and be fast asleep by sundown.

August 28, 2019

Mountain Meditation / Ponto

I bend in the wind
hold strong to my path
that ends in the foothills.
I look up at the summit
and do not seek to reach it.
but rather to love the ground
I stand on, the place
where I plant my seeds...
daisies and desires.
I smile at sunshine and
dance in the moonlight

2019

Plein Air

Pretty ladies of the Plein Air Painters
posed for a photo
found on a page of the morning paper.

The ladies with smiling faces seem to
invite me to join them,
so I pick up my pen and enter into

a hazy landscape of weedy words and
fern-like phrases,
draw inky scrawls across lined paper,

paint lyrical bouquets with bold strokes,
but soon feel faint from
heady scent of assonance, and so I put

down my pen and turn to the Obituaries
(which I used to ignore
before my eighties) as a poem fades into ...

2019

DATE
UNKNOWN

Barbie & Trish

Barbie overhears Mimi
talking to Nana Trish.
Barbie is shocked to discover
Trish never had a Barbie.
She wonders how Trish
learned about life and stuff
without a Barbie and a Ken.

Poor Trish! No one to
teach her fine points
of wardrobe planning
and accessorizing.
No wonder she's so tacky.

Oh sure, thinks Barbie,
Trish had Patsy Ann,
but she was a baby doll,
not a hip chick like me.
Patsy Ann didn't even talk
like Chatty Cathy who
came along when Trish
was grown and having fun
with guys instead of dolls.

Barbie, buried under a pile
of clothes in the back of Mimi's
closet, secretly wishes Trish
would rescue her.

She is feeling neglected
by Mimi who has taken up
roller blades and
rock climbing and softball.
Sports Sports Sports

Barbie wants to cry, but her
mascara would smear.
Barbie thinks she and Trish
might have a future together.
Barbie could help Trish be
stylish and hip. Trish could
teach Barbie what?

Not cooking or salsa dancing.
Not yoga or guitar.
O.K. So forget about Trish
teaching Barbie anything.
They could just hang
and groove, dress up and
do whatever nanas do.

If Barbie only knew!

Date Unknown

Four Thirty A.M.

and the child
breathes in
and the child
breathes out
deeply evenly
and my arm lays
over the child
my eyes
are closed
but my mind
is open
cradling
a poem under
my arm
and I breathe
deeply evenly

Date Unknown

Gluteous Beauteous

I have ample padding on my rump.
Some folks would say that I am rather plump.
And model types with buns so lean and flat
Would tend to think that I'm a trifle fat.
Yet there are those with generous derrieres
Who'd willingly trade my round rump for theirs.
When studying body shapes one soon surmises
That bodies come in lots of different sizes.
And though I've excess poundage on my butt,
If I feel good about myself ... so what!

Date Unknown

Goodbye

Intervening hours
spilling down the glass
lullaby senses,
wash away tears, and I
no longer reach out for you,
slipping from my mind.
Awareness of you
going
going
gone
as I ease into sunshine.
Only once in a while,
sudden as a bee sting,
a flash of your smile
and it hurts so much
that it no longer hurts.

Date Unknown

Hot Tub Syndrome

If you're planning to install a hot tub at your home,
You should be aware of the Hot Tub Syndrome:

Consider the rub-a-dub-dubbing and such going on in hot tubbing:
As water jets circulate bones and swish around erogenous zones,
One's blood pressure is rising and it hardly can be surprising
If a man is suddenly knowing his manhood's undoubtedly growing.

You further may find the jacuzzi contributes to make you feel woozy,
Along with the requisite brandy. Conversation will tend to get randy.
Those hot water jets go on bubbling and nobody seems to be troubling
Or giving much thought, I will bet, to proper hot tub etiquette.

For instance, a drunk in the drink. Should one merely allow him to sink?
As your muscles relax and unloose, guard against the possible goose.
Don't stare at exposed pulchritude. Refrain from remarks that are lewd.
Prolonging your soaking will soon lead to skin puckered up like a prune.

There's threat of a possible stroke. You simmer and steam as you croak.
But the bottom line question is whether we immerse in the altogether.
In spite of the perils I'll try it as soon as I've finished my diet..
I'm opposed to baring my blubber to the gaze of a fellow hot tubber.

Date Unknown

Is Sitting Befitting?

Episcopalians with weak knees endure
Discomfort with small hope of cure
As they kneel with a moan and creaking of bone,
But in humble devotion, I'm sure.

Though sometime before the last blessing,
When the aching becomes more distressing,
As attention diverts to the joint that hurts,
Saving knees instead of souls is more pressing.

And the thought maybe crosses their minds
That in some worship places one finds
Those, devout in feeling without any kneeling.
They pray sitting on their behinds!

But to worship in comfort and ease
Without getting down on his knees
Would be a bit alien to an Episcopalian,
And unheard of in most dioceses.

Date Unknown

Layover in L.A.

This room is perfect
in it's languor:

white plisse´ shade
drawn against late
afternoon sun

creamy satin negligee
draped on a velvet chaise
of pastel green

Casablanca lilies
in loose arrangement
adorn a dresser

melting ice
in a silver bucket
overturned flutes
and spilled champagne
on the Persian carpet

melange of
limp arms and pale legs
in lush repose
on rumpled sheets

and the scent
the musky scent
of passion spent

soft whir whir of
a ceiling fan and in a corner
near the door a crumpled
Virgin Airways ticket
discarded on the floor.

Date Unknown

The Man in the Full Moon

The man in the moon
will pull me into his
full embrace tonight.
I will not resist.
He will place a string
of stars around my neck.
I will feel his hot
breath on my throat.
He will whisper in his
hazy golden voice that he
is mine, only mine,
and it will be true
for one hour of rapture.
He cannot be constant.
Other lovers await him
as have I since
he last came by.

Date Unknown

Metamorphosis

Now you are
a tiny white
butterfly
fluttering
in and out
of my mind
where you
were once
cocooned.

Date Unknown

Not My Cat

Are you a cat person?
Not me.
Though Skooter seems
to think I am...fluffy little
black and white creature.
Some people say she's pretty.
Well, maybe...
though I didn't pick her out.
She found *me*.
...showed up one day
and started hanging around.
I named her Skooter.
Had to call her *something*,
didn't I?
Skooter likes dry food,
especially FRISKIES and
won't let anyone brush her,
except me and
today she caught a rat.
I guess I'll let her stay,
even though
I am not a cat person
and she is *not* my cat.

Date Unknown

Outsider on the Inside

hey you outsider don't fit in never win
not part of the group out of the loop
not quite hip can't get a grip
don't know the buzz words
don't know the slang not part of the gang

hey you outsider don't fit in too fat too thin
nobody wants you on their side
looking for a place you can hide

know the feeling? not quite good enough
never where it's at too thin too fat
not the right clothes big bumpy nose

know the feeling?
standing in the dark when everybody
else is dancin' in the park
not quite fast enough clumsy slow
don't know the lingo never get bingo
you're the only fish not in the swim
not part of the school not hip not cool

know the feeling? you wanna belong
join their chorus and sing their song
well fuck their song sing your own
stand alone wing it sing it
say what you gotta say your own way

anyone tells you it's not ok
screw it just do it
doesn't have to be pretty or sweet

find your own words drum your own beat
off key or not give all you've got
don't try to be like all the rest
be your own best sing your own tune
shoot for the moon the full moon

Date Unknown

Reaching for Heaven

I am haunted by a row of empty swings,
suspended in silence,
waiting to be played like instruments,
ready to make the music of laughter
and sounds of *WHEE!*
Where are the young musicians?
Are all of them grown and gone
like Davey and Jeff?

I walk a pathway in the park
and I remember:
The boys and I were swinging,
Davey and Jeff and me.
We sailed high into the sky,
reaching for heaven.

And I remember:
appreciating the passage from
Push me! Push me! to solo flight.
It happened suddenly...overnight.
And just as swiftly it seems they found
the swings were way too low to the ground.
And then the boys were gone.

Davey and Jeff, this is for you...
Wherever you are, whatever you do,
I hope you will always
reach for heaven.

Date Unknown

Special Delivery

I am an appropriate piece of rock,
a pebble from the shore of the Pacific.
I have tumbled through time to
become appropriately smooth and flat.
She found me on the beach
where I was one of an aggregation.
It was a Sunday afternoon
and he was surf fishing.
She was keeping him company,
basking in the sun.
He cast his line into the surf.
She cast pebbles.
They left for home when
the sun touched down and
the wind came up chilly,
he with an empty bucket,
she with a pebble in her pocket.
I am a pebble of singular beauty,
black as the deep, satin smooth
and sleek, small and flat and
appropriate for an envelope to
send flying to a friend
on the shore of the Atlantic.

Date Unknown

The State of Real Estate in a So Cal Coastal Community

Took a walk to the tumble down
part of town. Saw little square
stucco bungalows...gray faded
to white, white tinged to tan,
steadfast patches of scraggly
grass bordered by lipstick red
geraniums with sturdy stems
and invincible cheerfulness
even in seedy circumstances.
Saw an interloper townhouse
or two, here and there, evidence
of what the neighborhood will
eventually become, when nobody
I know will have the price
of even a little stucco bungalow
in the tumble down part of town.

Date Unknown

Tea Time

She carries her love to him
on an antique silver tray
laden with steaming teapot,
cup and saucer,
and a serving of toast.
He wraps his love
around her like
a cloud-soft shawl of
sunset colors, laced
with threads of gold.
He offers her a sip
from his cup.
She envelops him
in her love shawl and
they smile at each other.
His fingertips
trace her smile. The toast
is sprinkled with cinnamon
and unspoken secrets.
The orange spice tea,
soon lukewarm,
will be reheated.

Date Unknown

The Ghost of Love Lost

I see sly demons blindfolding
lovers, prompting them to make
promises they will never keep.

I see all the unkept promises
littering the ground like mustard
stained crumpled paper napkins

after a ball game. I see stolen
kisses creeping out sidedoors,
lovers sighing, parting, crying.

I see glass shards of smashed
dreams pierce through bone.
I see jagged scars of those alone.

Date Unknown

Three Purple Orchids

each in its own pot...
No, for these pricey divas
let's say celadon green
ceramic container
with crackled glaze. There!

They seem to stand taller now
on center stage of the buffet
beneath my dining room window,

each an exquisite extravagance,
though I wonder whether
three of them could be considered
ostentatious.

No matter.
It's a temporary placement.
I have a son

whose business is plants.
Exotic blossoms appear overnight
in corners of my house
like mushrooms in the lawn.

I am a foster mother to plants
meant for grander mansions.
Graceful palms displace my car
in the garage. *Leave the lights on,
Mom,* (For the plants, you know).

Flats of colorful flowers
line the side of my driveway,
bedded jewels glowing
in the sunlight.
I'm not a bit blasé about this.

I love having a floral way station,
and even if this is not a region
of obvious seasons,
when I wade into red poinsettias,
I know 'tis time for jolly.
Ho! Ho! Ho!

Date Unknown

Tundra

The key to her heart
is covered with rust.
The latch is hidden
by cobwebs and dust.
The key has been
stolen once or twice,
but that was before
her heart turned to ice.
Her frozen heart will
never more break,
and nobody nowhere
can make it ache.
Of course, her heart
no longer sings,
but she's safe from all
the hurt love brings

Date Unknown

Walk With Me a Way

Walk with me a way,
holding hands a while.
Lean your head to mine.
Let me see you smile.
Let me feel the warm
of your shining eyes.

Will you lend me time
so I can memorize
all the wonder hues
of a rainbow day?
Let us linger now.
Make the moment stay.

Walk with me a way,
touching as we go,
feeling sad for hours
that we'll never know.
Still, without regret
for a star we shared,
something precious seen,
something scarcely bared.

Walk with me a way.
Laugh a little too.
When at last you're gone
I'll remember you
with a rush of glad
and an inner glow.
Walk with me a way.
Must you really go?

Then ...
walk from me away.
Leave before I know.

Date Unknown

INDEX

(1996) Left to Right: (Top Row) Dean Dugger, Teresa Inman, John Mehlhop, Diana Dugger, Tyree Grant Dugger,

(Middle Row) Jeff Barnett, Trish Dugger, Dave Barnett, Claudia Barnett, Estelle Mehlhop, Tim Dugger, Betsy Bowman Dugger,

(Bottom Row) Grant Dugger, Kevin Dugger, Mimi Dugger, Andrew Dugger, David Dugger

CPSIA information can be obtained
at www.ICGtesting.com
Printed in the USA
BVHW011516031119
562744BV00005B/12/P